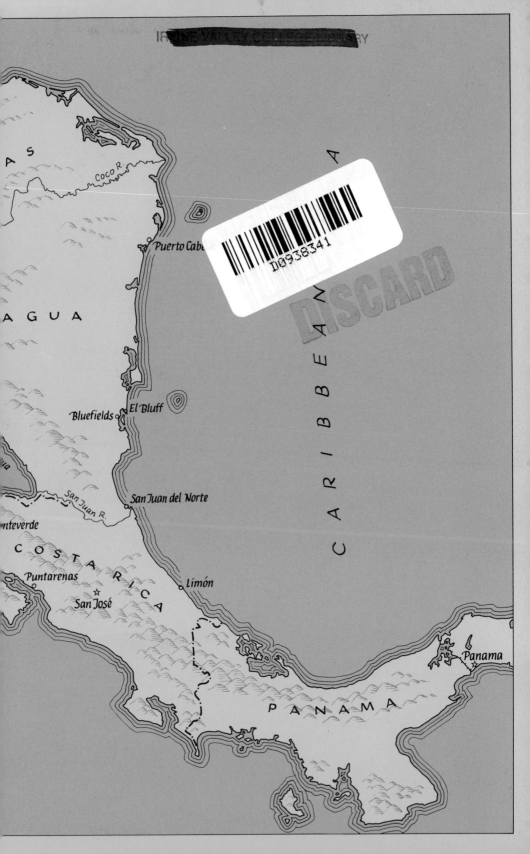

Central America: The Real Stakes

Other Books by Lester D. Langley:

The Banana Wars: An Inner History of American Empire, 1900–1934 (1983)

The United States and the Caribbean in the Twentieth Century (1982)

The United States and the Caribbean, 1900–1970 (1980)

Struggle for the American Mediterranean: United States-European Rivalry in the Gulf-Caribbean, 1776–1904 (1976)

The United States and Latin America, with E. T. Glauert (1971)

The United States, Cuba, and the Cold War (1970)

The Cuban Policy of the United States: A Brief History (1968)

Central America: The Real Stakes

UNDERSTANDING CENTRAL AMERICA BEFORE IT'S TOO LATE

Lester D. Langley

Crown Publishers, Inc.
New York

For "Guato," a Costa Rican boy who
  shared his candy with me
  on the San José–Cartago bus

Copyright © 1985 by Lester D. Langley

Published by Crown Publishers, Inc., One Park Avenue, New York, New York 10016 and simultaneously in Canada by General Publishing Company Limited
Manufactured in the United States of America
CROWN is a trademark of Crown Publishers, Inc.

Library of Congress Cataloging in Publication Data
Langley, Lester D.
  Central America.
  Bibliography: p.
  Includes index.
  1. Central America—Politics and government—
1979–   2. Central America—Foreign relations—
United States.   3. United States—Foreign relations—
Central America.   I. Title.
F1488.3.L36   1985   327.728073   84-23873
ISBN 0-517-55706-1
Design by Lauren Dong
10 9 8 7 6 5 4 3 2 1
First Edition

Contents

Preface

I N AN AGE WHEN THE PUBLISHERS ARE DISGORGING one book after another on Central America, this is yet another. But it is not a detailed analysis of the Central America of the past few years, nor an indictment of American policy, nor an inside account of the infuriatingly complex power struggle going on there. Rather, this book is a guide to Central America's salient features, its politics, its culture, and its conflicts.

In some instances, the characterizations of persons or events or places relate to the present; in others, they extend back as far as the sixteenth century, when the Spanish conquerors imposed their rule over that domain of mountain and tropics that links the two Americas. But whether the account reaches back four or four hundred years, it is, I believe, timely and necessary for understanding modern Central America, what its people are enduring and what is at stake there for the United States.

One's interpretations often depend on one's angle of vision. As a historian, I have sometimes taken the historian's view of men and events, yet in the course of writing this book, I have often found myself playing the role of sociologist, journalist, anthropologist, economist, and, quite simply, an American citizen alert to Central America's problems and U.S. involvement in its affairs. The perspective is from the level of those who rule, those who want power, and those twenty million or so *centroamericanos* on the bottom who have never had power nor economic security. It is they, frankly, by their numbers who are charting the isthmian future.

My first introduction to Central America came a generation ago when I was a graduate student working on a dissertation on the strategic importance of the Panama Canal in the years before World War II, an era when the American government believed, as it still does today, that its security interests in the region stood threatened by an external menace (then Germany, now the USSR and Cuba) and the internal challenge of nationalism. Since the early 1960s, when sentiment for John F. Kennedy's Alliance for Progress encouraged a generation of *centroamericanos* to look for a brighter day when their daily lives would be better and they would no longer suffer the rule of tinpot dictators, I have undertaken several trips to the isthmus. The latest came in February–March 1984 at the height of the Salvadoran presidential campaign.

The issues seem different now, but the old fears and the dreams have not abated. Where once only the Canal was the "jugular vein" of continental defense, now all Central America, it appears, has become a battleground of armies, ideologies, factions, and causes, in such numbers and varieties that few Americans have the time or patience to sort them out and try to make some meaning of what is happening there. This book tries to do so.

My thanks to Julian Bach, my agent; to Jim Wade, whose editorial talents reflect the best traditions of Harvard; and the many *centroamericanos* who befriended me. May they find nationhood and peace.

Part I

1 "Take Your Revolution Someplace Else"

A HIGH-RANKING STATE DEPARTMENT OFFICER, A fastidious man with precise notions about his country's role in the tropics, sat disconsolately reading the latest reports from Central America. His government's lofty plans for isthmian peace, expressed in a series of treaties drawn up three years before by the Central Americans themselves, had apparently collapsed. As before, in other isthmian political crises, Nicaragua was the culpable party. Its government, intent on dominating affairs in neighboring states, was again destroying the system peaceable Central American statesmen, following the wise guidance of the United States, had been striving to preserve.

But now, Nicaragua appeared to be disintegrating from within. The regime's enemies, some former adherents to the cause, had raised the flag of revolt in the isolated east. Their cause had roused political and, more concretely, economic support from American concerns engaged in tropical enterprise. And just as the revolution faltered, American troops, exercising a "policing" operation in what America characteristically described as a "disorderly society where lives and property were imperiled," landed to erect a protective cordon around "its" Nicaraguan rebels.

The prominent State Department official, mulling over the

alternatives, was heartened by the turn of events a dramatic—and decisive—military maneuver had wrought. But in the course of affairs in troubled Nicaragua the victorious rebel chieftain, shielded by the firepower of American gunboats and the authoritative presence of Marines, fared no better than the anti-American leader he had turned out. Within a year the new government found itself fragmented, facing conspiracy at every turn, in every ministry, as if revolt were endemic in the political system. And just as quickly the State Department official resolved that a military solution seemed the only *immediate* cure to deal with such a lamentable state of affairs.

The preceding description, with slight modification, could very well fit the pattern of American policy toward Central America as it appears to be developing in the 1980s. An anti-American regime dominates Nicaragua, its leaders hostile to the North American colossus and fearful of its intentions. The menacing presence of American military might surrounds this government, only a few years in power, confronted with the awesome task of reconstructing a society from the ravages of civil war. Its enemies, operating from the protective enclave established by a hostile neighbor, armed and financed by the seemingly limitless wealth of the United States, constitute a daily threat to the life of the regime, yet, somehow, it survives by exhorting the populace to maintain the faith and prepare for the inevitable Yankee invasion.

The State Department official described above is not George P. Shultz, but F. M. Huntington Wilson, and the parlous state of affairs he is assessing represents not the Nicaragua of today but the Nicaragua of almost three-quarters of a century ago, when the American government, frustrated over a seeming Nicaraguan menace to its peace plans for the isthmus, capitalized on the breakdown of Nicaragua's internal authority. First, American businesses on Nicaragua's isolated eastern shore financed the revolt, then, when the cause faltered, timely landings by American Marines sustained it. And afterward, when the revolution had won power, then suddenly confronted a new array of enemies, an even larger, and more decisive, number of American troops had arrived to set affairs in order. By the time their sojourn ended, more than a thousand Nicaraguans had perished in almost three years of civil war and American intervention. But Washington's prescription for isthmian peace had been sustained.[1]

Very few of the more than one thousand Americans who settled affairs in the Nicaragua of 1912 knew very much about the revolution that had brought them to the torrid Central American coast. Not even their officers, and there were some legendary representatives of America's imperial army in this intervention, were even remotely knowledgeable about Central America and its century-old struggle for unity. They knew only that these were "turbulent little countries" whose persistent wars endangered American security in the Caribbean. After all, theirs was the hallowed American tradition, picked up quite willingly from the British before them, of peacekeepers of the sea lanes and dingy tropical ports in the American Mediterranean. They were not imperial conquerors, charting some new landed empire for annexation in the wilds of the isthmus, but policemen keeping order, like the Irish cop on the block back in the Bronx.

It is well to remember the great American expedition into Nicaragua in 1912, for that was the *last* successful American military intervention *inside* Central America.

The Americans blamed Nicaragua's troubles on a few holdovers from the regime of José Santos Zelaya, the avuncular Nicaraguan Liberal who had tried to unite the country and then all Central America under his sway, and then resolved to get Americans out of his country by executing two American good old boys (Lee Roy Cannon and Leonard Groce) who had come down to lay dynamite charges in the San Juan River. The mines had endangered Zelaya's warships in his campaign against the rebels in the east, so the dictator (called the Pepper Man by his enemies for his putative use of pepper thrown in the eyes of prisoners during interrogation) had decided to make an example of the Americans by sentencing them to a firing squad. "I'm going to pluck the American president's plume," Zelaya had boasted to his foreign minister. The American secretary of state responded by solemnly declaring that Nicaragua was "beyond the pale of civilization" and dispatched a military expedition to chastise him.[2]

Zelaya left the country and ultimately died penniless in New York, but some of his anti-American coterie of Nicaraguan nationalists held on. And when the American government finally got a pro-American Nicaraguan in power in Nicaragua, a few of them decided to put up a fight against American intrusion. One of their leaders, now considered a great Nicaraguan nationalist, was General Benjamín Zeledón.

But General Zeledón had not counted on the resolve of the American government to avenge the deaths of Lee Roy and Leonard. When Zeledón threatened "our man in Managua" the American government promptly dispatched a landing force into Corinto, then and now Nicaragua's major Pacific port, that began a conquering campaign along the rail line from the coast down through the major towns of the country all the way to Granada on Lake Nicaragua.

The conquerors were America's imperial campaigners, Marine Corps officers Joseph P. Pendleton and Smedley Butler. Neither was an emissary of American capitalism. Pendleton, affectionately called "Uncle Joe" by the Marines who served under him, was in fact something of a fellow traveler, a disciple of Henry George, the famous nineteenth-century American socialist who advocated the single tax. Butler, son of a powerful Pennsylvania congressman, was an angular Quaker kid who had joined the Corps in the great war against heathen Spain and gone on to glory in the sack of Peking during the Boxer rebellion of 1900. He often wrote detailed letters describing his campaigns of pillage in remote places to his father, signing each "Thy Loving Son, Smedley."

Butler was America's archetypal imperial warrior. Dispatched to remote Bluefields, Nicaragua, with the Marines' Panama battalion in May 1910, Butler had saved the faltering rebellion against the dictator Zelaya. But he had little regard for the Nicaraguan rebels or the Americans who fought with them, regarding both as the "scum" of the tropics. "But I knew," he said later, "which side my government wanted to win." And in the Nicaraguan campaign of 1912 (despite suffering from a 102-degree fever) he commandeered a train and took it through Zeledón's territory all the way to Granada. In the course of this drive, he encountered the rebel leader. Taken blindfolded to Zeledón's hideout, Butler displayed an unqualified American righteousness about the cure for Central America's troubles. "General," Butler warned the Nicaraguan, "you've got to take your revolution someplace else."[3]

In those days American presumptions about Central Americans were strikingly similar to those of today. They had an unsettling habit of settling political feuds with firearms, of "recounting" ballots that did not validate the cause of those already in power, and of placing social stability and tradition, especially as these were symbolized by the family, ahead of such abstractions as nation or constitution. If there were American doubts about the capability of Central Americans to establish "decent, orderly" governments, there was certainly no ambiguity in American prescription when Central Americans threatened our interests. As Theodore Roosevelt might have said a few years earlier, "When they misbehave, we have an obligation to police them."[4]

Then, the United States had determined that certain political leaders and their followers were unworthy of ruling Nicaragua, even if Nicaragua was *their* country. Then, the American government went far beyond the strategic imperatives it had invoked to keep the European military presence out of the Caribbean, to protect the American southern flank (the country's "weak underbelly"), or to safeguard the sea approaches to the yet uncompleted Panama Canal. More than these, it convinced itself, if few Nicaraguans, that its mission of policing the tropics was a civilizing process the ultimate aim of which was to teach the Nicaraguans "to elect good men."

Since those days Nicaragua has experienced two even bloodier civil wars; the first elicited a massive intervention of five thousand American Marines, leaving as their legacy the Somoza family dictatorship that survived almost half a century; the second, nourished in the opposition to the crass despotism of that family, culminated in the victory over Somoza in our time. Its triumph has unleashed the suppressed Nicaraguan hatred of American meddling, patronizing, and military interference in Nicaraguan affairs.

While much has changed in the American imperial view in the past three-quarters of a century (the demonstrative self-righteousness of Theodore Roosevelt, still attractive as a biographical subject, does not have much appeal to Americans nowadays), there remains an unsettling similarity in the official assessments—in both the United States *and* Nicaragua—of the isthmian crisis of the age of Roosevelt and that of Reagan. Then, and now, each blamed the other for excessive meddling, the United States accusing Nicaragua of disturbing the "tranquillity" of its neighbors, Nicaragua condemning the United States for disturbing isthmian "internal" political affairs. Then, as now, each vowed its goal was isthmian peace, principally by resolution of political grievances among the isthmian nations, yet each attributed the failure to achieve this goal to the interfering policies of the other. And, more ominously, in the isthmian disputes of that earlier time each ultimately sought a military solution. There exists in the present circumstances of the United States–Central American relationship the unsettling prospect that those who direct the course of affairs may repeat that earlier and unfortunate "solution."

For what is happening currently in American policy toward Central America is the seemingly inevitable conclusion of the "worst possible scenario." In Washington it is conventional wisdom to hold that if the Sandinistas persevere in Nicaragua and the rebels triumph in El Salvador, then all Central America, including the model democracy of Costa Rica, will ultimately fall under the sway of Cuban-style governments. In the process, of course, the gruesome conflicts that would accompany these isthmian movements of national liberation would, in domino fashion, flood the United States with Central American refugees and precipitate a second Mexican revolution, and, conceivably, a second Mexican-American war.

Viewed in such ominous terms, it is fairly easy to see why the United States government exhibits a hair-trigger response to the latest anti-American diatribe emanating from Managua's coterie of revolutionaries or nervously assesses the latest battle report from an obscure Salvadoran village. For in the often vitriolic debate about Central America, unlike that over Southeast Asia a generation ago, there persists the troubling uncertainty that if Central America is "lost" to the communists it will mean more than the shift of five or six nations, though relatively small ones, into the Marxist camp. More than that, it is argued, a communist isthmus, in the heart of the Americas, will exercise a disruptive influence on the great landmasses of South and especially North America. Given the precarious state of the Mexican government and the rapid growth of Hispanic peoples in this country, the prospects for this eventuality, though improbable, cannot be considered as too farfetched to warrant ridicule. Put another way, the "domino theory" about the fall of Saigon leading to the collapse of Manila and then imperiling Honolulu proved to be a fallacy; an analogous scenario about the fall of Managua, San Salvador, Tegucigalpa, San José, and Guatemala City leading to the demise of Mexico City and threatening Houston may be an exaggeration but cannot be casually dismissed.

While the "worse possible scenario" described above is unlikely, the prospect of more discord and American military involvement in Central America is not only a probability but indisputably an actuality. And given the likelihood that the Central American situation may worsen, it seems appropriate that the American people, woefully ill-informed about Southeast Asia on the eve of massive American involvement in that Cold War arena, should at least have a guide, a modern Baedeker, to a complex but *understandable* part of what is, in fact, their world, the link between the Americas, Middle America.

Lamentably, the level of public knowledge about Central America appears to be not much more advanced in our day than it was before World War I, when a vigorous United States gloried in the construction of the Panama Canal and American readers had ample reference to Central American geography, society, and especially politics in dozens of newspapers. In 1910 it was generally believed that New Orleans was, in effect, the "capital" of Central America, and accounts of what happened on the isthmus regularly appeared on the front page of American newspapers.

Though in these times Americans focus most intently on Central America only when American lives are sacrificed, as in the brutal murder of three nuns and a Catholic lay volunteer in El Salvador, or when strategic considerations warrant our attention, the isthmian crisis of today poses a far graver threat to our political and social institutions than the instability of seventy-five years ago. For then the dominating American concerns were a secure isthmus that did not threaten American control of the transisthmian canal and an environment where banana entrepreneurs from the United States could carve out their fortunes without the harassment of "native" governments. Today the banana domains are joined by the great multinationals, the Canal is headed for Panamanian control (if still under American guarantee of its "neutrality"), and the great migration is composed of Central Americans on the move—agricultural laborers in El Salvador fleeing to Honduras, Salvadoran political refugees sheltering in midwestern American churches, Nicaraguan rebels plotting in the armed camp of Honduras and in the tolerant climate of Costa Rica. The visible crisis represents the cumulative impact of the Central American human crisis.

Our ability to direct the affairs of Central America is demonstrably more limited than it was seventy-five years ago. In those days the United States could virtually make—or unmake—Central American governments that it considered friendly or hostile. Its warships, merely by their presence off Central America's coast, could intimidate fragile governments a hundred miles away in the isthmian interior. Even the rapidly expanding banana empires of United Fruit, the Vaccaro brothers, or the flamboyant Sam "the Banana Man" Zemurray could, by shifting their financial support from one faction to another, determine the outcome of bitter political struggles within a Central American country. Nowadays, American war vessels still hover off the isthmian coast, and the banana companies still operate, but the political and economic realities of modern Central America, though still noticeably affected by American actions, are not readily manipulated by Washington. "The tail," to quote an old bromide, "is now wagging the dog."

Three-quarters of a century ago Central American politics inspired jocose commentaries in the United States about "Hatfield-McCoy feuds." One proper Anglo-Saxon observer, Henry Stimson, dispatched by President Calvin Coolidge to mediate a bloody Nicaraguan civil war in 1927, suggested that Central Americans might profit by looking on their political animosities in a spirit akin to American sports contests. If the game is lost, there will always be another. Nowadays Central American political contests are waged with abusive rhetoric, the old-line political parties have disintegrated into highly ideological factions, and Washington is virtually a captive of pro-American isthmian political power groups. The stakes are still political power, but the field of contest has been extended beyond Central America's borders. American emissaries in San Salvador castigate the Salvadoran death squads and call for land reform while Salvadoran exiles in Miami, physically secure in the land of the free and the home of the brave, fund their mercenaries and impede the most rudimentary social change. In the protective embrace of American churches scattered across the United States, their intended victims are sheltered, their sanctuary, in many minds, a vindication of Emma Lazarus' words carved on the Statue of Liberty.

In this disturbing way Central America's political life has become internationalized, the political factions linked in one way or another to the interests of the Cold War adversaries. While such a condition evokes the predictable commentary about Central America's not being "able to determine its own destiny without outside interference," it represents the historical reprise of isthmian life even more. The outside world has been interfering in Central American affairs since the early sixteenth century. Indeed, the isthmus was one of the first great real estate squabbles between competing Spanish conquerors. While the Spanish dons settled in the mountain valleys, shielded from the outside, less than two hundred miles away, on the pestilential Caribbean coast English and French buccaneers roamed at will, ravaging coastal towns or, later, establishing scabrous little villages for exploiting the vast timber resources of the Spanish empire. More than its neighbors, Nicaragua was the victim of economic pressures and political adventurers from the outside, notably those from the United States, early in its independent life. Canal promoters swooped down on the country with grandiose plans for charting a passage across the isthmus from the clapboard town of San Juan del Norte up the San Juan River to the lakes that dominate western Nicaragua and from there to the Pacific coast. The Nicaraguan canal never became a reality, but in the 1840s and 1850s, when the country was entering a formative period in its political development, Nicaragua experienced what no other Central American country has had to suffer. Britain and the United States vied for its favor and then, in a classic case of big powers dealing at the expense of a small country, agreed to what was in fact shared dominion over any Central American passageway.

The Nicaraguans and the others who dreamed of isthmian unity now had to stand by as the agents of international enterprise flocked to their shores with treaties and business agreements. Outsiders, British and American mostly, including the shipping tycoon Cornelius Vanderbilt, profited from these ventures. In a few years Vanderbilt turned the Nicaraguan route to the California goldfields into a highly profitable business. At the treacherous sandbars along the mouth of the San Juan River, steamers from New Orleans and Mobile deposited American gentlemen and their ladies. Husky black immigrants from the West Indies waded out in the surf to carry them and their belongings to shore for transfer to one of Vanderbilt's river vessels that plied the San Juan.

When the Panama railroad was completed in 1855, the Nicaragua route began to lose out, but the country, now highly publicized back in the United States as a place where aspiring southern gentlemen might make their mark, suffered yet another invasion. A Nicaraguan Liberal politician, in a standoff with his Conservative enemies, decided to import American gunmen to help out. The Americans who came lured others, among them an effeminate

Tennessean who had migrated to the California goldfields, William Walker. In California Walker had organized an expedition against the Mexican state of Sonora. When that failed, he and his immortals, as they liked to call themselves, headed for Nicaragua. For two years Walker ravaged the country, betraying his Nicaraguan ally and recruiting even larger numbers from the United States with promises of a southern tropical empire.

For a brief moment in its tormented, divisive history, Central America was united. Led by the Costa Ricans, who did not then exhibit their peculiar lofty detachment from their neighbors, Central Americans succeeded in driving Walker and his "invading infidels," as the Central Americans often referred to such invaders, from the isthmus.

But Walker had exacted a heavy toll. In one campaign he burned the old city of Granada and left a marker reading "Here Was Granada" as his only monument. He returned to the United States to enjoy the status of celebrity, appearing at the Metropolitan Opera in New York, gesturing to the ladies below. In 1860 he organized his third and last invasion, landing on the north Honduran coast. The Hondurans provided a stiffer resistance than he had anticipated, and Walker decided to surrender to a patrolling British warship. Its captain, thoroughly aware of the Central Americans' desire for vengeance, turned him over to a Honduran firing squad.

Walker passed into legend in the American south as a noble adventurer who had tried to "civilize" the tropics. But in Central America and especially in Nicaragua, the Walker episode left a deep mark on the Central American psyche. It was the result of fear of the outsider and his disruptive ways on isthmian life *and* a historical lesson—that the Central American republics, so very different, can unite against the invader, whatever his cause.

Americans of that age misinterpreted the war against Walker as a repudiation of political principles and institutions Americans cherished.[5] On the contrary, the first leaders of Central America in the 1820s and 1830s consciously emulated the federal system of the United States. And, like the founding fathers of the American constitution a generation before, they proclaimed their bold new political experiment and invited the "industrious foreigner," as the great Central American unionist Francisco Morazán declared in 1830, to share in its growth. The rambunctious republic to the north found—through expansion and bitter disunity—its nationhood on the battlefield. Central America's grand design began to disintegrate in the 1830s, and the isthmian wars that have raged off and on ever since, including those of our time, have in some way been linked to this frustrated, deep yearning for isthmian nationhood. The war between the states ended in this country in 1865; in Central America it is still going on.

A casual glance at Central America in these times only vaguely suggests that its troubles stem from this failure to achieve nationhood. More apparently, the origin of its agonies would appear to emanate from more easily recognizable problems—the glaring disparity between haves and have-nots and between city and country, the procession of bickering political leaders more interested in self-aggrandizement than in the needs of the nation, fears among the propertied that Marxism, introduced in Nicaragua and prophesied for El Salvador, is the fate of the isthmus, and the transformation of Central America into the next battleground of the Cold War.

All these and more are symptoms of the Central American condition, yet collectively they fail to add up to a persuasive explanation of Central America's malaise. If the lot of country people in Honduras or El Salvador could somehow improve dramatically, the enormous shift of income from the cities required for the task would inevitably turn their citizens into the new discontented or perhaps even urban guerrillas. If a handful of "good men," as Woodrow Wilson's generation believed possible, assumed power in the isthmian capitals, the authoritarian military structures, on which most of the states rely, would remain, assuring the fragility of civilian rule. A socialist Nicaragua, a possibility as long as the Sandinistas remain in power in that country, may represent less a threat to private property in Honduras than to the way of life in Costa Rica. But the Costa Ricans, who abetted the Sandinista cause in 1979, have managed to help create this threat for themselves. And if the Nicaraguans draw even closer to the Cubans or the Soviets, a corresponding move by the United States toward propping up the Hondurans will not necessarily make for *long-run* stability in the region. It will only signal yet another American response triggered by fear or apprehension, just as Zelaya's "pricking the American plume" three generations ago so infuriated a pompous American secretary of state that he called on the American military to retaliate.

The most deficient aspect of all the reams of analysis now disgorged from the presses on the Central American situation is that isthmian problems are of relatively recent origin. Some, like the guerrilla movement in El Salvador, give the deceptive appearance of immediacy. If that were so, then such problems *might* be curable with something on the order of the Caribbean Basin Initiative or the recommendations of the Kissinger Commission or, more forthrightly, by a dramatic American military or diplomatic initiative.

But what outside analysts define as a Central American "problem" with an obvious "solution"—such as having "honest elections" which place "good men" in charge of the affairs of state—is often for Central Americans something that seems quite natural or logical. To replace or alter their political or social values with an American prescription means far more than giving advice or giving money with strings attached. Such policies mean asking the Central American countries and societies to be something different, and for Central Americans that often creates even more difficulties than they're contending with now. Actually, Central Americans have been debating their problems, *as they define them,* for five centuries.

The United States, sensing a threat to its own security from the Sandinista triumph in Nicaragua and the rebellious left in El Salvador, has responded to this modern turbulence in Central America with policies that combine historic American concern with military might. The result, as in past isthmian troubles that have precipitated American action, is a growing conviction within the American government that if we can no longer direct the course of history in this region, the United States at least can prevent leftist domination there.

The truth of the matter, as this book attempts to establish, is that the isthmian convulsions of our times do not represent so much a clash of American power with Marxist forces as a modern manifestation of Central America's striving for nationhood.

That goal, unrealized for one hundred and forty years, is nonetheless an inevitability. Whether or not the United States stands ultimately with isthmian nationhood, as its traditions and interests dictate, remains a deeply disturbing uncertainty.

2 "They May Be SOBs, but They're Our SOBs"

I N HIS BRILLIANTLY SATIRICAL NOVEL *CABBAGES AND Kings,* William Sydney Porter (O. Henry), observing turn-of-the-century Central American politics from his hideaway at Puerto Cortés, Honduras, described a mythical land in which revolutions occurred off and on in the capital without disturbing the tranquillity of the countryside. The reason was not so much that the people did not participate or didn't care but that they simply did not get word about the latest shenanigans of the republic's political contestants, usually a high-minded civilian with persuasive oratory but without a reliable army versus a tight-lipped and scheming general backed up by shabbily clad but steadfastly loyal soldiers.

A president might survive an election or manipulate the national assembly or both, at least for a few years. But more often he would dispense too many favors to too few friends or antagonize the "foreign community," which generally conducted its lumbering or mining or, in Porter's day, its banana operations on the isolated coast. Confronted with a hefty tariff or squeezed for a "loan," the oppressed entrepreneurs, incensed over paying duties on everything from creosoted ties for their bastard-gauge railroads to ice to cool their drinks in the murderous tropical heat, would search for a "native" champion to fight for their cause. Usually their selection

17

would be a disgruntled governor of some isolated province or a troublemaking general from the capital who had been exiled to the boondocks, someone who had good connections to the banana barons and who knew his way around the Vieux Carré of New Orleans. Liberally financed by his foreign friends in the tropics, the revolutionary pretender could find in the Crescent City guns and mercenaries, capable artillerymen and especially machine gunners, men who had not yet settled down to steady work.

For the American entrepreneur bankrolling this revolution, the guiding principle was not "no taxation without representation" but simply "no taxation." For the disgruntled revolutionary chieftain, the reward was political power. For the American mercenary manning a Maxim gun in some ramshackle village like Rama or Namasigüe or La Ceiba it was a chance for some permissible looting or, as an incensed New Orleans journalist wrote in 1911, to engage in the business of "revoluting."

He was referring to one of the numerous Central American revolutions—this one in Honduras—of the era before the American government launched its military occupations to put an unromantic end to these doings and the isthmus came under the sway of modern armies directed by crass dictators capable of crushing resistance anywhere in their domain. In late 1910, four men—two American soldiers of fortune, Lee Christmas and Guy "Machine gun" Molony, and two Hondurans, one a swarthy mulatto named General Manuel Bonilla—plotted the invasion of Honduras in a New Orleans bordello, Madam May Evans' place in Storyville, a section of the French Quarter where New Orleans aldermen had decreed prostitution would be tolerated. As U.S. federal agents alerted to their plan waited outside, they caroused well into the night, and when the government men finally got tired and left, Christmas roared to the burly Bonilla, "Well, general, this is the first time anybody's gone from a whorehouse to the White House. Let's go!" They raced to a Lake Pontchartrain wharf, where a gasoline launch awaited them, sped through the Rigolets connecting the lake to the Gulf of Mexico, and at a tiny island off Pass Christian, Mississippi, rendezvoused with their invasion ship, a converted yacht, the *Hornet*, and their benefactor, the banana entrepreneur Samuel Zemurray.[1]

Christmas was already a legendary figure in Honduras, where he had once been director of police and a *general de brigada* in the national army. Bonilla, president of the republic from 1903 until 1907, had been rudely kicked out by another Honduran general and had found sanctuary on an American warship and, later, in British Honduras. Molony at age sixteen had run away to the Boer War and later joined the American expeditionary force that crushed the Filipino rebellion. Before this latest fracas he worked on the New Orleans dock for two dollars a day.

But the financier of this conspiratorial group was the most mysterious. Zemurray had arrived in the United States a penniless immigrant from Bessarabia, anglicized his name, and settled in Mobile. He began buying overripe bananas from United Fruit Company and shipping them upcountry to small Alabama towns. In the trade he acquired the nickname "the Banana Man," and before long, with some financial assistance from United, he started a steamship company, the Hubbard-Zemurray Line, to transport fruit from the isthmian coast to the Gulf ports. Five years later, in 1910, he broke with United, whose stuffy Boston director called him a "man of speculative ideas," and started his own banana business, Cuyamel.

The problem was that Zemurray was launching Cuyamel just as the American government, determined to assert "proper" financial supervision over the Central American republics, was enthusiastically touting "dollar diplomacy." That meant, as Manuel Bonilla knew, stricter (read "honest") supervision of Honduran customs collection. For Zemurray, faced with the task of competing with United, it meant paying a cent a pound for *everything* he imported for Cuyamel's operation.

So he bankrolled Bonilla's invasion, even giving his coat to his Honduran confederate, who was shivering in the December Gulf air. He explained, "I've shot the whole wad on you, I might as well shoot the coat too."[2] In the madcap affair the invaders lost the

Hornet to a patrolling U.S. naval vessel but triumphed when Christmas and Molony and their curious band of bedraggled Honduran soldiers and American tropical tramps took La Ceiba in a glorious battle on January 25, 1911. To the onlooking American and British naval officers, steeped in the traditions of policing the sea lanes and protecting their citizens in fetid tropical posts, La Ceiba figured no more importantly in history than, say, the gunfight at the OK Corral in Tombstone, Arizona. But the victory reinstated Bonilla and his *norteamericano* allies in power in Honduras.

Moreover, the battle marked the start of profitable years for the Banana Man. Zemurray transformed his little enterprise into a worthy rival to powerful United and in the late 1920s forced the Boston-based company into a showdown. UFCo bought Zemurray's company, paying him off in United stock. Anticipating such a move, Zemurray had been buying United shares over several years. The Banana Man walked away from the transaction with the stuffy New England accountants holding a controlling interest in the biggest banana enterprise in history. For a year or so he ransacked the bloated UFCo bureaucracy, then retired to a magnificent estate outside Hammond, Louisiana, with $30 million of United Fruit shares. That was in 1930. Two years later the relentless plunge of the stock market destroyed 90 percent of his fortune. Zemurray blamed everything on United's administrative stupidities. He stormed into the sedate Boston office of the company, threw his shares on the table, and yelled to the startled directors: "You've been [fucking] up this business long enough. I'm going to straighten it out."[3]

When the Banana Man returned to the north Honduran coast in the mid-1930s, Central America had already fallen under the sway of the "strong men"—Tiburcio Carías Andino in Honduras, Jorge Ubico in Guatemala, Maximiliano Hernández Martínez in El Salvador, and the most blatantly oppressive of all, Anastasio Somoza García in Nicaragua. Only Costa Rica escaped the caesarism that prevailed throughout the isthmus.

The tyranny of the Somozas was laid squarely at the doorstep of the United States. The other tropical tyrants, quite frankly, had seemingly acquired their power without direct Yankee influence, though Carías Andino had managed to crush a rebellion in the early thirties with some timely assistance from Machine Gun Molony, who had returned to Honduras after a stint as police chief in New Orleans a decade before. Ubico owed little to Washington in his seizure of power, and Martínez in neighboring El Salvador had actually defied the American government's "rules of behavior" for isthmian revolutionaries after he took over in El Salvador.

But Nicaragua and its ruling dynasty offered observers (and critics) an example of the dangers and effects of American intervention. In the twenty-five years between Sam Zemurray's investment in some Honduran "revoluting" and his return to the isthmian banana domains of UFCo, the United States twice massively intervened in Nicaragua, in 1912 and again in late 1926, to crush a rebellion that defied its political solution.

The leader of this rebellion, Augusto C. Sandino, reigns as the patron saint of the present Nicaraguan government, and the struggle the Sandinistas waged against the Somoza dynasty in the 1970s is in their minds directly linked to Augusto César Sandino's war against the Yankee invaders more than a half-century ago. They blame the machinations of American imperialism for the forty-year tyranny of the Somozas. Americans of this generation may not feel guilty about what their grandparents wrought in Nicaragua, but the Sandinistas are less forgiving. To them, the heightened American military presence in Central America is a replay of the last episodes of American imperialism of another age.

Americans of that era associated isthmian politics with endless disorder, frequent revolutions, and, most damningly, an incapacity to provide community well-being, in other words, "law and order." They viewed Central America's republics not as exotic and diminutive models of their own country but as somehow similar to American communities that had not yet achieved orderliness in their political affairs. When the Americans had their Marines chasing Sandino's army in the bush in the late 1920s, they were rapidly wearying of policing the tropics. They did not trust the old families that had ruled Central America for decades, yet they really feared what Sandino represented, a curious blend of romantic, revolutionary, and anti-imperialist impulses.

Trying to comprehend Central America's familial political parties was still a confusing matter for American observers. A century before, the Liberals had been the champions of economic "modernism," which meant emulating the English and American models of capitalism and promoting isthmian unity. The Conservative parties represented more a social club that cherished the Hispanic tradition and resisted the alien doctrines of the Anglo-Saxon world. At midcentury, however, the Liberals miscalculated, allying their fortunes in a bitter Nicaraguan civil war with Yankee adventurers like William Walker. The result was that for two generations the Liberals had to stand aside while Conservatives laid claim as the standardbearers of patriotism. When Zelaya came along late in the nineteenth century, he tried (and for several years succeeded) to unite isthmian Liberalism with anti-foreignism, especially anti-Americanism. Zelaya's Conservative enemies in Nicaragua now looked more favorably to American entrepreneurs and, when necessary, American troops to restore them.

The elder Somoza, though linked by marriage to one of the country's prominent social families, was a Liberal, and in an earlier day might have been expected to oppose American meddling in his country. But Somoza wanted power, and he quickly realized that Americans wanted to get their own troops out of Nicaragua if only they could find somebody reliable to run the country. Under Somoza, the American-created national guard, it was persuasively argued, would provide Nicaragua with an orderly society where private property was respected, elections conducted, and political violence ceased. What happened, of course, was that the national guard very soon became *Somoza's* police, and one of his first official acts as its head was political: the arrest and execution of Sandino, a deed carried out if not with American participation at least with American acquiescence.

By the end of the decade, with "Tacho" Somoza safely installed in the presidential office, the United States appeared inextricably tied to the Somozas. But, as Franklin D. Roosevelt commented when a curious aide inquired about his government's cozy association with Caribbean tyrants, including Tacho Somoza: "They may be SOBs, but they're *our* SOBs."[4]

FDR's sardonic comment, applicable as much to the Democratic machine bosses of the thirties as to the Caribbean tyrants of the same era, illustrated a deeper problem about Washington's unsavory links to the Caribbean despots. For Roosevelt's generation they offered an alternative to an exasperating role of dispatching Marines to police small countries that Americans believed were incapable of policing themselves. And, in a curiously perverse way, the rise of the Caribbean tyrants—Fulgencio Batista in Cuba, Rafael Trujillo in the Dominican Republic, and the Somozas and the other strong men of Central America—symbolized the triumph of *nonintervention*. More explicitly, the success of the Caribbean despots represented more than ample evidence that the smaller Central American and Caribbean republics were poor examples for democratic experiments. The Somozas, in this sense, stood for the failure, not the success, of American empire. As a Haitian informed a Marine officer in 1934 when nineteen years of American tutelage was ending: "You have accomplished much here, but this is our country and we had rather run it ourselves."[5]

Franklin Roosevelt tolerated the corrupt city bosses and racist demagogues in this country because they turned out a solidly Democratic vote and, even through corrupt practices, helped people on the bottom. The Central American tyrants, certainly the Somozas, helped only themselves and their hireling armies. Tacho Somoza transformed the national guard of Nicaragua into a virtually private army to sustain his own family. He made a country the size of Iowa over into a family business, and when the Sandinistas finally drove his son, "Tacho II," from power in 1979 they confiscated the family holdings and thus inherited almost 50 percent of the productive enterprises of the country. With his fall ended the "second" American empire in the tropics. And for its long association with Somoza and his fellow Caribbean tyrants the United States must assume some blame and bear some guilt.

But, regrettably, modern American policy toward Central America betrays a view of affairs not much more advanced than that of a half-century ago. This version of the proper course for U.S. policy, according to Jeane Kirkpatrick, holds that, faced with choosing either authoritarian or totalitarian governments in Central America, we must choose the former. The basic, and apparently decisive, consideration is that authoritarian regimes (like that of the Somozas and, by implication, of the other rightist governments of the isthmus) are corrupt, but their capacity to interfere in the daily *political* life of the individual is effectively limited by their consuming interest in self-perpetuation. In other words, authoritarian governments are too busy pocketing the economic rewards of power to care all that much about their critics—as long as their opponents do not get too close to the national coffers.

By contrast, totalitarian regimes are, according to Ms. Kirkpatrick, composed of ideologically narrow and puritanically severe leaders who busy themselves making sure that everybody is a true believer. With them you get bureaucrats who are uninterested in stuffing their pockets but religiously dedicated to sticking their noses into everybody's business. Neither is a palatable choice, but for the American government the first, however unsavory, is definitely preferable to the second. Fifty years ago, the choice seemed to be intervention, with troops if necessary, and a promise of elections, honestly conducted, with all the attendant expenses and animosities; *or* nonintervention, rejecting the use of troops, with the probability of authoritarian rule.

More than two decades ago, John F. Kennedy realized the excruciating complexity of such an "either-or" approach. In the aftermath of the demise of one of the Caribbean's most tyrannical rulers, Rafael Trujillo in the Dominican Republic, Kennedy told an aide: "We have three choices in descending order of acceptability—a decent democratic regime, another dictatorship, a communist government. We should strive for the first but we can't reject the second until we're sure we can prevent the third."[6]

Fundamental to Kennedy's maxim, then, was the belief that "decent democratic regimes," if not immediately attainable, should nonetheless be the goal of American policy in the Caribbean. The passing of twenty-five years and the retrenchment of American power have diluted his prescription for our priorities from three to two priorities, authoritarian governments over totalitarian regimes.

Two errors emanate from such thinking.[7] The first is the omission of "decent democratic societies" from the American scale of priorities for the kinds of governments we would *prefer* to deal with in Central America. Such regimes are not only achievable in the isthmus but have existed in Costa Rica for more than thirty years. And these laudable political achievements came about without massive American aid or military alliances. While Costa Rica enjoys certain democratic traditions not so readily apparent among its neighbors and is presently experiencing the economic pains attendant on running a modern welfare state, the *ticos*, as Costa Ricans call themselves, offer a symbol preferable to the American government's authoritarian allies in Guatemala, Honduras, and El Salvador.

Second, the announced preference of authoritarian to totalitarian regimes implies a permanency in our commitment to the former. And this also locks us into such an obligation at a time when strong-man authoritarian, "personalist" rule is going out of fashion; it has been in trouble in Central America since 1944, when Ubico in Guatemala and Hernández in El Salvador perished before reformist movements. Carías in Honduras fell a few years later. When Somoza died two decades later, his brand of authoritarianism was obsolete.

Current American policy toward Central America is apparently based on the belief that the rightist elements, to which we have become more attached, are, because of a shared animosity to the Central American left, amenable to *our* prescription for political survival. Rather than lose power, we believe, they will share it with their critics. Confronted with the demands for economic reform, they will spread the wealth more equitably rather than relinquish power to the left. In other words, they will run their country the way Mayor Daley ran Chicago.

The scientific model of the kind of regimes now emerging in Guatemala, Honduras, and El Salvador is not the personalist style but bureaucratic authoritarianism. It is not characterized by one-man rule but by brutish machine politics dedicated to self-preservation, the service of *its* constituency, and the harassment (and if deemed necessary, the extermination) of *its* enemies. Unlike the personalist style of the old Caribbean tyrants, whose corruption and inefficiency arguably permitted a semblance of political liberty, these modern authoritarians have mobilized the resources of the state to penetrate the remotest villages and impose their new order. They will politely listen to American sermons about "death squads" in El Salvador and unseemly "antiterrorist" campaigns in Guatemala, but they are no more convinced of the wisdom of American advice on how to run a government than were the fascist bureaucrats of Mussolini's Italy or Hitler's Germany a half-century ago.

The modern military chieftains of Central America obligingly dispatch their junior officers to the United States for antiguerrilla training and sullenly tolerate American lectures about the primacy of civilian rule. They do so because in their own struggle for survival they must placate, if only by some gesture of deference to the concept of civilian rule, their American benefactors. But they long ago learned American priorities, that the American government quite frankly prefers them in power to the Salvadoran left or the Sandinistas. They know that *their* war against *their* enemies must be continued pretty much with the methodical thoroughness they have demonstrated throughout the past half-dozen years in El Salvador and, in a less publicized way, for almost thirty years in Guatemala. They know Americans will get more upset over the deaths of four *American* churchwomen than over those of tens of thousands of nameless illiterate peasants or a score of petty political reformers.

Who can blame them for adopting such a murderous strategy? If El Salvador falls to the left, the United States will have to rethink its strategic calculations in the region, but hundreds of highly placed officers in the regular army and the various paramilitary units that proliferate will not suffer simply demotion or retirement to a coffee finca. They will, if they stick around for the new order to settle old accounts, quite probably get a punishment similar to the sort their minions have been meting out to the left for a generation. In the

Salvadoran left's repository of postvictory acts of justice, the military must atone not only for its more recent indignities but also for its slaughtering of leftist labor organizers and peasants in the bloody crushing of the *matanza* ("massacre") revolt in 1932.

Nor is there much prospect for a "populist" military course in Central America similar to the one that prevailed in Peru after the generals seized power in 1968. There are reformist elements among Central America's military cadres, certainly, but the traditions of their politics do not readily accommodate leftist solutions. Central America's military chieftains have grown accustomed to running the affairs of state, and the rising officer class, though more professional than, say, that of twenty or thirty years ago, remains very impressionable. The ultimate perquisite of rank in these armies is the satisfaction of knowing that the higher you rise the larger your political shadow. At the pinnacle you and your fellow generals can not only run the military, you can run the state. American-style military judgments about deferring to civilian authority or accommodating your leftist critics are not likely to get you there.

Yet there remains embedded in the American military psyche the notion that an intensive course in counterinsurgency tactics or military-civilian relations at Fort Benning will work wonders in the Central American military establishment. After all, twenty-five years ago Latin American junior officers were going through the presumably rigorous training in counterinsurgency in the Panama Canal Zone and then returning to their respective countries and chastising the guerrillas. Their most notable success came in Bolivia with the elimination of Ernesto "Che" Guevara. In Guatemala a few years later the ruling establishment, determined to make its point about its authority in the countryside, unleashed a counterinsurgency program that is still going on. El Salvador's dispatch of officers to the United States in the past few years is merely the latest episode in perpetuating the myth that American tutelage will somehow encourage a more enlightened view of the proper political role for Central America's colonels, namely, that they will see the wisdom of allowing the civilians to run things and confine themselves to suppressing insurrection and supporting constitutionally elected authority.

Three-quarters of a century ago, Central American armies were made up of illiterate banana workers or coffee laborers commandeered by some general to make war against a rival or provide his *presidente* with the shock troops for invading a neighboring country. There were no volunteers, despite the backbreaking work of agricultural labor in those days. Of course, country boys were always "volunteering" for service in this or that war. An astonished American consul watched them troop into dusty Managua in the days of the dictator Zelaya, who spent an inordinate amount of the national treasury making war on his neighbors. A general had dispatched a recruiting squad onto a banana plantation and seized forty men. Their hands were tied and then each was lashed with rope to the man trailing. With their commander the obliging general sent a curt message to the president: "I send you forty volunteers. Please return the ropes."

The American observing this depressing sight was understandably shocked; he made the astute observation that armies relying on forced recruiting are rarely composed of the most committed. Central America's military establishment has come a long way since those days, admittedly, but the generals still get their volunteers by scarcely more enlightened methods. In Honduras, whose twentieth-century armies have acquired a lamentably embarrassing record in warfare, recruiting gangs pull up outside theaters in late afternoon just in time to snatch bleary-eyed teenage boys emerging from matinees. And in Guatemala, whose commanders have considered themselves at war in the countryside for the past thirty years, the regular military has established the "Popular Forces" in highland villages to advance into guerrilla terrain ahead of its soldiers. A Guatemalan teenager who refuses to "volunteer" for this hazardous assignment is presumed to be a guerrilla.

The harsh reality of Central American society is its militarism. Americans long accustomed to expressing their admiration for the military by erecting statues to war heroes or welcoming their armies back home from a foreign war are thoroughly convinced the generals are not running the affairs of state. The United States is an antimilitaristic, not an antimilitary, country. The distinction is crucial. In Central America, save for Costa Rica, which abolished its army after the civil war of 1948, the military continually intrudes in civilian affairs, into each of the traditional structures of government—executive, legislative, and judicial—from the presidential palace, national assembly, and supreme court all the way down to the mayor of a one-street village. Indeed, the ubiquity of uniformed men in civilian business is such that it is the civilian and not the soldier who constitutes the appurtenance. There may very well be a civilian wearing the presidential sash, but he is ordinarily a showcase leader of limited power who very well understands that when the soldier speaks he must listen.

This is not to say that the military in Central America is a monolithic entity top-heavy with right-wing senior officers who never disagree on anything save the relative severity of the next campaign against the enemies of the state. On the contrary, some of the most spirited political debates have occurred within the officer corps, and defections from the military have occasionally supplied the armed left with its leadership. Guatemala's first major insurgency after the 1954 coup came from a group of officers frustrated by their failure to overturn the corrupt Manuel Ydígoras in 1960. When the generals finally tossed him out in 1963, the officers-turned-guerrillas had stayed so long in the bush they couldn't return to the fold, even when a civilian reformist president tried to woo them back with an amnesty several years later.

These episodes of internal squabbling and debate within the Central American military almost always turn on such questions as how great is the corruption in the military government and who must be purged to clean house or whether or not to turn soldiers accused of misdeeds against civilians (as in the case of the murder of the four Americans in El Salvador) over to civilian courts for trial and punishment. The inescapable outcome of these debates and related incidents has been the willingness of Central America's officer corps to accommodate critics up to a point, to put on a more respectable face by cashiering a few brutes from the ranks or sending a colonel with a knack for alienating the American embassy into "exile" as the consul in Madrid, or, if he is particularly notorious, to Upper Volta. Just as clear is the determination of the generals to draw the line when the question involves their putative *right* to interfere in affairs of state. As one prominent Guatemalan said when outsiders condemned his government's especially severe campaign against "leftist agitators": "If we want to kill each other off, it's our business. The United States has no right to interfere."[8] When Jimmy Carter, in a much-publicized criticism of the human-rights record of Guatemala's successive military regimes, tried to straighten them out with threats of withholding military assistance, the Guatemalan generals broke the country's military pact with the Americans and started buying their guns elsewhere.

Central America's military cadres do not believe their role is to serve the state; they believe they are the state. Their ultimate duty is the defense of the institution of the military and those identifiable interests the state is committed to protect; they feel much less obliged to defend constitution or nation. It's not a question of indifference to political ideals but essentially a matter of traditional priorities not all that dissimilar to those of John F. Kennedy.

And they are more than befuddled at our disapproval of the severity of their methods in the political arena after years of lecturing them about the need for "stability" in their politics. But politics dictates different rules for Central Americans than for us. After all, for Americans "politics" is business and rather profitable business at that, but the rules assure that when you lose there will be another contest. For Central Americans—even the amiable Costa Ricans—politics means personal confrontation, and if you lose there may be no second chance—probably not if you're tortured or exiled and certainly not if you lose your life. No Central American would have completely understood what FDR really meant when, referring to a squabble with the Republican opposition, he said, "I love a good fight." Not knowing his sometimes jocular way of commenting on rough-and-tumble politics, they might have believed he was talking about a shootout with the leader of the opposition.

They may be SOBs, but they *aren't* ours.

3 "You Can't Shoot Him, He's My Brother-in-Law"

I N THE 1920s, MANAGUA, NICARAGUA, HAD THE reputation among diplomats and soldiers as a backwater in America's informal empire, lacking the charm of San José or the power of Guatemala City before the 1918 earthquake. The American legation, an unimposing stucco edifice, stood on one of the town's dusty thoroughfares. The legation's main office was illuminated by a single bulb dangling from a wire. Outside, a guard of one hundred Marines symbolized the American presence in the country, a legacy from the 1912 military intervention aimed at putting an end to what American observers considered a Nicaraguan tragedy—the seemingly perpetual warring among the country's familial party factions.

In the dozen or so years since then Nicaragua's politicians had readily accommodated American prescriptions for "proper" political behavior. The old family animosities between Liberal and Conservative, between the "Reds" and the "Blues," rooted in the colonial antagonism between the cities of León and Granada, had apparently dissolved before the overriding issue of the country's relationship to the United States—as Nicaraguans put it, "the American Question." In the 1850s, the Liberals opened Nicaragua to Yankee adventurers and suffered the consequences for a generation, during which time they were regarded as foreign stooges. Yet at the end of the century, under the recklessly defiant rule of the

Liberal Zelaya, who vilified the big powers, Nicaragua atoned for the Liberals' earlier error. According to legend, Zelaya once stunned a Peruvian diplomat who threatened to protest his expulsion from Nicaragua: "Appeal by all means! When I ridicule the United States, laugh at Germany, and spit on England, what do you suppose I care for your beggarly little Peru?"[1]

Vowing to atone for the old Liberal guilt about selling out Nicaragua to the foreigners, Zelaya built his own antiforeign political family in Central America. In 1895, after less than two years in power, he fashioned a solidarity pact with the presidents of El Salvador and Honduras, the purpose of which was to revive the old Central American confederation. Naturally, it would be under Nicaraguan domination. This meant Zelaya had to implant his own brand of unity inside the country. His rule became increasingly more arbitrary and capricious. The government began intruding deeper into the businesses of the old commercial elements, traditionally Liberal in their politics. When the treasury still ran low, Zelaya authorized new taxes, especially resented by those on the eastern coast, where his harassed Conservative enemies had fled seeking refuge in the protective embrace of the banana companies. Even there the Conservatives felt the scourge of their persecutor in Managua. Zelaya would virtually order them to the capital with an invitation to one of his infamous "Borgia dinners." At the end of an elegant meal the president would request a "contribution to the cause of national unity." Refusal meant exile.

The banana companies on the coast sensed, with good reason, a kindred spirit among the frustrated Conservative families of Nicaragua. And, exploiting the bitterness against Zelaya and his crowd that welled up among them, in 1910 the American government clearly indicated which side it approved.

Of all the old Conservative families the Chamorros were probably the most conspicuous enemies of the Zelaya regime. In the American intervention of 1912 the family threw in with the Yankee invaders and in the aftermath profited politically in an arrangement their fathers would have thought ignoble if not treasonous. Emiliano Chamorro, known as the General, fought along-side the Americans in the military campaign to squash his Nicaraguan enemies. When his ally Smedley Butler stood in the square of Granada, the old Conservative citadel, and received a medal from the "ladies of Granada" for saving *their* way of life, Chamorro and the rest of his Conservative family must have had few doubts about where Washington's priorities lay. Naturally, the United States must be committed to *his* Nicaragua.

In the aftermath of the intervention, the General's star zoomed even higher. He became Nicaragua's emissary to Washington, where he signed a treaty with the American secretary of state, William Jennings Bryan, granting the United States the right to construct an isthmian canal across the country. (The United States retained the right of canal construction until the early 1970s.) Two years later he returned to Nicaragua aboard an American warship, an unspoken signal to his enemies that he was the choice of the United States to be Nicaragua's leader. Barred from a consecutive term by the constitution, he nonetheless maneuvered his uncle, Don Diego, into the national palace.

Events seemed to point toward a great Chamorro dynasty when, in October 1923, as Emiliano was sailing home from a conference in Washington, his uncle suddenly collapsed and died. The opposition Liberals, sensing opportunity, began maneuvering, their cause bolstered by an unambiguous American declaration that the United States intended to withdraw the Marine guard from the country. Señor Bartolomé Martínez, from another of the country's ruling dynasties, had, as vice-president, succeeded to the presidency. He was a staunch Conservative determined to keep on running Nicaraguan affairs. Pressed by overbearing Anglo-Saxon observers of Nicaragua's familial political system, Martínez acquiesced in an American-crafted electoral law and a proposal for the setting up of a national constabulary. The United States, which had established a similar institution in its eight-year military rule in the Dominican Republic, had lofty ambitions for the success of a similar institution in Nicaragua. Martínez rather graciously demurred on the ticklish question of American supervision of the upcoming election.

Sounding out the American embassy, Martínez soon became

convinced he could not be elected in 1924, and he decided that Emiliano Chamorro was not going to be elected either. He fashioned a coalition between his Conservatives and the León Liberals, the Conservative-Republicans, as the makeshift alliance was known, which nominated a retired capitalist, Carlos Solórzano, an affable Conservative more than willing to spend his own money to get elected, for president, and Dr. Juan Sacasa, a Columbia-educated physician and prominent Liberal, for vice-president. Chamorro pleaded for American supervision but was politely informed that the United States saw no reason to interfere in Nicaragua's "internal" affairs. Martínez ran the election and made sure Chamorro lost. In Chamorro's home district of Chontales, where the General was almost a cult figure, the president declared martial law and nullified the vote.

Safely and constitutionally installed as Nicaragua's new chief executive, Solórzano proved no match for the schemers who had manipulated his election. His wife had two brothers, General Alfredo Rivas and Colonel Luís Rivas, members of yet another of the country's powerful clans, entrusted with Managuas's military defenses. The congenial but terrified Solórzano anticipated Chamorro would try to avenge the political wrong, which in Nicaraguan politics was the equivalent of a social *faux pas* as well, so he begged the American government to retain its legation guard in the capital. In a sympathetic response the State Department agreed, if Solórzano would move quickly toward organizing a constabulary. The compliant national assembly hastily passed a law authorizing a four-hundred-member Guardia Nacional, and a veteran American officer, Major Calvin Carter of Elgin, Texas, arrived to assume responsibility for training its recruits.

A short time later the Marines boarded a train for Corinto, their departure captured by a newsreel crew filming the waving "grunts" in the car windows. In the enthusiasm of the moment, former president Martínez jumped in front of the whirring camera and flourished a Nicaraguan banner.

As far as the Conservatives were concerned, the last obstacle to their assault on the government's coffers had sailed away. They now turned their attention to the affable but dim-witted Solórzano, who busied himself placating the Liberals with such convincing gestures of atonement that his Conservative friends—*his* family—began turning against him. In the assembly they disrupted his plan for a sorely needed restructuring of the banking system. Even his cabinet members grew hostile.

But the most degrading incident occurred at the International Club, only a few blocks from the national palace, where on a balmy August evening in 1925 Managua's social elite gathered for a sumptuous banquet honoring the minister of instruction. The president and Señora de Solórzano headed the guest list, which included the American minister, the diplomatic corps, and the city's most prominent Liberals. The Solórzanos departed early, but the merriment continued. It was rudely disrupted by a swaggering interloper, Gabry Rivas, a Conservative party dandy, who held a revolver in each hand. In his entourage were shabbily clad but well-armed men who stretched in a line out of the building and into the street. Shouting that he was the representative of General Alfredo Rivas, the intruder proclaimed his mission to liberate the beleaguered *presidente* from the clutches of his Liberal associates. He fired shots into the ceiling, roaring, "Down with the Liberals!" The hubbub caused women to faint and fistfights to erupt. A few sought refuge underneath a massive billiard table, as Rivas roamed the elegant halls looking for prominent Liberals to arrest. The American minister, politely informed he might leave unharmed, declined, and was quickly surrounded by frightened Nicaraguans beseeching his protection. One, Larga Espada, grabbed the minister's coattails as he was dragged away by his captors.

Once their quarry had been escorted outside, the armed men politely allowed the remaining guests to depart. Major Carter dutifully supplied President Solórzano with an extra guard and offered to accompany the harassed Nicaraguan leader for a confrontation with General Rivas. Obviously exasperated by this demonstration that one of Nicaragua's highest-ranking military officers would place his political convictions above his sworn duty to safeguard the republic and its leader, the American offered to shoot Rivas.

"You can't shoot him," Solórzano solemnly responded, "he's my brother-in-law."[2]

Matters of course got worse. Within a year Solórzano found himself maneuvered out of the presidency by the ever-conspiring Chamorro, who gave the frantic Nicaraguan executive a choice— resign the presidential office and take an extended leave outside the country or be declared insane by the Chamorro-dominated assembly. Solórzano took his leave, and Chamorro drove the Liberal vice-president into revolt by cleverly arranging for his own elevation to the national palace. By the tacit rules of Central American politics, the Nicaraguan presidency was, after all, rightfully his, but the American government, particularly the flinty Calvin Coolidge, would have none of these shenanigans. The powerful moral disapprobation of the State Department's Latin American division, backed up by patrolling U.S. Navy gunboats, imposed a new government in Managua.

The dutiful Major Carter stayed long enough in Central America to acquire an education in isthmian politics, and when he finally returned to the United States, as his countrymen were reading daily of Washington's latest military crusade in the tropics, he described the Nicaraguan conflict that Coolidge seemed intent on settling as a "Hatfield-McCoy feud."[3]

This characterization, which bespeaks a contempt for Central American politics, perhaps unintentionally conveys another truth: isthmian politics cannot be measured by the standards of this society. It is not a matter of inferiority or superiority but of difference, in origin, meaning, and purpose.

American political parties have evolved from the competing factions of property holders into powerful competitive coalitions whose ultimate goal is control of the social-service state. If one counts the federal government, there are fifty-one prizes up for grabs. The crucial consideration is how the bounty will be divided.

Politics in the United States is more than the art of the possible. It is business, and serious business at that.

Central America's political heritage, like that of its concerned northern onlooker, also lies in property, the landed estates of a feudal past where titles are traced not to the Homestead Act or a similar dispensation of public lands but to grants from the King of Spain in the sixteenth century. But Central America has a cultural heritage that counts for much more in political life. The isthmus' first European overlords, born in Spain, were called *peninsulares*, those from the Iberian peninsula. Their children *born in the New World* formed its first post-Columbian aristocracy, the Creoles, also Spanish but with an inherited sense of inferiority toward the *peninsulares* and a lasting feeling of superiority over the *ladinos*, the offspring of Spanish-Indian unions. The *ladinos* have reciprocated by keeping their bootheels on the necks of the descendants of Central America's *first* aristocracy, the Mayas.

And the enormous political and economic power that went with the crown's grants was not seriously challenged by democratic movements or corporate capitalism until after World War II. Throughout the isthmus—even in Costa Rica—the Central American republics at the turn of this century were the domain of extended families, their economic base the landed estate. In Guatemala there was the García Granados clan, in El Salvador the Araujos and Meléndez families. Anastasio Somoza García joined this elite by marrying into one of the country's long-standing prominent families and acquiring extensive holdings in the countryside. The rural plot of several hundred acres (which in diminutive Central America takes on the aura of "estate") remains a major way to obtain membership in the elite for the ambitious military man.

In colonial times the large landowners obtained quite liberal privileges from the Spanish crown to use Indian labor; after independence they prevailed on national governments for the same authority. If defied, they armed their followers and raised the flag of revolt. When foreign concessionaires entered the country, as the banana entrepreneurs did before World War I, they in turn readily adopted the traditional rules of national politics.

Ultimately, of course, there were challenges to the prevailing order. The most frightening occurred in El Salvador, where in 1932 communists organized peasant labor unions on the coffee fincas and launched a revolt. In retaliation the oligarchy visited a gruesome justice upon the conspirators. The Salvadoran military, commanded by the fearsome General Maximiliano Hernández Martínez, swept through the countryside, rounded up leftist suspects, and systematically shot them. When the campaign ended, ten thousand had perished.

Out of this and less sanguinary confrontations in neighboring countries the ruling order learned a lesson in some elementary rules of political survival. The peasants' league that provided the shock troops for the 1932 revolt was a signal that the tradition of master-man relationship (the *patrón* system) was disintegrating. If the oligarchy was going to persevere it would need the protection of the military. In the nineteenth century the officer class had claimed the younger sons of the ruling families, but after World War I an increasing proportion of the senior officer ranks has been composed of men from humbler social stations. In El Salvador, as in several of the other isthmian republics, the ruling families, fearing insurrection or reformist social movements, have looked to the modern military officer as the guardian of their power and influence.

As a reward for its policing role, of course, the Central American military has demanded a price. Its ambitious senior officer cliques have aspired to social status in the old order, and if they cannot be provided with an honored family title they can at least be offered the opportunity to profit from office by a lucrative concession on this or that service so they can acquire the ultimate symbol of political *and* economic *and* social respectability in Central America—the country place, the "estate." When General Martínez ruled El Salvador he provided his officers with separate clubs and institutions, so as to create a kind of elite officer corps similar to that of Nazi Germany or Japan. In such manner new family dynasties are born, and the sons and daughters soon find their niche in the established order via a colonelcy or a well-made marriage with a member of one of the republic's social clans. Predictably this process has meant a certain democratization among the elite. El Salvador's proverbial "fourteen families" have in modern times escalated to 244, more or less.

Yet even here the established families' dominance of national life has only recently begun to diminish. The nineteenth-century Salvadoran planter class, which constituted a kind of baronial aristocracy in its time, has diversified in this century by shifting the family fortune into the agro-export market. In all the republics save perhaps Panama, which Omar Torrijos transformed into a western hemispheric banking center, the export of agricultural products earns the largest proportion of national income. Retailing and manufacturing, which rose significantly in the past several decades, tend to be dominated by *nouveau riche* families, yet among them are persons who can trace their lineage to the old commercial classes in the Central American cities of the Spanish empire.

In Nicaragua the antagonism between these two powerful groups, represented by the family estates of the countryside versus the commercial houses of the cities, became so intense as to provoke fratricidal conflicts. The family animosities provided a major part of the explanation for the division of political party loyalties in the nineteenth century: Conservatives were "country" families; Liberals, urban clans. León, the Spanish administrative capital for Nicaragua, became the symbol of Liberal politics. Granada, a more rustic place, was adopted as the center of Conservative strength. In an effort to compromise by geography, these warring factions located the national capital at Managua, roughly halfway between the two.

Even when an aspirant to high social or political standing has achieved sufficient wealth (through what country barons in the old days termed "crass" endeavors like retailing or commerce), he will readily sink some of the new-made wealth into the land. In Central America, where the amount of arable soil is generally about 10 percent (in El Salvador, it is a munificent 30 percent) of the national domain, the possession of two or three hundred acres commands impressive social attention. A colonel in the armed forces who cannot trace his blood line back to the conquistadores or even to a

nineteenth-century country family will be sorely tempted to aug-
ment his salary with a sufficient amount of graft just to be able to buy
some country property. He is not buying a place in the hills far from
the urban din; he's purchasing his way into the family club that runs
the country. The elder Somoza in Nicaragua (grandnephew of a
notorious outlaw, Bernabé Somoza, hanged in 1849) used his position as head of the national guard and later as president to build a
family dynasty founded ultimately on land acquisitions. After the
elder Somoza died from an assassin's bullet in 1956, his sons
transformed their inherited wealth into a family business that owned
or controlled, it was estimated, 50 percent of the country's agricultural, commercial, and manufacturing wealth.

In Guatemala, the sway of the ruling classes may be less visible
to the outsider than in El Salvador because of the focus of recent
events, but the encrusted power of the elite is just as solidly
attached to the landed oligarchy as well as its modern industrial and
commercial allies. Thomas and Marjorie Melville, in a scathing
indictment of Guatemalan life, have delineated the country's classes into the following categories: upper, 1 percent (of almost eight
million people); middle, 17 percent; and "popular," 82 percent.[4]
What this has meant, among other things, is that the consequential
decisions and actions of national political, social, and economic
affairs are determined by fewer than 100,000 persons. Even the
middle classes, which in Guatemala usually denote a small farmer,
petty bureaucrat, or shopkeeper, exhibit far too little class con-
sciousness to act as a buffer against the power and influence of the
ruling elite. More often than not, the Guatemalan middle-class
representative is either desperately trying to escape from sinking
into the mass of the 82 percent who have virtually no political clout
or scrambling for a passport into the elite, a diploma from the
military academy, or a university degree.

The family political system that still prevails in the Central
American states has, in the past fifty years, been buffeted by the
currents of social change and the disruptive shock of civil war. In
those countries where it is strongest—El Salvador and Guatemala—
it has persevered by incorporating the military into a new order.

When revolutionaries in El Salvador describe politics in their country as "fifty years of military rule" they unintentionally simplify the situation. A more accurate description is a "military guardianship of the prevailing order." The generals who may be running the country are not politically neutral or disinterested soldiers who have seized power, as the military often justifies its takeovers of governments, "to save the nation from chaos." Rather they are more visible associates of the ruling landed and commercial classes. They are the recently admitted members of the family who wear uniforms and dispatch squads of illiterate draftees to guard the coffee fincas or round up the leaders of a peasant cooperative and shoot them. The leaders of the cooperatives or the missionaries and priests who counsel them threaten not only property but the social order as well. To remove them is to protect the family.

The link between the civilian elite and its military guardians is one of mutual dependence, not blood trust. In the 1932 communist uprising in El Salvador the coffee barons called upon General Martínez and his troops to crush the revolt, and the general complied in a thoroughly bloody fashion. But after defending the estates of El Salvador's finest families against the Red peril, Martínez retained the presidential palace as his residence for another dozen years. And for its decisive role in bringing down the reformist Arbenz regime in Guatemala in 1954 (by the expedient of *not* supporting the government in its moment of peril), the Guatemalan military assumed for itself the "obligation" of running the country ever since.

The generals might very well turn control of the affairs of state over to a civilian, even one with reformist notions like José Napoleón Duarte in El Salvador, but the recipient of their largesse knows only too well that if he shifts too abruptly left—by, let us say, calling for negotiations with the rebels in the countryside or more than cosmetic agrarian reform legislation—the gold-braided keepers of the national patrimony will almost certainly step in. Ordinarily the official reason is to "save the country from the communists," but a more apt characterization would be to prevent the state from interfering too much in the national economy, i.e., in family business.

In other words, to keep the civilian bureaucrats from expanding the meager social services of the government by squeezing a few more colones or quetzales or lempiras from the moneyed classes to pay for them.

American observers of Central American life are sometimes befuddled by the ability of the propertied order to get support from those on the bottom. In the 1982 Salvadoran election, for example, rightist candidates for the constituent assembly fared rather well, the most conspicuous among them the ruggedly handsome Roberto d'Aubuisson, reputedly one of those controlling the country's notorious death squads and an outspoken, even threatening, critic of middle-of-the-road Salvadoran politicians who call for negotiations with the rebels. In the Salvadoran presidential elections of 1984 the charismatic d'Aubuisson and his fellow ARENA (National Republican Alliance) candidates, calling for a military solution to the civil war and a dilution of the land reform program, got the votes of the propertied elite. But their votes would not have produced the impressive electoral return ARENA garnered without support from the bottom of the electorate as well.

Liberal critics rightly observe that Central American elections, where voter participation is much higher than in the United States, are rarely conducted "fairly." In the countryside illiterate peasants nervously line up at balloting stations under the suspicious eye of a local army officer and the stern gaze of soldiers who are there to "keep order." The local communist or reformist party organizer has long since been routed from the area, and the watchful army officer is only too attentive to the distinctive markings—a rooster or a fish or other symbol—that differentiate the ballots deposited in a transparent box (necessitated, it is said, to prevent ballot-box stuffing). In the cities, predictably, such casual intimidation is much less obvious but persists.

But the have-nots often sustain the rule of the haves because they feel a need to perpetuate family rule, to vote as their parents or grandparents did. In this way they gain a sense of importance, even a fleeting sense of power, by perpetuating those who *are* in power. It is not that they fail to sense the patent injustice of so few people having so much power or money or land while they have so little. Their family traditions, habits, and beliefs, reinforced by the traditional church doctrine that in the final summing up they will be the equal of their masters on this earth, compel them to sustain the status quo. They are inured against the promises of middle-class reformers. They know if a reformist government promises a new era for them it will have to crack down on the generals with their $200,000 houses in the palatial residential sections of the capital or deprive too many of the sons of the republic's social elite of their Mercedeses. And then there will be *real* trouble for everyone.

The sometimes violent, sometimes benevolent style of the ruling order, despite its patent unfairness and unbreakable determination to perpetuate its rule, reminds those on the bottom who is in charge. In Guatemala he may be the country *patrón* waited on by a dozen or so servile Indians, in Honduras the army colonel with the right connections to afford a Mercedes and a spacious home (with guards) in the suburbs of east Tegucigalpa, in El Salvador the exporter who must drive to work in a bulletproof four-wheel-drive Chevy. In differing ways each represents inherited authority and interests, and when these are at stake, the ruling familial order will denigrate almost any political principle or justify the elimination of virtually anybody threatening that authority. This has been gruesomely illustrated with the succession of midnight arrests, torture, and murders committed by officials in the name of state security but in reality at the behest of higher authority. Even prominent churchmen who condemn this ritual of death are not immune from harm. There is, alas, no exact way to identify the carriers of the virus of disruption.

The state does not try to supplant the values of family solidarity with loftier ideals of nation.[5] This heritage of Central Americans runs as deep as the seventeenth century, when the withering economy of Spain, its empire harassed by its European enemies and its finances controlled by outsiders, compelled Spaniards, from aristocrat on down to petty municipal official, to depend on family and kinship to sustain economic and social rank in the larger society. Even the imperial bureaucracy absorbed its members by tests of familial ties, not dedication to task nor loyalty to nation. The

Spanish empire was not the empire of an abstraction but the domain of the crown. Conquerors and clerics, inspectors and governors, all the way down the line, represented the crown's, the king's, authority, not that of the nation. And the most influential families in Spain had their scions scattered throughout the colonial bureaucracy, the military, or the church. Even in the mercantile realm businessmen and traders looked to the extended family and its reinforcing values rather than unquestioning loyalty to the corporate abstraction of the firm as a more reliable indicator of human worth.

Such traditions of family loyalties easily converted to the Hispanic settlements of the New World and shaped the social character of the Spanish empire in Central America and the first generation of rulers after independence. The social stability of Central America in the nineteenth century depended not on political institutions, which were riddled with controversy and division, but on the solidarity and paternalism of a small number of dominant families. They married their daughters off to second or third cousins and sent their sons to private academies and then on to the professions of law or medicine. This was the preparation for national political life, not the vulgar hubbub of local politics but the reassuring traditions of family. Avoidance of involvement in all but the most exclusive social clubs and marriages, arranged with special attention to family status, ensured that the class system of these extended families perpetuated itself well into the twentieth century.

The family-centered social aristocracy, then, set the model for Central America's nineteenth-century political development. Institutions of governance naturally embedded cherished familial values and loyalties in the bureaucracies of the modern state. Continuity with the past—not the past of abstract political principles but the enduring values of family and comradeship, *compadrazgo*—is thus assured. Even in Costa Rica with its middle-class patina, the legacy of the *first* ruling families has not yet run its course. A sociologist working in San José (the grandson of Sam the Banana Man Zemurray), in an otherwise tedious study of the *tico* elite, has traced the lineage of Costa Rica's social and political aristocracy back through the years, beyond the coffee-growing barons of the nineteenth century, to the conquistadores. He found that the marriage of Juan Vázquez de Coronado, one of the first venturers into the idyllic Meseta Central (the central highlands), and Isabel Arias Dávila, sister of the fierce Panamanian governor, produced a lineage that has included twenty-one presidents and 220 deputies of the republic![6]

Not a few democratically minded Costa Ricans were taken aback by his findings, but they have managed to rationalize matters by pointing out that Costa Rica had no significant Indian minority— and until the late nineteenth century by law and into the twentieth by custom, the West Indian black banana pickers were confined to eastern Limón province, so the settlers of the Meseta Central mated within the extended family.

The *ladinos,* who now rule elsewhere in Central America, have values strikingly comparable to those of the Costa Ricans about family, values just as deeply influential in their political lives. In the nineteenth century, when prospective *ladino* leaders began extending their influence beyond their isolated valleys to the world beyond the mountain, they had to rely on older, tested values of family to survive. After the disruption of the Central American union and the fratricidal wars that accompanied them, the old Creole aristocracy—those Spaniards born in the New World and their descendants—drifted into mercantile affairs along with other foreigners, Europeans and, later on, Americans, and preserved their way of life behind the imposing walls of their courtyards. *Ladinos,* upstarts, took on the task of shaping national political life. For such an awesome task they were ill equipped, by either tradition or education. So they crafted their own political movements around friends, the extended family, who could be counted on for support in a crisis or revolution not because the constitution or the nation must endure but because the leader of the family must retain his power and his access to the national purse in order to help his family get along. Every now and then a political figure with a broader vision and deeper philosophy came along—Policarpo Bonilla in Honduras in the early twentieth century probably qualified—but more often

Central America's leaders possessed other traits, bravura, an iron will, and more important, loyalty to friends. In return, of course, the friends were expected to remain unswervingly loyal to the *jefe*, the boss. It's a variation on "My country, right or wrong," where leader substitutes for country.

Very little of this makes much sense to outsiders, particularly Americans, who genuinely want to give Central Americans some good advice about running a republic and have naturally concluded that what has worked reasonably well for them—compromise, give-and-take (even among enemies), and laws and institutions grounded in ageless political principles rather than government by personality—might also be preferable for Central Americans. Or, at least, they might give it a try.

In the *ladino* psychology, each person is unique and implants his personality on the offices or roles he undertakes in life. So institutions like the "presidency of the republic" (or political parties) necessarily are molded into whatever they may be at a given time by the personality of the man who happens to be in charge. And once you get your chance at power, what counts most is your determination to stand by your family, to remember your friends and close ranks with them against their enemies because *their* enemies are by the natural order of affairs *your* enemies. There's no such thing as the man not being "big enough for the job." The office, whether it be president or municipal clerk, is what one can make of it, always remembering that friendship and family occupy a higher place on the scale of values than honesty and efficiency in public service.

Naturally what this has often led to is inordinate favoritism and corruption in public service. But the leader who finally gets to the top through blood ties and friendships and suddenly decides to name cabinet ministers or the director of this or that agency on the basis of professional qualification or experience regardless of political affiliation is in jeopardy of losing his support system. "Government" is an abstraction. In no Central American country does it possess the imposing physical and institutional manifestation of the Capitol and the White House, edifices and entities that reassure us that government is permanent even if the persons running it are not. What is permanent to the Central American political leader is not public office, which is temporary and sometimes very dangerous, but one's extended family, its lasting values and its needs.

Early in the twentieth century, when the United States began interfering more directly in Central American affairs, there was widespread conviction in Washington that "undesirable" elements could be expunged from isthmian governments. As Woodrow Wilson once explained to a skeptical British diplomat perturbed about heavy-handed American diplomatic and military pressures on Mexico, "we are going to teach them to elect good men."[7]

The problem lay in the definition of a "good man" in politics. Wilson had in mind the philosophical liberal Francisco Madero, whose noble struggle to achieve the idea and reality of an elected leader had ended the ignoble rule of the old dictator Porfirio Díaz. Madero had then swept into office on a democratic tide only to be assassinated two years later on the orders of a conspiring general whom he had trusted to defend the state. In Wilson's view Madero had perished because he had tried to change a system founded on favoritism and corruption. In fact the dimunitive Mexican *político* had played favorites in his appointments just as his predecessor had and in doing so had aroused the jealousy of other ambitious men because he had passed out too many jobs to *his* political family and not enough to other aspirants. Wilson had presumed, as have successive presidents who have grappled with Latin America's arcane politics, that Madero's election by the rules would inevitably change Mexican thinking about their political priorities. But for Madero, family came first, as any "good" Mexican politician knew then and knows today.

Just as the American government has habitually used the term "good men" to characterize what it wants as leaders of Central American governments, its officials continually invoke "professionalism" as a laudable goal of our efforts to influence Central America's military officers. Back in the twenties Washington undertook considerable interest in trying to limit isthmian armaments as a realistic means of reducing the number of occasionally bloody wars among the republics. In the past generation, the American government has been heavily arming these governments, then expressing anguished disclaimers when the governments turn their weaponry on their own peoples. The practice reached such notorious levels in Guatemala in the 1970s that its government won the unenviable distinction of being the worst abuser of human rights in the world.

The policy seemed to work better in neighboring El Salvador, whose military chieftains were even more dependent on Washington's largesse. With considerable fanfare the Defense Department and the American mission in that country undertook to transform the Salvadoran military into a trim fighting unit. At the American embassy, advisers gave enthusiastic talks about ridding the Salvadoran military of its incompetent officers who could not mount search-and-destroy campaigns. The Americans attributed this reluctance to wage more than a "nine-to-five" war against guerrillas to traditional familial and adolescent bonds among the Salvadoran officer class. At one point the American ambassador, speaking with more conviction than judgment, argued that an "entire generation" of young Salvadoran officers, drilled in American military techniques and values for ninety days at Fort Benning, could replace these cliquish elements.[8] In the future the modern Salvadoran officer would lead his men into battle to defend republican government. But when the young cadets and lieutenants got back to their country, their commanders quickly began reinforcing *Salvadoran* military traditions.

None of the Central American states is really a nation, nor do their governments project the rule of law rather than the authority of men. So the ageless principle of loyalty to family over loyalty to nation or constitution has survived into modern times.[9] The challenge from the left—whether the organizers of Indian cooperatives in Guatemala, the guerrilla bands in eastern and northern El Salvador, or the Marxist ideologues in Managua—represents something far more ominous than loss of property through agrarian reform or nationalization of business. Quite correctly the ruling familial orders sense that the isthmian turmoil of the past generation is resurrecting older and quite dangerous loyalties—not to them but to the larger Central American family of those on the bottom who are enduring a common suffering and who are dimly perceiving they do not have to make sacrifices to the gods of the old order's familial political quarrels.

4 "A Pretty Hot Number"

Central America's familial political rivalries that American troops were dispatched to settle produced, in the late 1920s, yet another anti-American Nicaraguan nationalist.

H E WAS AN IMPROBABLE HERO, AUGUSTO CÉSAR Sandino. On a Hollywood back lot in 1920s America he could easily have passed for an extra in a Tom Mix movie. The United States Marine Corps officially described Sandino as just a "mule thief," a Nicaraguan epithet on a par with "horse thief" in the United States. Yet privately Marine officers, some on their first tour of duty in America's tropical empire, developed a grudging admiration for this diminutive Nicaraguan rebel with his western-style hat and Smith & Wesson revolver strapped to his waist.

In summer 1927, repudiating the old-fashioned political deal President Coolidge's personal emissary Henry Stimson had fashioned underneath a blackthorn tree on the banks of the Tipitapa River with Nicaragua's most prominent Liberal general, Sandino organized an army of men, women, and children and proclaimed his defiance of American power. Anti-American sentiment already ran deep among Latin Americans in this decade, and Sandino received recruits from every hemispheric country save Peru. In China nationalist soldiers named a brigade for him. For five years he eluded the Marines, despite their ready adaptation to bush warfare. His reputation grew despite the concentrated efforts of Washington to portray him as not much more than a nuisance in its grand design for Nicaragua's political rehabilitation.

Sandino had a quality about him that in a later era would have been called "charismatic." He attracted attention to his cause by making pronouncements against what he considered the bane of Nicaragua, indeed all Latin America—the callous manipulation of its affairs by the great powers, most recently by the United States. Interviewed in his Nicaraguan lair by the radical journalist Carleton Beals, Sandino boasted that his political purpose was in many respects similar to George Washington's in 1776. But in other incidents of the long war, particularly during his raids on the foreign-dominated east coast in 1931, Sandino incorporated a noticeably anticapitalist tone in his rhetoric. He sacked a mine belonging to La Luz y Los Angeles Company, an American concern, and informed the owners they could collect for damages from Calvin Coolidge. Such talk, in an age when the American government placed considerable credence in stories of Sandino's links to revolutionary Mexico and, allegedly, to the "international Bolshevik conspiracy," merely reinforced American suspicions.

Mr. Coolidge, given to occasional warnings about the Red menace, would have been hard pressed to trace the global ties of Sandino's cause to Moscow. Apart from the international representation in his army and the modest flow of supplies from Mexico, Sandino's cause, though laced with vaguely socialist condemnations about capitalism and its attendant evils in Latin America, was quintessentially Nicaraguan in its origins. He indicted the United States for its interfering ways, however well intentioned, in the republic's internal affairs, and he castigated his fellow Liberals for consorting with their persecutors. That his intention was a Marxist Nicaragua is unprovable, given the ideological shallowness of his thinking and his willingness to negotiate with the Nicaraguan beneficiaries of American intervention, a gesture that led to his betrayal and death.

A crusty old Marine veteran of the Nicaraguan campaign, remembering Sandino and the war he waged against the United States, described him in succinct and unambiguous words: "He was a pretty hot number. The establishment was afraid of him."[1]

The principal plotter against Sandino (and, it is generally acknowledged, the man who gave the final order for his death) was the elder Somoza, Tacho I, chief of the newly established Guardia Nacional and confidant of the American mission in the country. Earlier, when the Marine campaign against Somoza was faltering, Somoza had boldly chided a Marine officer: "You Americans are a bunch of damn fools. You've got five thousand soldiers down here chasing this guy, but you'll never catch him."[2] Somoza spoke idiomatic English, acquired during his stint at a Philadelphia business college. The Marines had come to trust him as a guy who "played square with us."

He had accompanied Henry Stimson as interpreter during that reluctant emissary's mission to arrange a peace between the country's warring factions in spring 1927, and his ingratiating manner and "no-nonsense" approach had impressed those Americans understandably befuddled by the arcane world of Nicaraguan family politics. When the American Marine casually inquired how Somoza would deal with this elusive "bandit," Somoza did not mince his words: "Simple. I'd invite him to dinner, have a few drinks and good food, then I'd have my men take him out and shoot him."

Several years later, after the Marines had pulled out and returned to a depression-wracked America that had suddenly wearied of Mr. Coolidge's jungle war, Somoza made good on his boast. Satisfied that his former Liberal allies had finally rid themselves of their American protectors, Sandino boldly entered Managua and publicly embraced the new president, on whose behalf he had begun the war seven years before. Already Somoza's plan for his elimination, which two generations of Latin America's left devoutly believe found its final approbation in the American embassy, was unfolding. On a February evening in 1934, Somoza's guardsmen snatched Sandino and his associates as they left a sumptuous dinner expressly ordered for the rebel's reconciliation with the country's Liberal elite.

Sandino was taken to a grassy airstrip and shot, his executioners aiming by the glare of truck headlights. He was denied even the ritualistic giving of souvenirs to his assassins. Reaching into his pockets he found nothing. "Screwed!" he said. "My political leaders have already emptied me of my contents."[3]

The machine-gun blast that swept Sandino out of Somoza's way did not eliminate him from Nicaraguan mythology. Before long stories about the guerrilla leader took hold, and inevitably they were transformed into legend. Not even Tacho I, the founder of the dynasty who pushed aside the once venerated Sacasa in 1936 and took over the presidency, could dispel the myth. Ironically the elder Somoza perpetuated Sandino's fame by publishing a collection of documents portraying the slain rebel in a more flattering way than Somoza had intended.

In the first glorious months after the fall of the Somoza dynasty in summer 1979, the victorious Sandinistas jubilantly placarded the bombed-out cities of Nicaragua with banners and posters with the benign likeness of their hero. Everywhere, they were determined to revive the legend, as if it were symbolic evidence that their struggle had brought the victory that the Marines had denied to Sandino and that, at last, the scales of historical justice were balancing. Countless streets, a major port, and the international airport bear his name. Cadres of work parties bearing pickaxes and shovels even dug up a sizable quantity of stone and dirt in Managua, still suffering from the devastation of the 1972 earthquake, looking for his bones. They hoped to enshrine them and provide the people with a tangible link to the man who began their long struggle against American power.

The Sandinista plan for Nicaragua took its inspiration, then, not from the German philosopher who had prophesied the collapse of the capitalist order more than a century before but from the rather simplistic economic analyses of their canonized revolutionary patron saint. Sandino's guiding principle had been that Nicaragua had never been permitted to control its own destiny and that those in power were lackeys of the United States. That was not an uncommon lament in the Caribbean and Central American backwaters of the American empire in the twenties, though in Nicaragua the imprint of American rule, perpetuated by the Somoza dynasty, the argument ran, seemed much more deeply inscribed than in other places. Thus the view that the overthrow of the dynasty installed by the Americans would lead ineluctably toward the self-determination that Sandino had championed.

In the beginning of the revolution, before the victors had taken to quarreling among themselves, there persisted the belief that the appropriation of the Somoza family holdings would obviate the severe course the Cuban revolution had taken in 1960. Unlike pre-Castro Cuba, Nicaragua had not labored with an economy heavily controlled by foreigners. The Somozas had demanded too high a price to suit prospective foreign investors.

Daniel Ortega, a prominent member of the Sandinista ruling junta, speaking before the Sixth Summit Conference of Nonaligned Countries in Havana a few months after the triumph over Somoza, invoked Sandino's 1928 appeal ("Our Country and Freedom") to the delegates of the Sixth Pan-American Conference, which had also met in Havana. Then the American delegation, headed by Charles Evans Hughes, former secretary of state, managed to head off rising Latin American criticism of American intervention in Nicaragua with somber warnings about decent people "butchered in the jungle" if the Americans left Nicaragua. Disposing of Somoza as the "last American Marine," Ortega recited a list of economic measures that the Sandinistas had already accomplished: nationalization of 50 percent of Nicaragua's arable land (1,350,000 acres), 180 commercial and industrial firms, 400 homes belonging to fleeing Somocistas, and the country's banks. He followed with a litany on the government's takeover of national resources and agricultural exports, the beginning of agrarian reform, and an intensive program in housing, health, and education. The comparison with the early ambitious plans of the Cuban revolution was unmistakable (and doubtless intended), and before long Cuban doctors and teachers began filtering into the new Nicaragua, heading for the countryside in the service of a state Castro has called a new comrade in his quarter-century war with the Americans.

The Sandinistas of those days still retained enough of their wartime unity and purpose to undertake what prudent observers considered an insurmountable task. Had they not overthrown a despicable tyranny, one armed with the most modern weapons Somoza could purchase? Unlike the Cuban revolutionaries who had marched into Havana in early 1959 with no bloody final push (largely because the Cuban urban middle class had withdrawn its support of the dictator), the Sandinistas had to depend on the active collaboration of Nicaragua's commercial and professional classes against the family. Even with their aid the last battles for victory were sickeningly gruesome. In driving out the Somozas the impossible had been achieved.

No program of those early months was more infused with alacrity and ambition than the literacy crusade. Sandino himself had called for such an effort, even in wartime, and had personally instructed one of his generals. Somoza had calmly tolerated press criticism because of the simple fact that more than 50 percent of urban Nicaraguans were illiterate. But they could see and hear, and radio and television were severely controlled. In the countryside illiteracy was much higher. The Sandinistas began nonetheless with noticeable enthusiasm. Since they owed $1.6 billion to international creditors, paying teachers for such a crusade was out of the question. They enlisted volunteers, outsiders (mostly Cubans) and Nicaraguan high school students, many of them ignorant about country people and their daily trials. The Ministry of Education adjured them "to take up arms of pencils and primers and do battle with ignorance in order to learn about country life." Fifty-five thousand tromped into the Nicaraguan thicket with the alacrity of Civilian Conservation Corps volunteers in the 1930s in this country. They complained of mosquitoes and soaking rains, but they managed to persevere and even gain from the experience. One volunteer boasted, "Today I learned to milk a cow."[4]

But even as middle-class high school students were venturing into remote areas of the country in the service of the government's literacy crusade, the unity of the National Liberation Front was already showing noticeable strain. The stresses had appeared before the hour of victory over the deposed Somoza. In the aftermath the urban middle-class professionals had turned against the regime, largely out of their disgust over Somoza's blatant pocketing (at their loss) of aid money sent to the country after the 1972 earthquake. They soon came to fear that the revolution was already shifting perceptibly to the left. Some departed the country, but most chose to stick it out, accepting the Sandinista pledge to a pluralistic society (a term much used in Nicaragua nowadays) in which private enterprise and state socialism coexist. The most publicized confrontation has been the government's censorship of the press, especially *La Prensa*, a distinguished Central American daily published by the Chamorro family. The assassination of Pedro Joaquín Chamorro, an outspoken opponent of the Somoza clan, in early 1978 helped galvanize the urban reformers in support of the insurrection that finally toppled the dynasty. *La Prensa*'s persistent criticism of the Sandinista directorate, particularly for its stalling on the issue of elections, had merely heightened Washington's suspicions that an inner circle of dedicated Marxists in the government intended the creation of a Cuban-style economy.

There are compelling similarities between Castro's Cuba and Sandinista Nicaragua. Each can lay claim to a history of political turbulence and revolutionary aspiration ultimately quelled and then distorted by repeated American military interventions. Each, shaped by a Spanish colonial policy that starved the countryside to serve the city, has confronted awesome obstacles in bringing country people, who produce the country's export wealth, to the level of city dwellers. And the Cubans do not have to remind their triumphant brethren in Managua that their countries share the humiliation wrought by American power. They can (and most certainly have) reminded the Nicaraguans that they can (and must) resist American manipulation of their revolution.

So far, the Sandinistas have not adopted the Cuban tactic of provoking Washington into breaking diplomatic relations, as Castro did in the twilight days of the Eisenhower presidency. They might well take this course, given the American cutoff in economic aid and the persistent American support of the incursions and raids by the state's enemies based on the Costa Rican and Honduran borders.

While they have gone far in fashioning the new economic Nicaragua without the predicted demise of private property, the Sandinistas have not yet molded the new "political" Nicaraguan. How well they succeed will depend on three elements touching on Sandinista rule—its relationship to the military, the peasantry, and the middle class. In each of these there are persistent, troublesome aspects that bode ill for the pluralistic society to which the Sandinistas are pledged.

When the modern Sandinistas fashioned their revolutionary front in 1961, they drew on two models, Sandino's war against the Marines in the late twenties and Castro's successful guerrilla campaign against the Batista government three decades later. Ernesto "Che" Guevara's Bolivian incursion in the mid-sixties, designed to incite "one, two, many Vietnams" in Latin America, had proved an ignominious failure, for Bolivian forces had shown the effectiveness of U.S. counterinsurgency training. Somoza's guardsmen, they correctly surmised, were comparably equipped and trained. They began, then, by adopting Sandino's strategy of operating in the bush, waging hit-and-run strikes of the type originally designed to lure the guard and Marines into the countryside.

The problem with this strategy lay in the ability of Somoza's troops to protect the urban centers. Ultimately, the Sandinistas organized raids into the cities to undermine the authority of the dictatorship. Their most spectacular assault occurred in December 1974, when they literally crashed a sumptuous party in honor of Turner Shelton, the American amabassador to Nicaragua and an obsequious defender of the Somoza regime.

Somoza retaliated in a savage campaign, throwing the Sandinistas into inner turmoil and bitter division. One faction wanted to wage a guerrilla war *à la cubana;* a second favored an urban uprising by the abused Nicaraguan proletariat. But the strategy eventually settled on was a makeshift alliance of the country guerrillas, the urban warriors, and the bourgeois political opponents, known as the Third Force. Hardline Sandinistas, fearful of a premature confrontation with Somoza's guard, demurred, but the Third Force sparked a truly popular insurrection in Nicaragua's cities, drawing the Sandinistas into the struggle. By the time the dictatorship finally collapsed, the guerrillas, by the decisiveness of their military campaign, were firmly back in command of the armed revolutionary front.

They have retained a firm hold on the new Nicaraguan army. One undisputable justification for this is the persistent menace of counterrevolution. But the Sandinastas have given no clear indication that when the revolution is secure they will permit a truly apolitical military. When a critic of the new order questioned, among other things, the political indoctrination of troops, Tomás Borge, minister of the interior in charge of police and state security, responded unequivocally: "There are no apolitical armies: everyone serves some determinant political purpose."[5] Such a narrow focus may be necessary in a society under siege, but it reflects, ironically, more the military philosophy of the elder Somoza when he took control of the national guard a half-century ago than that of Sandino, who perished opposing such a concept.

Just as the Sandinistas have infused their new army with an ideological spirit, they have made a conscious attempt to incorporate, for the first time in Nicaragua's history, the working class into the new Nicaragua. In his eastern campaigns, Sandino exploited workers' grievances against the foreign-owned companies dotting the Caribbean coast and enlisted their laborers in his army. There was little place for unions in Somoza's Nicaragua, though in the popular-front atmosphere that prevailed in the forties the beefy Tacho I would regularly show up for May Day rallies. In what would doubtless appear as a paradox in these days, the Communist Party, organizing in Managua in 1944, offered its support to the regime. Such displays of unity vanished with the rapid growth of the agro-export economy in the fifties and sixties, which brought added wealth to the Somozas and to the small but influential Nicaraguan middle class. Most of them despised the family for its crass manners and perpetuated corruption, but Somoza permitted a sufficient amount of the wealth thrown their way to keep bourgeois elements quiet.

Somoza's blatant theft of money, food, medicine, and other goods sent as aid after the 1972 earthquake, the savagery of the counterinsurgency by the guard several years later, and the assassination of Pedro Joaquín Chamorro (ordered, it was believed, by Antonio Somoza Portocarrera, Tacho III, "the Kid"), who had been unremitting in his attacks on the flaws of the dynasty—all combined to bring the middle class into the opposition. Somoza had gambled that he could defeat the Sandinistas with a grisly but justifiable campaign and placate his urban business and commercial critics with philanthropic gestures and reminders that however distasteful his family was to the proud old-school elements of Nicaragua, he stood for order. For a few years the strategy worked, but Chamorro's death galvanized Somoza's bourgeois enemies into an organized protest movement. They fashioned an alliance between their Union for Democratic Liberation and the working-class opposition. It was a bold maneuver Somoza had not reckoned on. In the first pronouncements of the alliance appeared far-reaching economic reforms (of a kind guaranteed to jolt the middle class) phrased in anti-imperialist rhetoric. The true believers in the Sandinista leadership saw their hold on the anti-Somoza elements among the working classes rapidly slipping.

But within the final year of the civil war the Sandinistas regained their control on the direction of the crusade. Second thoughts about the economic changes they had called for in their early pronouncements prompted the professional and middle-class faction to dilute its program for a new order. There were even calls, motivated in part by Jimmy Carter's famous letter praising the dramatic improvement in human rights in Nicaragua, for "Somozaism without Somoza." The Sandinistas countered with military actions and a pledge for national reconstruction, yet they could not afford to reject the aid proffered by the middle classes in the final months of struggle against the hated regime. Neither did they have to pledge that the new Nicaragua would disavow socialism. As the commander in chief of the Sandinista Popular Army, Humberto Ortega, declared, "We did not sustain any agreements. We simply established the rules of the game and acted accordingly."

After five years in power the Sandinistas have not yet transformed Nicaragua into a Cuban-style society. But neither have they repudiated socialism as an ultimate answer. Most of the major economic questions about the settlement of the Somoza state structure have been settled. But there remains an uncertainty about the new political order. In a society faced with external threat, internal dissent is subject to close scrutiny. Thus the sometimes bewildering maneuvering of the Sandinistas, simultaneously making peaceful gestures to their domestic and international critics and waving a flag of defiance before them.

The explanation lies in a maze of ideological justification, political necessity, and historical experience. The Sandinistas have compromised their ambitious economic program for the masses by a frank admission that the working classes, now better organized and demanding much more than ever before, must sacrifice in the revolution's hour of peril. Yet they have incorporated the workers, through the Sandinista Workers Confederation, into the new order and granted them an unparalleled status in affairs of the state. And they have maintained, though not without considerable political animosities, their link with the country's wary middle class. Merely by expropriation of the Somoza family's holdings the state has been able to avoid the wholesale confiscations that sent a generation of middle-class Cubans packing for the United States. Laboring under internal grumbling and external scrutiny, the Sandinistas pledged elections for 1985 and then surprised the world by holding them a few days before Reagan's stupendous November 1984 electoral triumph. That they were willing to do so showed *some* faith in the democratic process. More likely, their gamble demonstrated a commitment to survive adversity.

Predictably, just as they had difficulty understanding the depth of anti-Americanism in Cuba, Americans have been occasionally befuddled by the Sandinista condemnation. One credible argument is that the Sandinistas are dedicated Marxists taking Nicaragua down the road to a Cuban-style socialism and, naturally, are following Castro's model. First, they antagonize the Yankees with offensive decrees. They have managed to upset Americans by cracking down on the middle-class opposition to the regime. Very quickly, since 1979, the American government has become a champion of freedom of the press in Nicaragua. Second, if this scenario runs parallel to what happened to Cuba a generation ago, the Sandinistas will commit some international misdeed intended to provoke the Yankees into breaking diplomatic relations. Yet, it is acknowledged, the Cubans have warned the Nicaraguans "not to make our mistakes." These include a break with the Americans.

The Sandinistas may ultimately impose a socialist order in Nicaragua, but Marxist ideology is not the fuel for the anti-American fire sweeping the country. *Nicas* draw their animosity toward us from the heart of their own experience, the historic antagonism Nicaraguans have felt toward outsiders as far back as the seventeenth century. For most of the twentieth century, in one way or another, the foreigner has ruled Nicaragua—the Americans directly with their troops or through hirelings like the Somozas, "the last Marines," as the Nicaraguans call them. It is not Sandino's frankly vague socialism that inspires the Sandinista firebrands nearly as much as his unequivocal opposition to American interference in Nicaraguan affairs for whatever goal—freedom of the press, free elections, and so on. Not every Nicaraguan is a Sandinista, but every *nica* is a nationalist.

And, more than any political force in Nicaraguan history, the Sandinistas have exploited the latent antiforeign passion of the ordinary Nicaraguan. In kicking out Somoza they proclaimed the expulsion of, not a *Nicaraguan* tyrant, but an *American* lackey. They have created an armed populace, many of them adolescents who scurry about Managua with carbines and a steely look that signals a fiery determination to die for the cause. And the cause these grim-faced teenagers will sacrifice themselves for is not the blissful socialist paradise of Marx but the ravaged homeland of Sandino.

Nicaragua is a terribly battered country. Its suffering from natural and man-made disasters for two centuries has been greater and has left deeper scars than the experiences of its neighbors. Earthquakes have devastated every Central American capital except Tegucigalpa in Honduras, yet only Managua retains the look of a bombed-out city still not recovered from the last quake. Nicaragua's civil wars have taken a grim human toll, not just in numbers far greater than the civil convulsions of the other republics, but in the enduring trauma that has persisted long afterward.

The Sandinistas have become the tough guys on the block, displaying a combativeness honed by generations of collective guilt at the suffering they understandably attribute to the outside, especially the United States. And like battered children they have grown up with a seemingly natural pugilistic style. As battered children often do at maturity, the Nicaraguans may very well become the batterers.

5 Matanza: *The Little Man with the Red Star in His Lapel*

"El Salvador" means "The Savior," but the professed saviors in that country's tormented history haunt modern Salvadoran society like specters.

A MONG THE VETERANS OF THE *MATANZA*, THE massacre of communists in El Salvador in early 1932, mention of his name still provokes outrage against the left and fears of class revolt. Augustín Farabundo Martí, who has left his name and a goodly portion of his ideology to one of El Salvador's largest guerrilla bands, was, like Sandino, an enemy of the political order that ruled Central America a half-century ago. And, like the Nicaraguan rebel, he had known a relatively comfortable childhood but had chosen a moment in his early adulthood to raise his flag of defiance. For Sandino, the time had come when he returned from revolutionary Mexico with a few hundred dollars and a revolver, bent on ensuring that the rightful candidate for the Nicaraguan presidency wore the distinguished sash of office. For Martí (and his well-educated fellow students in San Salvador in the early twenties) the act of protest against the social system came with their expulsion from the country. Martí had committed no crime. He and several others, most of them sons of the capital's establishment, had been arrested at a student rally for a visiting delegation of Guatemalan radicals. When the president of the republic, a member of the country's "fourteen families," offered to settle the matter by dispatching the ringleader to prison but letting the rest go with an avuncular lecture on the evils of radical activity, Martí protested they were all guilty, so all should receive the same punishment. The startled president, indignant over the remarks of this unprepossessing *ladino*, decided to send the ringleader *and* Martí into exile.

Thus was born the legend of "El Negro," Farabundo Martí, who looked more the village merchant than the disciple of Lenin. At the national university his philosophy professors had taught the positivism of Comte and Spencer, whose writrings reinforced with "social science" the rigidly class notions of the Salvadoran aristocracy. But Martí preferred the dialetic of Hegel and Marx.

He was a visible figure in Central American radical circles in the twenties. In Guatemala City, where dissident intellectuals formed the Central American Socialist Party, Martí was a charter member, but in this and later radical activities in the isthmus he always seemed to stand apart from his fellow travelers, more determined to think for himself and less disposed to bend to party dictates. His comrades found it difficult to get to the left of him on anything. At gatherings of literati in San Salvador in the late twenties, in an era when coffee prosperity had seemingly decreed perpetual rule for the landed aristocracy, he appeared at poetry readings and literary forums wearing a red star on his jacket lapel. In the center of the star was a tiny picture of Leon Trotsky.

Even in the more liberal atmosphere that prevailed under the Salvadoran gentleman president, Pío Romero Bosque, or *don* Pío, as he was affectionately called, and who considered the communists mostly a humorous nuisance, Martí remained an outcast. He disinherited himself from a not insignificant estate in the countryside and migrated to New York. There he labored on behalf of the Anti-Imperialist League, which busied itself mostly by cranking out pamphlets denouncing the American intervention in Nicaragua. But the real struggle, he believed, was back in Central America, and he sailed for the isthmus by a bafflingly haphazard route to Mexico, Cuba, Jamaica, and finally British Honduras. From Tegucigalpa, Honduras, which he reached after a tortuous journey through Guatemala, Sandino's agents spirited him into the mountains of northern Nicaragua. Sandino's war against the Marines was then in full swing, and Martí hoped to join the crusade to expel the Yankees from the isthmus. But within a year Sandino was in flight to Mexico, and Martí, disillusioned over his inability to convert Sandino to communism, was a man without a champion.

He got back to El Salvador in 1930, in time for the collapse of the coffee prosperity and the rapid onset of trouble in the countryside, where for years itinerant communists had been circulating among the plantation workers, seasonal laborers who worked the harvests for a few months and survived the rest of the year on their trifling garden plots and the begruding philanthropy of the big landowners. The agitators were a hardy breed. They got little support from international communism, surviving as laborers and disseminating the message of revolution to illiterate peasants. Like most country people in Central America, the coffee workers had been initially suspicious of outsiders, particularly the fair-skinned young intellectuals from the capital. Oblivious to Marxian economic thought, they despised the masters of the coffee fincas and their arrogant ways.

Now an agent of the Socorro Rojo Internacional (SRI), the "Red Aid Society," Martí succored the demonstrators the government had tossed in jail for protesting the severe economic conditions, and he distributed reports of workers' unrest to the world press. Even the benign *don* Pío was angered, and Martí shortly found himself in a jail cell with country peasants. But the president had in mind a punishment befitting his social status—exile as far from Central America as a steamer would carry him. He jumped ship in California, making his way back down the Pacific coast to Puntarenas, Costa Rica, where an alerted Salvadoran agent waited with a steamship ticket for Peru. But when the ship docked in Nicaragua he again slipped away, heading across northern Nicaragua into Honduras and, with the timely assistance of Salvadoran communists in Tegucigalpa, back into El Salvador. In February 1931 *don* Pío, now in his last frustrating month as president, thinking himself rid of El Salvador's leading agitator, was startled to read in a letter-to-the-editor column in the newspaper that Farabundo Martí was back in the country.

For a year Martí and his radical associates in SRI kept up a propaganda war against the government. In the countryside, especially around Sonsonate, workers' strikes and peasant disturbances began occurring with such frequency that local officials all the way up to the president were soon convinced they were a communist plot. In many instances the precipitating issue was the abuse of a landowner toward an Indian village, whose inhabitants, roused to destructive fury by an agitator long enough with them to be trusted, stormed into the provincial capital seeking revenge. The country squires of El Salvador regularly called upon guardsmen to stop this kind of "agitation" and, if necessary, plied them with liquor to inspire them into murderous revenge. In such confrontations Martí found gruesome details for his propaganda crusade against the government and calls for solidarity of worker and peasant.

The weary civilian rulers of the country even permitted the communists to participate in an election, but widespread fraud in balloting, a perennial bane in Central American elections, cost them heavily. For the coffee aristocracy, the gesture indicated a dangerous democratic weakness, and in early 1932 the military, acting on the elite's appeal, tossed out the civilian government. The new president of the republic was now General Maximiliano Hernández Martínez (remembered to this day as General Martínez), a stern-minded disciplinarian with a deeply religious antipathy to the communists.

When the communists made a final appeal for peaceful solutions to the crisis, Martínez coldly rejected them. They began talking about revolution, even plotting among presumably sympathetic junior officers in the army. A delegation of conspirators called on the secretary of war and boldly informed him that "the peasants will win with their machetes the rights you are denying them." The unruffled minister responded, "You have machetes, we have machine guns."[1] But the rhetoric coming from Martí and his comrades now appeared as dangerously provocative and sufficiently seditious to convince General Martínez that exile for these Marxist-minded sons of the established would no longer do. In the aftermath the government produced as evidence Martí's directive to revolutionary units in their assault on the bourgeoisie: "Use against them the most opportune means; kill them in some other way without delay; do away with all of them, saving only the lives of children."

In the revolutionary cells of San Salvador the revolt of January 1932 unfolded as a series of disasters. The barracks uprising never developed beyond tough talk. Martí himself and his fellow urban conspirators quickly fell into General Martínez' expertly tossed anticommunist net. So rapidly did the conspiracy disintegrate that the Salvadoran communist leaders were on the verge of calling everything off until word came about spontaneous peasant attacks against petty officials and property owners in the countryside.

There was little coordination of the revolution in the country, no well-planned seizures of key government posts but rather random assaults of machete-bearing laborers against the rich. In some of these the rebels undeniably committed atrocities. One prominent Italian merchant, who had displayed a philanthropy toward less fortunate Salvadorans, was overpowered in his home and forced to watch as the invading gang raped his wife. Afterward the peasants dragged him about town by his thumbs. When he begged for water, one chronicler of the revolt states, his persecutors urinated in his mouth. They systematically tortured him for a day before a rebel put him out of his misery with a machete blow.

The peasants took their revenge against the landowners who had abused them and the town merchants who, they believed, had cheated them. They took few lives but put many houses to the torch. The best estimates of deaths attributable to the roaming mobs reached not much more than two dozen. But the savagery of these killings and the inflammatory rhetoric churned out by Salvadoran communists were literally a waving of the Red flag before polite society. Around Sonsonate, the hardest-hit province, the burnings occurred during a spectacular eruption of Izalco, the "lighthouse of the Pacific," the republic's famous volcano.

General Martínez required no further inducements to retaliate. In the countryside military squads, their soldiers inspired by fanatical speeches from their commanders about saving the country from the Red menace and Salvadoran women from gang rapes, methodically rounded up communist organizers and Indian laborers and slaughtered them. The most conservative estimate of those killed in the General's revenge stands at ten thousand, though others persuasively argue that numbers reached much higher. Bodies lay along the roadsides for days, turkey buzzards feasting on the carcasses. Around Izalco the military arrested anybody carrying a machete and quickly marched him before a firing squad.

In the capital the police compiled names of communists from voting lists and swept through the *barrios*, ferrying their prisoners aboard trucks in the middle of the night to the Acelhuate River and shooting them. Bodies were interred in mass graves on the riverbank. In San Salvador's hotels the soldiers arrested blond-haired guests on the presumption they were Russian and dispatched them to the firing squads.

In the aftermath of the *matanza* General Martínez proved as resolute in justifying the carnage as he had been in ordering the extermination of at least ten thousand of his countrymen. Responding to criticism that compared the taking of so many lives with the thoughtless extermination one applies to ants, the General, a practicing Theosophist, commented, "It is a greater crime to kill an ant than a man, for when a man dies he becomes reincarnated, while an ant dies forever."

With equal conviction about the righteousness of his course, Martínez rejected the services proffered by commanders of American warships from the Special Service Squadron that patrolled Central America's Pacific coast to "show the flag" and, if called upon, to assist "native governments" in keeping order. The Salvadoran military and the planter-merchant class it served were then, as they are today, resentful of outsiders giving them advice on how to handle domestic affairs.

Martínez just as confidently demurred at the suggestion of quickly sending Martí and the other high officials of the Red Aid

Society to a midnight firing squad. The outspoken little man who adorned his coat lapel with Trotsky's face would have become a peasant hero. General Martínez resolved that Martí would be transformed into a villain, a conspirator against the state whose call for revolution had brought misery and death to ordinary Salvadorans.

The government provided Martí (and two other conspirators) with a fourth-year law student as defender and subjected them to a public trial before a military tribunal. One of Martí's fellow defendants attributed his participation in the revolt to the spirit of "rebellious youth." The second declared his only sin was the publication of leftist pieces in *Red Star*. By the time he finished pleading for his life it was midnight. The exhausted Martí tried to persuade the court that his fellow prisoners were indeed misguided and should be freed and readily accepted responsibility for the revolt, the details of which he learned mostly from the prosecutor's tabulation of evidence against him.

But his appeal had no persuasive effect on General Martínez. All three were taken by ambulance to the general cemetery, lined up against the north wall, and shot. Martí remained a true believer to the end, rejecting the supplication of a priest to hold his final "communion with God." Looking to the heavens, with a slight smile creasing his lips, his only utterance was "God."

The *matanza* had a curious impact on the international communist movement. Far from garnering praise as a martyr to a noble peasant cause that perished before the capitalists' machine guns, Martí was quickly dismissed as a well-intentioned but naive son of the establishment. The Communist Party of the United States, then enjoying a revival because of the collapse of the American economy, cited the Salvadoran revolt as illustration of the catastrophe wrought by what Stalinist bureaucrats labeled "deviationism." The sacrifice of so many lives of those on the bottom was attributable to the failure of the revolt's chieftains to prepare the people for armed struggle. If the *matanza* accomplished little else for the leftist cause in El Salvador, it instructed the next generation of communists that they must contribute not only the leaders but a more substantial number of the shock troops for the struggle.

As for the victors, the '32 revolt and its bloody aftermath have contributed an ineradicable legacy. The guilt for such a monstrously high death toll was joined in symbiotic union with recurring fears of a class war in the collective psyche of Salvadoran rulers. Once they were convinced that the danger had passed, the elite whose soldiers had just finished massacring ten thousand people now turned to somber analysis about doing something for the survivors. Though Martínez turned the country into a police state, laws appeared directed to changing the master-man relationship on the coffee fincas and even to breaking up the very large plantations.

These were generally accompanied by legislation designed to salvage the coffee economy with a modern, state-supported financial underpinning. Over the years reform movements surfaced—in 1944, when Martínez finally fell from power; in 1948, when young Turks in the military seized control and promised a new era; again in 1961, as John F. Kennedy was launching the Alliance for Progress with its lofty goals of peaceful revolution; and the coup of 1979. All of these sought reform in the countryside—and every one was followed by resistance from the still-powerful landed aristocracy.

Farabundo Martí's disciples had to wait forty-five years to avenge his death. In July 1977 a squad from the Popular Liberation Forces pulled up in front of the home of Osmín Aguirre y Salinas, former president of the republic and director of national police forces in the *matanza,* and gunned him down as he spoke with his grandchildren in the front yard. He was eighty-two. The execution represented the kind of justice Farabundo Martí and his generation in El Salvador would have approved.

His successors are not so naive as to believe that an isolated incident will spark the general insurrection against the people's oppressors Farabundo Martí longed for. In several respects the modern Salvadoran guerrillas have proved much more clever in their approach to changing Salvadoran society. While tolerating—even encouraging—spirited debate over the course of action at the bottom of the revolutionary files, they have been striving for unity at the top. The disenchantment brought on among Christian Democrats when José Napoléon Duarte joined the Salvadoran junta in 1980 shoved several prominent members of that party over to the Democratic Revolutionary Front, the umbrella political organization that represents the guerrillas internationally. As the Salvadoran oligarchy and military have adopted more extreme tactics to preserve their authority—as one landowner put it, referring to pressures for land reforms, Salvadorans now have the law of the jungle—the Front has acquired even greater international respectability on the grounds that lawless behavior by those in authority justifies the guerrilla struggle in the countryside.

But, as the *matanza* demonstrated, possessing the just cause means little if power is the only way the just society can be wrought. The Sandinistas had at least one clear advantage over the Salvadoran guerrillas in this regard. They could afford disagreement among their splinter groups because their revolution focused on a common enemy, the Somoza family, hated by elements on the Nicaraguan right almost as much as by the left. But the Salvadoran left faces a different, more deeply entrenched enemy, the persistently tenacious Salvadoran oligarchy that has demonstrated a remarkable capacity to survive and even tighten its grip. As long as the right keeps chanting that a leftist victory will mean the end of private property in El Salvador or similar horrors, it can maintain a powerful hold on the war-weary property holders.

In short, the Salvadoran left and even the reformers of the middle, as Duarte has discovered, face a formidable obstacle to change in the guise of a reborn Salvadoran fascism, whose spokesman trumpet home, property, church, and family. At leftist rallies in early 1981, when the guerrillas were talking of a general uprising in the cities, they shouted "Revolution or Death!" An inept military, buttressed by rapid infusions of U.S. aid, gave them death. At rightist political rallies vigorously youthful candidates like Roberto d'Aubuisson led enthusiastic crowds in patriotic songs and a stunningly effective slogan, "Nation, yes! Communism, no!" Not surprisingly the Front for National Liberation has incorporated some of its own fervently patriotic appeal in its plans for a new Salvador once military victory is achieved.

It is in the countryside, in the tiny villages where the reach of modern society is negligible and the state has done little for the Salvadoran *campesino*, that the guerrillas have their strongest appeal.[2] Popular support for a guerrilla movement, important for the survival of any guerrilla war, is absolutely vital in a country like El Salvador, jammed with five million persons with every border only a ninety-minute drive from the capital and no really isolated areas. Here the guerrilla must blend in with village culture, which is no easy accomplishment for someone accustomed to city ways.

The Salvadoran guerrillas have taken a clue from the 1967 Bolivian adventure, where Che Guevara, trying to create a "Vietnam in the Andes," failed to win the confidence of rural people and became a relatively easy target for Bolivia's U.S.-trained counterinsurgency forces. From the beginning of the Salvadoran war in 1979 the rebels have insinuated themselves into village life. Traditionally suspicious of outsiders, the Salvadoran *campesinos* have become more than passive spectators to the war: they shelter, feed, and protect the guerrillas. In return the rebels help them in the fields and provide educational and medical services, poor by urban standards yet more than Salvadoran governments have been willing or able to do.

What has happened in Chalatenango province, now almost completely under rebel control, provides a measure for the kind of society that lies in store for El Salvador if the revolution prevails in the rest of the country. Chalatenango lies north of the capital on the Honduran border. When the guerrillas firmly imposed their authority they organized collective farms, a decision bound to arouse resentment among a people with deep-seated attachments to their own plots, however minuscule. But in Chalatenango the guerrillas were able to prevail because they offered medical care and literacy courses to people who had never seen a doctor or learned to read and write. These fundamental services, coupled with pledges that the produce of the collective farms would go first toward alleviating hunger, allowed the guerrillas to penetrate a closed social order and begin changing its ways.

What the Salvadoran revolutionary ideologues have in mind,

then, is something different from the liberal democratic state of rival political parties common to western Europe and the United States. "Popular organizations" will be the foundation of the revolutionary order. In the cities, popular committees will dispense political education. And in the villages, if the Chalatenango experience may be used as an example, participation by every adult in the basic decisions of the community will be the order of the day. Through the administrative councils (named after Farabundo Martí) the guerrillas have organized civil administration under four sections. A civil registrar is charged with carrying out daily civil assignments and keeping statistical information. If there is no priest available or willing, a religious "agent" comes into play: he convinces people that the revolutionary and religious life are mutually supportive. Then, to fill things out, there are an economic sector charged with overseeing the collective farms and disseminating its produce, and self-defense units, taught by the guerrillas to dig tunnels in the hills to shield the villagers from aerial assault.

"Liberation," including the molding of a "new woman," is a fundamental tenet of Salvadoran revolutionary doctrine, as is "pluralism," by which the guerrillas mean a continual participation of the political and social sectors in the revolutionary order. By such constant reminders of the "imperialist chains" that once shackled them, the Salvadoran people will accept the "just restructuring" of society. Little wonder, then, that the families that have been running the country for so long have become so terrified at the prospect of even a diluted version of the plans the true believers have in mind for the country.

While the modern rulers of El Salvador speak of change and under American prodding have even grudgingly pursued agrarian reforms, they harbor age-old fears about willful little men with red stars and their plans for a restructured El Salvador. For those who hold power, vigilante justice against the left is ultimately acceptable if its intent is the prevention of the kind of society that Martí and his fellow travelers dreamed about some fifty years ago. The elite may privately admit their guilt of undeniable persecution and injustice meted out to the Salvadoran peasantry bequeathed to them by their parents. But they are not likely to accept solutions that endanger their inherited place in the social structure. They may share power, and even some of their wealth, with their critics for reasons ranging from philanthropic impulse to self-preservation in a hostile world.

But in their estimation the left is not, nor has it ever been, a "loyal opposition," willing to stop fighting its guerrilla war in return for a gaggle of seats in the national assembly and some impact on the crafting of social legislation. And by a similarly perverse but understandable logic the Salvadoran leftists know they cannot relinquish their guns and trustingly sit at the table of Salvadoran power brokers. Neither can enter into a public bond of peaceful competitiveness while privately each wants the other eliminated.

In El Salvador politics is not the art of the possible among parties competing for public approval. The political arena is more analogous to a bullfight, where the crowd's fears of the destructive capability of the enraged beast can be allayed only if the bull dies. It does not matter if the bull, his neck muscles pierced by the repeated attacks of the *picadores,* does not have any chance of survival. The contest is not supposed to represent a fair fight between crafty man and powerful animal but the triumph of a man foolish or brave enough to get into a ring with the bull.

6 A Man Named Napoleón

A
SARCASTIC REPORTER ONCE ASKED FRANKLIN D.
Roosevelt if he was a communist. "No," re-
plied the president. "Are you a socialist?"
The predictable response—"No." "A fascist?" And again the reply,
"No." Exasperated, the reporter finally blurted out, "Well, what are
you then?" "I'm a Christian and a Democrat," said FDR. Roosevelt
was a deeply religious man, but his politics were no-quarter and
blatantly partisan. He was a Christian and a Democrat, but not a
Christian Democrat (CD).

Americans who learn of this middle-of-the-road, sometimes
left-of-center, relatively new political movement are often puzzled
by its marblecake mixture of religious belief and social commitment. Its dynamism is drawn, not from traditional credos of separation of church and state or the privacy of one's religious faith, but
from the conviction that the noblest political values are religiously
inspired and the most convincing evidence of one's religious commitment lies in the political arena. The true Catholic is the public
man.

José Napoleón Duarte, the Salvadoran Christian Democrat and
currently probably the best-known figure of that persuasion to
Americans, looks neither philosophical nor pious. He more readily
resembles a battered pugilist who retired from the ring before

75

suffering permanent brain damage. He is tough and combative but displays an undeniable humanity and the reassuring mellowness that can come with age. The younger men on the make in El Salvador tend to the extreme, Roberto d'Aubuisson on the right, Guillermo Ungo on the left. Duarte and the few noteworthy Christian Democratic disciples in Central America, creators of the refreshingly new political movement of an earlier generation, are rapidly becoming a vanishing breed. Their decline is an ominous comment on the future of nonviolent reform in the isthmus. What they have had to do to get power is a somber comment on the prospects for "decent democratic regimes" there.

Christian Democracy in El Salvador—in all Latin America—is a movement of the middle and upper classes on behalf of the have-nots, particularly the urban dispossessed. From the beginning it has projected itself as an alternative to right-wing militarism (thus insisting on civilian rule of the military as fundamental) or rejecting Marxism (for its systematic degradation of the individual). For that reason alone its appearance in the early 1960s attracted considerable attention from the American government, especially from John F. Kennedy, who condemned Latin American generals for interfering in politics and Castroites for their insistent calls for violent revolution. Christian Democracy's first notable victory came the year after Kennedy died with the triumph of Eduardo Frei in Chile, an election where the United States had staked much because Frei's strongest opponent was the Marxist Salvador Allende. Frei was touted as the "last best hope," and when Allende finally won power in 1970 the American government undertook to bring him down with a concerted political and economic campaign that bordered, in the minds of liberal Americans, on subversion.

The celebrity status of Christian Democracy in the larger countries of South America in the 1960s overshadowed the fledgling CDs of El Salvador. After all, the turmoil lay elsewhere, and in Central America even Kennedy seemed willing to tolerate military regimes rather than run the risk of getting another leftist like Arbenz or Arévalo. The reformist Christian Democrats of the isthmus did not then get the kind of attention from Washington they now command,

at a time when their prospects for changing Central America peacefully are rapidly diminishing.

Duarte offers an excellent example of the isthmian reformist
whose image in this country is curiously different from what it is in
his own. He was not a founder but a convert to Salvador's Christian
Democratic movement. Typical of the Central American elite, he
went to the United States for his university education (to the University of Notre Dame, which awarded him an engineering degree in
1948). By his own admission he was not politically active after he
returned to El Salvador until 1960, when he showed up at a
Christian Democratic study group. Up to then his most visible
public role had been at Boy Scout and Red Cross functions.

El Salvador was then passing from one of its cyclical right-wing
phases to a brief civilian interlude, tolerant of the left, then back to a
vigorously anticommunist military order. As it was to demonstrate
in Guatemala and Honduras a few years later, the American government frankly welcomed the assurances offered by anticommunist
military regimes in Central America. The Christian Democrats in
those days, of course, posed no realistic alternative to the isthmian
parade of military regimes. Their leaders were little more than
isolated voices of disaffected sons of the establishment or middle-
class businessmen and professionals like Duarte who disliked the
military in politics but hated the communists even more.

Yet the times were propitious for their message for the undeniable reason that the CDs appeared as the proper anchor for the
middle class as against the intransigence of the right and the calls to
violence from the left. And they offered a program of social services
to meet the needs of the rapidly expanding urban proletariat fleeing
from the countryside to the Latin American capitals. Even Castro
sensed their significance. When Frei defeated Allende for the
Chilean presidency in 1964, despite the patent fraud of his victory,
the Cuban leader admitted, "Sometimes our opponents surpass us
in ability."

What explains men like Duarte, capable of surviving in the
tumultuous Salvadoran political arena where personality, "charisma," counts for so much more than ideology (Central Americans

consider Americans "ideological" rather than "practical" in their politics), where advocacy of social justice is routinely twisted by the right to mean selling out to the communists, and where support of pluralism in politics is routinely described by the left as sycophancy to the military? Is it toughness, perseverance, idealism, naiveté, or adaption, or some kind of synergistic combination of all of these qualities?

The Christian Democrats have been around for only one generation in Latin American politics, so brief a time that their ideology has never percolated down to the countryside, traditionally the breeding place for isthmian political movements. They have been in power so infrequently that the American government, which, sadly, measures the ability of Latin American political figures mostly in terms of staying power and anticommunist conviction, has not yet become convinced they are capable of surviving. There is, lamentably, a cynical view that men like Duarte may be too "Christian" to last, a judgment sadly reinforced when the beleaguered Salvadoran leader appeared on American network television on the eve of the 1982 elections to ask Americans to "pray for El Salvador."

Despite the pious tone of this appeal, Duarte is not a visionary, nor is he a cleric who happened to get his philosophical training in engineering. American observers of the Christian Democrats routinely—and mistakenly—assume the party is a *Catholic* political movement, an action-oriented Latin American Knights of Columbus. Marxists decry the Christian Democrats as namby-pamby servants of the entrenched church, which in their analysis has served as historic persecutor of the masses because in the past the clergy have so often importuned the people to suffer social and economic injustice while reassuring them they'll get to heaven ahead of their oppressors. The links between the Christian Democrats and the Catholic Church are tenuous; neither, paradoxically, has moved to strengthen what would appear to be natural ties. But the Catholic layman's traditional social concerns for the plight of the less fortunate has been a powerful motivation for political action. The Christian Democrats leave the afterlife to the priests; they are committed to improving the lot of people in the here and now.

On religious education and birth control, Christian Democratic positions are synonymous with traditional church doctrine; on social and economic programs and international issues they are often at variance with the church. They have condemned the Americans for intervening in the Dominican Republic in 1965 "to prevent another Cuba" and chastised the Cubans for accommodating Soviet imperialism. Their chosen political path, in other words, has been essentially middle-of-the-road, and they've caught considerable flack from both sides of the political spectrum.

But they have been almost perversely unpredictable, and their explanations for their behavior, in a society where personal magnetism counts for so much, suggest opportunism. Their philosophical convictions can be exasperatingly difficult to decipher. As a Nicaraguan disciple once explained:

If by left we understand the struggle for social justice, the great battle for the social and economic redemption of the people, the incorporation of workers and peasants into the mainstream of culture, then undoubtedly we are leftists. If, however, by left is understood historical materialism, communist totalitarianism, and the suppression of liberty, then in no way are we leftists. If by right is understood the conservation of the spiritual values of civilization, the historical legacy of humanity, and the dignity and liberty of man, then there can be no doubt that we are rightists. But if by right we understand the conservation of an economic order based on the exploitation of man by man, on social injustice, we energetically refuse the name of rightists. [1]

This description, a model of conviction and clarity, demonstrates the commitment of men like Duarte to what for Americans would be the most sensible approach to the political and economic dilemmas of Central America. Regrettably, the prospect of achieving it anywhere in the isthmus (with the notable exception of Costa Rica) in the foreseeable future is unlikely.

Yet in the political realities of Central America not even the Christian Democrats are exempt from the hallowed political axiom that what you stand for can mean a lot for your personal stature, but your political values, however noble, can do little for changing things if you have no power. If you're powerless you have to make arrangements with those who have power if you're going to get anywhere. If you're unwilling to compromise your principles and still want to govern, then there's always the revolutionary course, which Duarte has rejected. In this society, politics, as Dean Acheson described it in one of his memorable metaphors, is a horse trade. "I've got a horse, you want to buy my horse. I lower my asking price, you raise your giving price. You get my horse, I get your money. That's American politics." In Central America the powerless have few horses to trade.

In Duarte's case this has meant, ultimately, a gentleman's agreement with the right, a move Duarte made in the uncertain days after the 1979 reform junta collapsed and another, espousing reform with repression, took its place. The shift hurt Duarte considerably with leftist elements in El Salvador and disturbed liberals in this country, who concluded that his commitment to social change was circumscribed by conditions dictated by the Salvadoran military. Such a casual analysis overlooks the painful (figuratively and literally) experience Duarte has endured since the 1960s. He has not forsaken principle for power; he has, as I believe can be explained, diluted his principles in order to incorporate some principle in governance.

Duarte's political career began in urban politics. In the sixties he served as San Salvador's mayor, in an era when just about every Latin American capital was experiencing rapid overcrowding, overburdened public services, and, in the case of San Salvador, a noticeable decline in the quality of urban life. So Duarte launched a reform movement to clean up the capital, paying for it with a much-publicized "moral crusade" of taxation of night clubs, gambling dens, and whorehouses. Ultimately, of course, the city's entrenched business interests got the sympathetic ear of the president and he halted Duarte's crusade. But in the process Duarte managed to build a constituency among the thousands of petty vendors, refugees from the countryside, and displaced persons who clogged the sidewalks in the downtown selling bananas or combs or plastic billfolds. Duarte built new markets for these "centavo capitalists." He pushed "community action" organizations, local advisory groups demanding better garbage collections, improved street lighting, and the like—the kind of politics that irritated the old business community and aroused the suspicions of the ruling order.

To transfer local action programs from the city to the country in any Central America republic but especially in El Salvador, where rural reforms mean a confrontation with the old landed order, is a dangerous undertaking. In the late sixties, as Duarte began maneuvering for his presidential campaign, he did not make agrarian reform a paramount goal. As a matter of fact, Christian Democracy's position on that controversial issue in Salvadoran politics was then practically identical to that of the ruling party.

But a newborn leftist party, whose spokesmen wanted reconciliation with Castro, outspokenly championed land reform. In doing so, they aroused bitter memories of the 1932 communist revolt among the right. In the 1967 elections the communists were trounced, but the Christian Democrats fared well, and in the intervening years the ruling party (the Party of National Conciliation, PCN), as it has generally done over the years in El Salvador, genuinely worried about a coalition on the left. The 1969 war with Honduras brought a severe economic downturn for El Salvador, prompting calls—even from the ruling party—for expropriation of the larger plantations and a vigorous program of industrialization. Fearful that the Christian Democrats would steal its thunder on the issue of economic modernization, the PCN tolerated and even encouraged blatantly fraudulent practices in the 1970 elections for national assemblymen.

The Christian Democrats lost heavily, and Duarte, looking ahead toward the presidential election only two years away, sanctioned a pact with the communists to form a political coalition known as the Union of National Opposition. In the subsequent highly charged campaign the establishment ran a colorless but reliable army colonel. In the voting Duarte outpolled him by 72,000 votes, but a right-wing electoral commission "recounted" the ballots and sent the contest to the assembly for final decision, as the constitution required.

There, of course, Duarte lost. But he had followers, enthusiastic supporters, young idealistic officers with bitter memories of the incompetence of their superiors in the war with Honduras. On March 25 they arrested the president (in a polite call on his residence) and announced they controlled San Salvador. Duarte had not been an organizer of the revolt but under the circumstances joined in, expecting electoral justice and, shortly, the presidential sash across his chest. As luck would have it, just after Duarte gave his blessing to the revolt, crack units of the national guard and police restored order and liberated the president in a brief but fierce military confrontation that took two hundred lives. The forces of restoration then arrested Duarte and, to teach him a lesson, tortured him. Then they kicked him out of the country. For the next seven years, except for a brief visit in 1974, he remained an exile in Venezuela.

These years away from his homeland taught Duarte a lesson about the reality of Central American politics. In a society where the reformers in the middle are so few, the espousal of undeniable truths or the display of humanitarian ethics is no guarantee of getting power. Duarte had played by the rules, and he had lost. In the sixties the Salvadoran establishment had tolerated, even encouraged, the Christian Democrats, looking on them as a "loyal opposition" but always a minority, a nuisance but infinitely preferable to the communists. When Duarte had seriously challenged for real power, the establishment had brazenly and fraudulently stopped him, mostly out of fear of losing power. This was a fear motivated by the military's assessment of its place in Salvadoran politics for half a century. Over the years it has been able to shift leftward, adopting progressive views, then dramatically retrench when it faced the prospect of losing support from the economic magnates for its tolerance of what the Salvadoran right labels communist.

Thus the dilemma for the men in the middle. When Duarte returned to San Salvador in 1979, just as Somoza's dictatorship was perishing in Nicaragua and El Salvador was rapidly slipping into the political violence it has been experiencing ever since, Duarte the man of principle had become Duarte the available political aspirant. His was still a middle-class political philosophy. He still spoke in a tone of urgency for reform. He still mouthed the old bromides about political decency. But the experience of defeat, tempered by physical suffering and exile, had noticeably mellowed his formerly rock-hard convictions, especially the old Christian Democratic principle about civilian control of the military.

Duarte's relationship to the transitory juntas from 1979 to 1982 illustrated his ultimate dependence on the armed forces. He has chosen this most bloodstained element in Central American politics not out of conviction but out of necessity. If the choice is a just policy or an unjust policy, the middle-class reformer will choose the former; if the choice is continuing with the unjust society but holding on to the prospect for changing it or arriving at a just society only by tearing apart the society you have, then the choice is still the former. In October 1979 a progressive faction in the military tossed out its repressive superiors, then loftily declared it would not corrupt its military purity by taking over the country's governance. Another junta formed, a curious amalgam of right, middle, and left politics. There was included a communist as minister of labor. Shortly after its formation, as the Salvadoran economy worsened, Duarte returned from exile in 1979 to a thunderous reception at Ilopango airport (it has since been supplanted by the modern facility at Cuscutlán), and, to his surprise, a violent demonstration by leftist agitators who had long ago given up on pluralistic Christian Democracy as the solution to Salvadoran problems. Expecting to be swept into power by a grateful people (who were actually embittered over the fraudulence of the 1972 election and bruised by the heavy-handedness of seven years of military rule), Duarte found himself on the sidelines. There were two CDs on the junta, and they joined the leftists of the group in insisting on civilian control of the military. When the junta pressed the issue, its members threatening to quit if the generals refused to acquiesce, the commander of the powerful national guard curtly informed them, "We've been running this country for fifty years, and we are quite prepared to keep on running it." Salvadorans were already chiding their reformist governors as the junta of turkeys, meaning they would be soon roasted and served for Christmas dinner for the military.

The "turkeys" lasted till New Year's 1980.[2] A few days after Christmas they had again confronted the generals and, rebuffed a second time, decided there was no use in going on. For three days the capital was plunged in an urban convulsion punctuated by fierce clashes between the Popular Forces, a coalition of leftist groups, and the military. Then, dramatically, came announcement of a new government. Duarte was not a part of it, but he had taken a hand in its formation with a gentlemanly understanding beforehand that the important issue of civilian control of the military would not be raised.

During these troubled times the center of Salvadoran politics split apart. The rightist death squads, modeling themselves on their Guatemalan counterpart, began their systematic kidnapping and killing of organizers of peasant cooperatives. The leftists brought into the government by the October '79 coup fled into exile or joined the guerrillas. A prominent member of the Popular Forces announced that revolution was the only solution. In the reconstituted junta of January 1980, the Christian Democrats resurfaced, but their old allies on the left had departed, and pluralism was a dead issue.

Still, the rejuvenated right was not satisfied. Roberto d'Aubuisson appeared on national television to condemn the "com-symps" among the Christian Democrats. He named names. Soon after that, when one "named" Christian Democrat, the attorney general of welfare, Mario Zamora, was meeting at his home with his colleagues, among them Duarte, a vigilante squad broke in, dragged Zamora into the bathroom, and shot him dead.

Nothing was done to punish the murderers. The brother of the murdered man, Rubén Zamora, indignantly resigned from the Christian Democratic Party (and ultimately joined the liberation movement), and Hector Dada, then the CDs most prominent spokesman, quit the junta. Only by the narrowest of margins did the fractured junta avoid another coup. In the countryside the violence escalated, in a manner that befuddled Americans, who watched nightly television reports on Salvadoran troubles but could not understand why a new government land reform program should be accompanied by such increased violence.

Close observers of the Salvadoran scene understood what was happening. The government combined reform with repression. It confiscated one-fourth of the arable land in the country—376 estates belonging to 244 people—then entrusted the transfer to security forces. These military units, linked by blood and values to the Salvadoran right wing, distributed the seized lands to their friends or simply used their authority to identify the organizers of peasant cooperatives so they could be taken off and shot. Little wonder, then, that Amnesty International announced in spring 1980 that the Salvadoran situation was even worse than the one in Guatemala. When Archbishop Oscar Arnulfo Romero, who had given up on the Christian Democrats as offering any hope for peaceful reforms, announced that insurrection was the only alternative for the oppressed and urged soldiers not to fire on unarmed civilians, he paid for the advice with his life.

By the end of 1980 El Salvador was breaking new Central American records for political homicide. The gruesome character of the civil war that continues to this day took its essential form: increased guerrilla activity in the countryside that augured leftist triumph but could not deliver; an indecent and apparently unstoppable vigilantism on the right; search-and-destroy missions in the mountainous interior; assassination of leftist spokesmen in the capital. The ghastliest episodes occurred in November, when security forces dragged away five National Democratic Front leaders meeting secretly at a school near the American embassy, tortured them, and shot them; and in December, when four American women, three nuns and a layworker, were intercepted after leaving the airport, tortured, and killed. Their bodies were unearthed from a shallow grave a short time later, and all America was horrified.

Embarrassed, the junta of reform/repression (mostly repression) had to find someone with sufficiently respectable credentials to convince the American people that its Salvadoran allies were not brutes, just tough-minded characters who out of necessity had to employ repression to keep the communists from taking over. The military was now quite prepared to accept a civilian president, as long as he didn't insist on telling the generals how to fight *their* war.

Given the murderous ferocity of the right and the acknowledged terrorism of the left, Duarte appears to outside observers as the last best hope for his country. He had joined the junta of "reform and repression," as the government of 1980–1982 was known, only a few weeks after a right-wing assassin had gunned down Archbishop Romero in reprisal for his condemnation of the government's savage campaign in the countryside. With Romero's death Duarte became, for Americans, the only source of moral authority in the Salvadoran government; it was as if his mere presence in power among men who had seemingly lost control of a social order obsessed with fears of its own destruction could somehow lend a semblance of legitimacy to that government.

Predictably, since he had no other choice, Duarte tried to analyze the Salvadoran political situation in terms palatable to Americans. In halting English, which he insisted on speaking among American reporters who got along well enough in Spanish to understand, he explained the death of Romero as an event so despicable that no one person could be liable and in the same breath tried manfully to transfer the blame away from the military or the government. Always he spoke of the paramount need to "control" affairs, in tones of a firm but essentially decent man who has had the misfortune of being forced into associating with a gang of cutthroats who need an honest man up front. Even in those tumultuous days he projected an optimism of being able to "control" the course of events. Once, in a session with reporters at the bar of a fashionable San Salvador hotel, he was explaining something when an obviously inebriated Salvadoran businessman intruded. To demonstrate his displeasure with Duarte, the man unzipped his pants and began urinating on a nearby chair. He was on the verge of saying a few words directly to Duarte when the guards tossed him to the floor. Duarte appeared unruffled: "We are *trying* to get control."[3]

The tragedy was he did not get control of the one institution of the country—the military—that has determined the course of Salvadoran history for the past fifty years. Perhaps he failed because the generals would not give in to a principle, once vital to Duarte and the Christian Democrats but always so odious to them—civilian control of the military. Perhaps, as Duarte has often stated, such a transfer of authority would have made little difference in a society where the men at the top have lost "control" over those under their command. In any event, when Duarte spoke of authority he had in mind "moral authority." That, apparently, was enough for the outgoing Carter administration. Despite the outrage over the murder of four American churchwomen in December 1980, early in January Duarte received a secret pledge of American aid. The following day a hit squad killed the head of the agrarian reform program and two American agricultural experts (representing the AFL-CIO's Latin American organization, the American Institute for Free Labor Development) as they sat drinking coffee in the Hotel Sheraton. These and the less publicized shooting of an American reporter (whose face and hands had been blown off to conceal his identity), subsequently traced to national guard squads, occurred only a few weeks before Ronald Reagan took office and signaled that El Salvador was a new battleground in the Cold War.

Duarte inherited the military and what it stands for, and the Reagan administration inherited Duarte. The presumption was that what Duarte stood for would be the order of the day. And in the early weeks of his "second chance," as Duarte called his experience in the junta of "reform and repression," matters seemed to be going his way. The guerrilla offensive, called for spring 1981, was beaten back with almost devastating results for the urban left. In the national assembly he called for nationalization of the banking and agro-export systems and won handily.

If he had possessed a mandate from the Salvadoran people, already war-weary, and a national assembly packed with Christian Democrats ready to do his bidding, Duarte might have been able to accomplish much in those two years he directed the Salvadoran junta. But the people had not chosen him: he had been permitted to exercise power by a military alert to the importance of maintaining the flow of foreign and military aid money from Washington. To be sure, the much-vaunted agrarian reform program, which the Carter administration had pushed following the October 1979 coup, continued, but whatever limited success it had in the expropriation of the largest estates (over five hundred hectares) paled when measured against the frenzied efforts of the oligarchy and its minions in the assembly to stifle legislation directed at redistributing the much more numerous holdings of one hundred to five hundred hectares and implementing the "Land to the Tiller" plan, designed to give Salvadoran *campesinos* title to plots they farmed.

In its eagerness to inspire the Salvadoran military to take the guerrillas head-on, the Reagan administration expressed a noticeably flagging enthusiasm for a program that Duarte's political enemies characterized as "communistic." And, as Duarte himself often explained to the droves of American reporters who followed him around in search of a story, his power was not "legitimate." Thus he could not be expected to have "control" over the death squads or guardsmen who carried out reprisals on *campesinos* trying to organize their own cooperatives or take possession of land they believed rightfully theirs.

In March 1982 Duarte tried to obtain that legitimacy in the elections for a constituent assembly. He soon found himself outmaneuvered by anticommunist zealots who had a no-quarter platform ("Fatherland, yes; communism, no!") and their champion, Roberto d'Aubuisson. When the balloting was over Duarte had lost. Had the American embassy not brought its considerable influence on the newly elected assembly d'Aubuisson would have become provisional president.

But Duarte refused to drop out of the increasingly violent Salvadoran political arena. More than ever, he comported himself as the "man in the middle," the "last, best hope," in an emotionally charged political campaign for the 1984 Salvadoran presidential office. He has won the grudging support of an anticommunist American president once doubtful of his abilities. He has survived an election and then a run-off against a younger, more vigorous political candidate who very nearly defeated him.

Duarte's triumph in the fierce Salvadoran presidential contest of 1984 has delivered his long-sought "legitimacy." But his victory has not legitimized the principles of Christian Democracy, only the survival of the man as just one of the ruling order. Clearly, he has learned some harsh rules about Central American politics. Arriving in Washington just a few weeks after his narrow victory over d'Aubuisson, Duarte captivated a suspicious Congress with reassuring words and pledges of justice despite revelations that CIA money had poured into his campaign. Congressmen who had relentlessly condemned American policy in Central America had to admit that if the charge was true, American dollars had at least assured the victory of a decent man (Duarte) over a putative killer (d'Aubuisson).

Duarte returned to San Salvador, talked about negotiations with the political wing of the guerrillas, and spoke firmly about dealing with their armed allies in the mountains of El Salvador. A jury in a Salvadoran village returned guilty verdicts against guardsmen implicated in the murder of the four American churchwomen. In the capital, Duarte removed a few conspicuous and embarrassing officers, known for their links to the death squads, from American scrutiny, but the military retains its status of equality, or, more precisely, autonomy.

Initially lukewarm about Duarte, the Reaganites have had to make some painful reassessments about this tough-looking Salvadoran with his guardedly optimistic approach to the problems of Central America. The ordeal of Duarte has taught a painful lesson about the complexities of isthmian, especially Salvadoran, politics. Though the prospect of falling dominoes that would begin with the Sandinista triumph in Nicaragua and be furthered by a guerrilla victory in El Salvador is unsettling for American calculations, that eventuality may pose a milder threat to our interests than the resurgence of the right.

Americans have become obsessed with Cold War examples of

leftist movements exploiting social injustices to discredit existing governments and win power for themselves, replacing, to use Kirkpatrick's phrase, a "mildly authoritarian regime with a totalitarian one." But the proper historical analogue for Central America may not be, say, Cuba in 1958, but Germany in 1932. El Salvador today, like Germany then, is undergoing a wrenching ordeal in which the stakes are not simply which political party will rule but which social values will dictate how society will be organized and governed. Like the Nazis defeated in the German elections of 1932, the Salvadoran rightists are shifting perceptibly to the view that they can "save" the nation from social destruction. Only men like Duarte stand in their way.

Duarte is not a man of Napoleonic abilities. Damned by the left for selling out to the right, grudgingly tolerated by the right because he represents the decent guy up front, thus ensuring the flow of money and arms from the Americans, Duarte and like-minded reformers of his tactical persuasion in Central America are men with an uncertain future. His political appeal in the past rested on his rejection of the charismatic leader, the leader who governs by virtue of personality, in favor of the champion of a practical philosophy, a program. He attracted attention as an idealist without illusion. Yet to snatch the elusive ring of power Duarte has had to project his tough personality, his scrappiness, and suppress his considerable intellectuality. There are men of thought and men of action, Woodrow Wilson once observed. Duarte and his kind can retain conviction, assailing the established order with righteous condemnation, and remain in opposition; or make a political pact with the right, suffering military meddling in politics, and at least possess the semblance of power if not the real thing.

They cannot have both.

7 Down in Tegoose

Honduras has become the bulwark of American power in Central America, a presumably steadfast ally in the Cold War and, in the past few years, our newest military outpost. When American troops began arriving in much larger numbers in 1981, a Green Beret sarcastically noted the country's geopolitical importance: "This dump is the center of the world now."

I N THE MID-1890S THE ADVENTUROUS REPORTER Richard Harding Davis, not yet famous, took a trip through Central America with a couple of pals. The lively ports of the Honduran north coast, with their generous international sampling of humanity—French boarding-houses, German businessmen, Americans on the lam from the law back in the states—reassured him that civilization was penetrating the tropics. But thirty miles or so inland, where the Honduran hills mark the boundary of the banana lands, Davis and his companions needed a guide to lead them through the monotonous trails that ended, after days on horseback, in Tegucigalpa, "inside" Central America.

Tegucigalpa* is the most remote of the Central American capitals, a backwater city hidden beneath towering mountains, but in recent years it has experienced a building boom. A luxury hotel, the Sheraton, has replaced the Honduran Maya as the city's swankiest guest house, and the influx of another generation of *norteamericanos*, soldiers and evangelicals, both committed to saving the country from the Red menace, has bequeathed a bilingual atmosphere to their lobbies. Like San Salvador and Guatemala City, sister capitals to the west and northwest, Tegucigalpa is daily reminded of its precariousness by the carbine-bearing guards at bridges and especially at the numerous banks downtown and in nearby Comayagüela. Tegucigalpa/Comayagüela is Minneapolis/Saint Paul, separated by the Choluteca River, a polluted stream littered with garbage and discarded automobile tires, yet the river boasts its tin shanties, and in the dry season Honduran waifs cavort along its broad sandy banks. But the Choluteca, unlike the Mississippi, does not drain a continent, nor leave much of a mark on Honduran culture.

As in San Salvador and Guatemala City, modernity and tradition are fused. Downtown "Tegoose" is actually a street of approximately four blocks closed to auto traffic, the Holiday Inn at one end and the Parque Central, a half block square dominated by a fading colonial church, at the other. Between are smart shops featuring the latest European fashions and pleasant restaurants and coffee shops where the city's government and professional people gather to chat in the Hispanic fashion about the "American presence." The *norteamericanos* who constitute the subject of their conversations are either holed up in the hotels or out in the countryside spreading the word of God. Around one corner from the Gran Vía, a pleasant cafeteria with a tiled floor reminiscent of a 1950s soda shop, stands the Crazy Horse Disco Dance. Not two blocks away is the pastel colonial edifice where Francisco Morazán, patron saint of Central American

---

*Hondurans often abbreviate Tegucigalpa to "Teguc," pronounced "Tāy *goose*," and spelled, in Spanglish, "Tegoose."

union, lived. It is now the repository of the National Archives and Library, containing probably no more volumes than the Harrisburg Public Library.

In none of the Central American capitals is the symbol of authority or nationhood represented by an urban setting similar to Pennsylvania Avenue with Congress at one end and the White House at the other. In Tegoose the Presidential Palace, an unimposing building, and the National Congress, a curious modern edifice built in the early fifties, stand a short block apart, separated appropriately by the national bank.

One hundred fifty years ago Tegoose had a faint hope of becoming the center of the Central American union, but Morazán, who might have become the isthmian George Washington, Thomas Jefferson, and Napoleon—all in the person of one determined *centroamericano*—realized only too soon in his career that Tegucigalpa, the ancient Spanish mining center untouched by earthquakes, was too isolated even from the rest of Honduras. So he carried his unifying crusade across the mountains into Guatemala and El Salvador. There he met his match in men who had no use for such lofty goals as isthmian union. One of them, Rafael Carrera, a *ladino caudillo* from Guatemala, broke Morazán's tenuous hold on the federation. By the early 1840s, when the rambunctious United States was preparing for its absorption of the old Spanish northwest, the United Provinces of Central America fell into disarray. Morazán perished before a firing squad, and Tegoose lost whatever prominence the George Washington of the isthmus had bequeathed to it. Comayagua, to the north, became the national capital. For another forty years Tegucigalpa remained what it had been under the Spanish, an isolated town in the mining district of inner Central America, guarded from the outside by looming hills and lost to history. In 1880, after years of haggling, the political barons decided that the national capital should be moved from Comayagua, lying in a pleasant valley between Tegucigalpa and San Pedro Sula, down to Tegoose.

In the years that followed, in what Hondurans proudly called the "Golden Age" of President Marco Aurelio Soto, Tegoose enjoyed a revival brought on by a mining boom. At the 1884 New Orleans Exposition the progressive president of rival Guatemala exhibited more than one thousand products his country exported. His counterpart from Honduras, Luís Bográn, displayed a 100,000-square-foot map showing the regions of greatest opportunity for enterprising Americans who might exploit the mineral riches of the mountainous Honduran interior. Honduras was already deeply in hock to certain British financial syndicates which had excited a succession of Honduran leaders with the prospect of laying a national railroad from the north coast to Tegoose. Now, as the century drew to a close, its leaders looked to eager American capitalists and fortune hunters as a way of escaping the grip of European finance.

And the Americans came, but it was not Tegoose that benefited so much as the isolated mining towns in Olancho and Yuscarán. A generation of ambitious entrepreneurs and down-and-outers discovered Honduras: the Valentine family, who moved from New York in 1879 and founded the Honduras and Rosario Mining Company; a larcenous Louisianan, Major Ed Burke, accused of fraud in a Louisiana bond scheme, who fled to Honduras to reestablish himself in mining (and politics); and the banana barons who transformed the north coast into American domain after the turn of the century. Most of this new wealth was siphoned off to New Orleans, Mobile, and Boston. Well into the twentieth century Tegoose remained an isolated capital of a country for which the term "geographical expression" would have been an accolade.

Until the 1960s the only spectacular urban growth in the republic lay over the mountains along the north coast where the big American banana companies, United and Standard, transformed backwater ports and havens for runaways and tropical tramps into bustling company towns. Any aspiring Honduran politician who wanted to wield power down in Tegoose had to come to terms with the banana barons (*la bananera*, as the Hondurans say), who bankrolled their candidates in direct proportion to the leniency the prospective president of the republic displayed toward their "special" needs, i.e., no customs duties. Sprawling free-port ware-houses still dominate the north-coast towns. And *norteños* looked to the *bananera* for work, political guidance, and authority. Teguci-galpa may have been the republic's capital, but the banana com-panies ruled the north and, it was said, the country.

And until the fifties Honduras was the quintessential banana republic. Obsequious to American wishes in international politics, it served as a staging area for the overthrow of an undesirable leftist regime in Guatemala in 1954. Yet in the same year coastal banana laborers, accustomed to years of browbeating and abuse, rallied against the *bananera* and in a celebrated strike wrung significant concessions from their American rulers. When it was over, a disgruntled American diplomat perhaps unintentionally com-plimented the Hondurans: "Hell, this place wasn't even a country until now."

What happened hardly constituted a revolution, but some things changed for the *hondureños*. San Pedro Sula, thirty miles from the north coast in a valley flanked by verdant hills, developed a go-getter spirit. Its leaders transformed a town of twenty thousand on the Chamelecón River into a modern inland city with probably the only significant industry in the entire country. And down in Tegoose (though the capital lies at three thousand feet above sea level) Hondurans had a modestly left-of-center civilian president, Ramón Villeda Morales, who had emerged in the wake of the old dictator, Tiburcio Carías Andino. Carías Andino had ruled the country for twenty-five years with a contract from the banana barons in one hand and a club in the other.

Villeda exhibited a refreshing sardonic humor about Honduras. "We are the country of the seventies," he would boast, "seventy percent illiteracy, seventy percent illegitimacy, seventy percent rural."[1] For a few years in the early sixties, when the Alliance for Progress sparked hopes for a brighter future, Hondurans showed an unnatural optimism about national politics. But the army grew tired of Villeda's reformist notions and in 1963 tossed him out. And though Kennedy publicly declared his displeasure with military rule and for a while even refused to recognize its legitimacy, the generals were not dismayed. "You'll be back," one of them bragged to an American diplomat. In six months he was proved right.

A decade later, as the Southeast Asian venture and Nixon's career were ending, Hondurans witnessed renewed American attention, similar to that it had attracted in the first decades of the twentieth century. The guerrilla movements that afflicted its neighbors largely bypassed Honduras. Its military government was comparatively benign when measured against the severe tactics of the Guatemalan generals or the crass opportunism of the Somozas in Nicaragua. And so Honduras acquired, almost by default, a certain distinction in American eyes. With the eighties has come a civilian president, Dr. Roberto Suazo Cordóva, an avuncular man from the country who makes pilgrimages to the remote towns and lets the generals run the country.

In the same span Tegoose has come of age as America's favorite capital among the Central American republics. It lacks the urban muscularity of Guatemala City or the human density of San Salvador, but San José, Costa Rica, is too far away (and presumed "safe") to serve as anticommunist bastion, and Managua, of course, has been lost as an outstation of American power. Belmopan, capital of the newest isthmian republic, Belize, would scarcely qualify as a county seat. The elevation of Panama into a third-world role in international politics, a change symbolized by the 1979 canal treaties and the emergence of Panama City as a great international banking center, disqualifies that capital. All this has meant that Tegucigalpa, which nominally governs the Caribbean bulge of the isthmus, now occupies a formidable place in American strategic calculations.

But it is a position that has devolved on Honduras only because of its geographical position, and the Hondurans know it. The Americans have struck their deal with a stridently anticommunist government in Tegoose because it is militarily expedient to do so, not because the United States has much commitment to elevating the lot of ordinary Hondurans.[2] There have been predictable aid packages for the second-poorest country in the western hemisphere—Haiti is at the bottom, and Honduras would have to sink a long way to replace it—with the concomitant obligation of turning the southern part of the country into a staging area for assaults by anti-Sandinistas against Nicaragua and the entire country over to the United States for military maneuvers. That Tegoose has profited is undeniable. For the first time in Honduran history the capital is exerting a political and economic sway that most Latin American capitals have been exercising over their national domains for most of this century.

Avenida Seis (Sixth Avenue) is the main drag in both Guatemala City and in Tegoose. In the former it runs straight through Zone 1, lined by modern shops with the latest American gadgetry and European fashion. Signs advertising Jordache and Wrangler and Sergio Valente extend over the street, creating a claustrophobic ambience. Guatemalans may flock to see Grade B movies (Joan Collins in *The Bitch* or *Violence in America,* a crudely fashioned collage of news reports on murder in the U.S.A.), but their sartorial tastes, at least for the middle and upper classes, are big-city. Hondurans have not yet acquired that sophistication, but they're catching up, American-style. Newspaper ads exhort them: "Get ahead! Learn English!"

Sixth Avenue in Tegoose rises up a modest incline (by Honduran standards) with Spanish-style pastel buildings set close to the street, winds in serpentine reflex down into the valley of a polluted creek past squalid restaurants and hotels, and then heads up again into Tegoose's most fashionable residential area. Here is the American embassy, an impressive, sprawling bastion perched on the hillside, guarded by machine-gun-bearing *hondureños* with stupefied expressions. Unlike its counterparts in Guatemala City and San Salvador, the embassy in Tegoose does not require the unwieldy concrete bunkers to protect against a Lebanon-style assault with a truck of explosives. No vehicle could acquire enough velocity or possess sufficient mass to overcome the angle of topography or ram through the stone fence and mound of earth behind it.

A short walk away (down one hill and up another) through a residential neighborhood of $200,000-and-up stylish houses with Mercedeses in the drives, there is a strip of American and European restaurants catering to foreigners. The elegant and famous Honduran Maya stands not far from here. It is lunchtime, American standard, and a small group of American soldiers, dressed in civilian clothes in a futile effort to be inconspicuous, are enjoying Wiener schnitzel in the next booth. Their discussion, audible throughout the *gemütlich* patio dining area, begins with the ill effects of drugs but soon drifts to the condition of the people they've come down to protect. They have recently arrived from the coast, on leave down in dry but cool Tegoose from maneuvers in the torrid north. The Hondurans are likable, a bit subservient, they agree, but not overly grateful for their presence.

A shoeshine boy is making the rounds, a smudged-face kid wearing ragged clothes but possessing an infectious smile. He represents, along with the newspaper peddlers and fruit-stand operators, the foundation of "centavo capitalism" in Central America. He approaches the Americans, but they're not interested in shiny shoes for the afternoon, so the kid wanders off to the steak house across the way with the expectation, probably, of finding some other Americans and making four lempiras (two dollars) and a significant contribution to his family's daily income. Perhaps *he* is the breadwinner of his family. The money he takes in is minuscule in comparison to the millions in dollars the Americans and their comrades represent to his country, but these are monies that will never filter down to the shoeshine boy.

Urban sprawl afflicts Tegucigalpa, and because the city lies in a valley surrounded by towering hills, the growth of new *colonias* occurs on an angle, in almost every direction. Low-slung shacks on twisting dirt streets inch up the hills, so that the suburbs look down on the city. Even the airport, now an obsolete installation that reminds arriving Americans of airfields on the milk run in the Dakotas, has been flanked by these mushrooming squatter villages that plague Latin American capitals. If the Hondurans build another, as the Salvadorans have in their sleek new jetport of Cuscutlán, connected to San Salvador by a four-lane *autopista*, they will probably have to go forty or fifty miles to the north to find enough level ground for a modern runway. Tegoose is not likely to relinquish its hold on the seat of government just in order to have a nearby airport that can accommodate 747s.

Life in Tegoose appears relaxed when measured against the hectic routine of sprawling "Guate" or congested San Salvador. On Sundays the capital practically shuts down, as if governed by some Honduran variation of midwestern American "blue-law" ordinances intent on punishing those who violate the Sabbath. Around the Hotel Ritz, in the center of San Salvador, the intensity of street life picks up. Middle-class Salvadoran families head for a popular fried-chicken outlet and the unwashed mill about a five-or-six-block market of stalls with plastic items, inexpensive clothing (no guayabera shirts here), overpriced tools, and the like, and listen to a beefy woman with a bullhorn who booms out nonstop for twelve hours in cadences matched only by southern livestock auctioneers.

By most accounts, Honduras is underpopulated. But the mayors of its only two large cities (Tegoose and San Pedro Sula) have become concerned in recent years over an "urban invasion" of country folk looking for the better life.[3] They speak in ominous terms about the ramshackle one-room huts inching up the side of El Picacho, the most famous of Tegoose's protective mountains, each containing four, five, sometimes more, illiterate, diseased, or malnourished dwellers, who, like their counterparts in Guatemala City or San Salvador, where they're even more numerous, are escaping the wretchedness of rural life. The prospects for them are bleak. The father stands little chance of becoming much more than a menial laborer who gets one day of work per week. If he's very lucky, he may acquire an old school bus, giving it a personal touch with a mixture of garish designs, and provide a service to his neighbors, people like himself. The mother may get out of the hovel and become an entrepreneur, presiding over a fly-infested fruit stand and exercising a dawn-to-dusk vigilance over two or three or more children who cavort on the sidewalk.

Yet still they come in from the country because they have hope. They dream of getting ahead, sending the son to the technical institute or betrothing the daughter to a university graduate headed for a job with the Banco de Londres or a slot in the government bureaucracy. That may give the children a chance at a modest two-bedroom stucco house with a gently sloping roof and a small patio and a Toyota or Datsun in the driveway in one of the diminutive "Levittowns" out from the city. It will mean that the daughter might be able to live the role of the traditional Hispanic woman and that *her* children can go far beyond the first or second grade, the educational level of her parents. She may even live the character she faithfully watches on her favorite "prime-time" soap opera, where the "young and the restless" are not quite so explicit in word and deed as their American counterparts but have the same problems—family troubles. The concerned, overly protective momma tries to warn her daughter, foolishly enamored of a rake, that she should enjoy her fantasies by reading "Jazmín" books, the Spanish-language equivalent of Harlequin romances.

Doubtless some of these things lay on the minds of the passengers on the 9:15 bus to San Pedro Sula, five hours and 165 twisting miles to the north. Buses to other parts of the country, in Honduras and in other isthmian capitals, depart from different places in the city, usually near the biggest market (in Tegoose, across the fetid Choluteca in Comayagüela), but almost always within reasonable walking distance from one terminal to another. Transportes Norteños takes you from Tegoose to San Pedro for $3.50. Naturally, if you want to go only to, say, Comayagua, about fifty miles up the road, you can buy a partial fare and be deposited on the highway at the Texaco station outside town; or you can walk over to the Tegucigalpa–Comayagua Transport Company and the driver will dump you in downtown Comayagua. The system gets even more complicated, and very little about it makes sense to an American, but it does guarantee that any Honduran equivalent of Greyhound will not have a monopoly on the main route across the country.

But unlike Greyhound the buses are not of uniform quality. One might get a powerful Mercedes cruiser (as I did on the trip back from San Pedro) or an aged rattletrap discarded years ago by a Louisiana school system. On the journey to San Pedro I wound up on the latter variety, though the driver, a husky black man who probably lived in

San Pedro, had decorated *his* bus, inside and out, with a personal touch. In artfully drawn letters, beneath "Transportes Norteños," he had inscribed "Dios Me Guarde" ("May God Guard Me"). Inside, along the narrow strip above the windshield, was a mural depicting the punk rock group Kiss and a ledge for his cassette player. On American buses the playing of a radio or cassette is generally prohibited; on Honduran buses it is socially mandatory for the driver to provide conversation and musical entertainment. In this case the driver had a Michael Jackson tape, which blared out for the first time as we sat waiting for him to finish his Salva Vida beer. We heard Michael Jackson off and on for 165 miles. There was a reassuring thought conjured up by this scene: the fifty or so people who put their lives in the hands of someone who beseeches the Almighty to guard him, likes Michael Jackson, and drinks a beer called Lifesaver before heading out on one of the most tortuous highways in Christendom, are not ready candidates for communism.

By tradition Central American bus drivers depart from one place to another when they have a full load. If operating on a published schedule, as does Transportes Norteños, they somehow manage to fill every seat before leaving, and if not, cruise slowly through town until they do. The 9:15 filled up quickly but did not leave for thirty minutes. The starter wouldn't turn the engine, a predicament unsettling to no one but the only *norteamericano* aboard, who sat wondering how long it would take Transportes Norteños to get another starter. The other passengers were apparently unperturbed, keeping up a constant chatter or buying cookies or chewing gum or dried bananas from the swarming peddlers who surround a halted bus. The driver called on a teenager in a grimy sweatshirt, armed only with a screwdriver, to bang on the starter solenoid. For twenty minutes or so there were futile efforts to get the engine started. Finally, the driver yelled for a few good men to get off and give this cumbersome contraption a shove. A few seconds later we were finally on our way north. When you're at the bottom of the capitalist order, where most Central Americans are, you depend on such spontaneous assistance, even from your customers, to keep going.

Leaving Tegoose by any direction means going up. The way north winds through Comayagüela up a hill flanked by poor *barrios* of shabby pastel houses with tin or ruddy tile roofs, roadside eating joints with one or two tables and a few chairs with torn plastic cushions, a Pentecostal tabernacle or Seventh Day Adventist Mission, neither of which looms mightily on the horizon. Only the hills and mountains rule Tegoose.

Already the driver has made three stops to pick up people who couldn't make it to Transportes Norteños' terminal but who have to go up the road toward San Pedro. Across the aisle is a frail mother of perhaps thirty but who looks forty-five or fifty. She weighs no more than a hundred pounds but has managed to carry her son aboard, a lad of perhaps ten, who has five pounds of braces strapped to his legs, and his crutches. She nestles him on her lap, allowing his legs to extend into the narrow aisle, but after a few miles, tiring, she asks the boy to stand, placating him with a *dulce*. Soon she is engaged in animated conversation with people around her, telling how her son had polio and passing a faded snapshot of him for everyone to see. "Yes," they agree, "he's a fine-looking boy." She is from a village fifteen miles from San Pedro and had brought her boy down to Tegoose to a clinic for treatment. Had she never heard of the vaccine? someone asked. Yes, she explained, but it had not been available in her village until a few years ago and by then it was too late for her son.

By this time the bus had wound up the mountainside and was plummeting into the next valley. Infrequent travelers on Central American buses should sit toward the rear, so as to avoid seeing ahead. In this way one is only occasionally perturbed by the realization that the driver is spending an inordinate amount of time on the left side of the road. To be seated in the front row is an experience in perpetual terror. Passing two or three trucks on a curve or a hill is, for these drivers, a casual maneuver. The operator of the 9:15 to San Pedro performed the feat four or five times with only one hand on the wheel, all the while engaged in effervescent chatter with a bosomy woman in a tight-fitting skirt seated strategically to his right. Passing two trucks on a blind curve (to the right!) going down one of these precipitous inclines requires two hands on the wheel, only furtive glances to the right, and the requisite two or three beeps on the horn to let the slower-moving trucks know you're passing *and* signal any oncoming Toyotas or Datsuns or the south-bound Transportes Norteños to slow down or pull over to the side of the road. The passenger may now be reflecting on the original purpose of the slogan "May God Guard Me" inscribed on the front of the bus. Thirty minutes out of Tegoose, SAHSA, the Honduran national airline, has erected a sign: "If you had flown with us, you'd already be there." But, then, SAHSA does not emblazon its planes with "May God Guard Me."

Thirty miles out there is a military checkpoint, a small cinder-block structure. The bus stops, and the hawkers materialize, thrusting plastic bags of melon slices, corn on the cob, or candy at the window, yelling out prices with a *"Quiere? Quiere?"* (Want one? Want one?) This is evidently a scheduled stop, which means there will be five minutes or so to allow men, women, and children to get off and scatter for a convenient boulder or tree or bush behind which they can heed nature's call. A beefy official, casually dressed, emerges from the cinder-block hut and steps aboard. The passengers extract smudged documents bearing the seal of the republic or plastic identity cards. He may be looking for Salvadorans or simply reminding these people about the reach of the national government back in Tegoose. Mine is a passport, scrutinized by the ponderous Honduran and returned with a reminder that I have only three more days in his country.

Two soldiers and a fat woman wearing a paper sun visor and sporting a flower in a mass of twisted black hair get aboard. One of the soldiers, his hat perched back on his head, gives her knowing looks, but at the next town only the soldiers get off. Two miles later the driver slams on the brakes, pulling over precariously near a rock ledge. A young woman in the front who had not relieved herself back at the checkpoint is provided an unscheduled rest stop, shielded from traffic by the bus and a mound of rock. Greyhound executives will doubtless wince at such personal service.

Winding through these interminable hills and isolated valleys, one is reminded of the burdens imposed by isthmian topography. This is *inside* Central America, where there is no vast Mississippi heartland, no great plains of farmland to feed the people, no mighty inland cities to draw the urbanbound away from national capitals packed with humanity, like San Salvador or Guatemala City or even Tegucigalpa.

Aside from Comayagua, which does not have the size to play such a role, there is only San Pedro Sula, the end of the line for Transportes Norteños. Hours ago the brown hills of Tegoose have given way to mountains clustered with tall pine. Thirty miles from San Pedro the landscape alters to dark tropical green, and the highway descends from the last mountain and passes an Alpine lake into a valley carved out by the Chamelecón River. This is the southern entry into the Honduras most Americans know best, the banana domains carved out years ago by Standard and United, a region that for decades looked north to New Orleans or Mobile and not down to Tegoose for its needs. The long twisting mountain highway has now straightened, passing through small villages with tin, tile, or thatch-roofed huts.

At one of them a scrofulous man carrying fifty pounds of onions in a mesh sack gets on. Trailing him is a boy with an LP gas canister, its valve wrapped with thin plastic tied snug with string. They deposit their cargo atop the huge spare tire that lies in the space next to the left-side emergency door. The man is going to San Pedro to sell his onions and get enough money to fill the gas canister, its leaky valve betrayed by a noxious rotten-egg odor. The boy is his son. He was married some years ago, but his wife turned out to be a no-account who ran off with a neighbor to Tegoose, leaving him to tend the onion patch. He personifies the Honduran lower-class male, what is still known in the American south as the good old boy. He talks incessantly about his life, much of which is bound up with his weekly excursion to San Pedro. But after a while, having recounted the big events in his life, he leans over and begins to drowse.

Twenty minutes out of San Pedro the bus driver with the Michael Jackson cassette slows and for several miles avoids his daring passing maneuvers. The reason for his more professional behavior is soon apparent. An American military convoy is passing, headed south, I learn later in San Pedro, for maneuvers with the Honduran army in the Comayagua Valley. The trucks are the familiar olive-drab Americans occasionally encounter on an interstate, where they pose little problem to the flow of traffic. But here, where the *main* highway across the country is not much wider than a farm-to-market road, these cumbersome vehicles are an overpowering presence.

The passengers are momentarily drawn from their animated conversations about daily frustrations by the convoy. They have, surprisingly, little to say about what these vehicles really mean for their country, perhaps because they and most Hondurans like them have had no part in the decision to bring the American military into their country. Their facial expressions are the look of resignation to events over which they have no control. Even the onion man, roused from his stupor by the slowing of the bus, who has far more consequential matters in his life than concerns about the American military presence in his country, does not seem much impressed by this show of might.

The convoy finally passes, and the driver resumes his normal—read fanatical—driving habits. Suddenly the bus lurches to the right, the emergency door bolts open, and the gas canister is on its way out when, quick as a cat, the onion man snatches it in midair. Then he drifts off into sleep. At the terminal he plops down to the ground, turns, and with a mighty heave pulls the onion bag onto his shoulder and, with the boy trotting ahead, trudges off to the San Pedro market. With the money from the onions he can buy a few bottles of Salva Vida and forget about his woman down in Tegoose.

San Pedro is the country's second city and still its most progressive. It is surrounded by small plants that manufacture steel rods and cement and other light industrial products. It is connected to the sea and, ultimately, the great markets of the southern United States, by railroad. San Pedro exudes a midwest boosterism. It has pleasant shaded streets that run true and a downtown of go-getter businesses. Everywhere there are symbols of the historical American entrepreneurial spirit that long ago penetrated the Honduran north coast. And there are statues to the benefactors of the American presence—General Manuel Bonilla, the burly mulatto who opened the country to Sam "the Banana Man" Zemurray in the early twentieth century; and Miguel Paz Barahona, the Masonic (an unusual affiliation for a Central American politician) president who in the mid-twenties placated Yankee business interests.

San Pedro is usually the first stopover for the southward bound from the states. Its citizens, long accustomed to the power of the American dollar, are hospitable, and its frequent American visitors are pleasantly lulled by its ambience into believing that San Pedro is typically Central American. To save such places from communists seems as undeniably compelling as saving Kansas City.

San Pedro boasts a luxury hotel, the Gran Hotel Sula, just across a comfortable square from downtown, a formidable building with the impressive awesomeness of a spa overlooking small shops. The Gran Hotel Sula has a friendly staff and manager, a beefy bilingual *norteño* who has placed his picture prominently in the lobby along-side a sign that reads, in English and Spanish, "Hello, My Name Is . . ." Here the incoming tourists and evangelicals and off-duty American military can feel at home. They will be properly pampered before heading out to save souls or go on maneuvers to the south or enjoy scuba-diving in the Bay Islands. In the gracious patio, where guests gather to drink or lunch, English is as commonly heard as Spanish. But San Pedro is not the real Central America nor an authentic replica of Honduran culture; it represents the accomplishments of imitative north-coast Hondurans who long ago learned to live with and profit from the banana companies lodged in the neighborhood and have modeled their town on American lines. It is atypical of Central America, and with its noticeable community pride and solidity is not easily duplicated elsewhere in Central America until one gets to the Costa Rican highlands.

On the day I arrived in San Pedro the Gran Hotel Sula was jammed with Americans—an evangelical group out of New Orleans, which at one time sent only guns and soldiers of fortune to these parts, and of course American military, some in uniform. For relaxation I chose the more sinful atmosphere of the hotel bar. A few stools away was another American fondling a bottle of Salva Vida, the ubiquitous Honduran elixir. He had the look of a man long at sea who has found a port. Some days before, the U.S.S. *Flately*, a minor vessel in America's naval armada, had docked in Trujillo, an ancient north-coast port of no great significance except that it was where, in 1860, a firing squad of illiterate Hondurans dispatched the American adventurer William Walker, conqueror of Nicaragua, into immortality.

"You an American?" he asked.

"Yes." Not an hour before I had passed for Costa Rican in the restaurant across the square. "I'm down here writing a book about Central America."

"This place is the dumps," he said. "Everything shuts down at ten o'clock at night. There's nothing to do. It's worse than Peoria."

I had not realized the U.S.S. *Flately* docked at Peoria but thought it better not to say so. He took another sip of his "Lifesaver." "Think I'll go down to Tegoose," he said. "It's got to be livelier there than around here. There's a flight out of San Pedro in the morning. I hear it takes only twenty minutes. Man, I need some excitement."

"Why don't you take the bus?"

8 Omaha, Central America

ICARAGUANS LIVE IN A STATE OF SIEGE AND deprivation, bitterly debating their future in a depressing environment wrought by natural disaster and civil war. Their southern neighbors, the Costa Ricans, live in a fertile valley of placid towns and a capital that reminds visitors of Omaha, a bustling overgrown city of go-getters. They continually fret over their declining standard of living and harbor fears about becoming the "next Lebanon."

Nicas and *ticos* are unalike in almost every respect, save for a Hispanic heritage, and at opposite ends of the spectrum in their posture toward the United States. Costa Ricans, who have suffered no American military penetration and only isolated cases of Washington's political chastisement, are the only truly pro-American people in Central America. Their admiration of American culture is a sobering reminder that cultural affinity and genuine friendship between two countries cannot be reinforced by policies of threat and intimidation. And Costa Rica's experience in our time offers an ominous warning about the prospect for what Kennedy called "decent democratic regimes" in Latin America.

I was reminded of their differences in a polite conversation with a distinguished gentleman from Madrid, retired from the World Health Organization but still much traveled, who sat next to me in the comfortable international departure lounge of Managua's Augusto César Sandino airport.

We had finished negotiating the last checkpoint—four coming in, four going out—this one full of stern-looking Sandinista customs officials. We had started through together, but his still-valid U.N. passport had expedited his passage, and I had delayed my own progress by trying to pay the departure tax (ten dollars and ten córdobas) with a twenty-dollar traveler's check. On top of that was a two-dollar visa fee for entry into Costa Rica, but since the córdoba was currently exchanging at thirty-eight to one, the official owed me money—in dollars. Two, then three and eventually four of these unsmiling guardians of the regime scurried about looking for a few stray dollars. The Nicaraguans are desperate for dollars; it is a matter of survival for their economy in a time of stringent measures against them by the American government. On entering the country the first greeting after *Viva Nicaragua Libre* and *Viva Sandino* is a sign explaining the emergency law requiring those carrying dollars to swear to the amount and convert at least sixty into córdobas, and to pledge on leaving that they're not carrying out more money than they brought into the country. In the past five years, $5 billion has fled Central America, and Nicaraguan emigrants trying to get their dollars out of the country can be subjected to unpleasant searches.

Exasperated, I finally blurted out that I'd be satisfied with córdobas, knowing I could still spend them down the way in the duty-free shop. But the harassed young Nicaraguan insisted I wait, as if it were a point of honor that no *yanquí*, whose government's economic policies were at least partly responsible for his country's predicament, was going to embarrass him. It took twenty minutes to provide my change, but he managed to get it—in dollars.

When I finally caught up with the Spanish gentleman he was nursing a rum and Coke. "I try to understand these people," he said sarcastically. "But look at the mess they've created." He continued with some condemnatory observations other critics of the Sandinistas have been harping on for several years—the severe economic measures, press censorship, harassment of the regime's political enemies, trouble with the church, and so on. I interjected random comments about the problems the Sandinistas encountered when they took over in 1979. After all, how much time does it take to restore a country shattered by civil war and natural disaster, and laboring under the threat of counterrevolution and hostility of the Americans? His tone softened a bit, but he had seen no signs the Sandinistas were trying to rebuild Nicaragua with any noticeable determination. As I had done, he had walked about downtown—or what once was downtown—Managua, past the desolate lots and near-collapsed shells of buildings.

"Did you see any construction going on?" he asked. "That should tell you a great deal about this new order. I've seen all this before, in Europe a generation ago. What these people want is power, nothing more."

It was obvious that our interpretations of the Sandinistas were on a collision course, so I was glad when the conversation shifted from "these people" to Costa Rica. He had never been there. By some inexplicable quirk, in his many years in W.H.O. his itinerary had taken him throughout Latin America but never to Costa Rica. He had read of this idyllic place where the people were friendly, cultured, civilized—traits he equated with being very Hispanic. The highlight of his visit would be a concert at the National Theater, a majestic edifice on the central square in downtown San José that symbolizes, the Costa Ricans will tell visitors to their country, the superiority of their way of life.

An hour later our Aéronica 727 descended into Juan Santamaría airport, named after a Costa Rican lad who sacrificed his life in the war against Walker. Costa Ricans well remember that story and many others about their crusade to rid Central America of invaders from the north. It is a tale that reminds them of the role they once played in shaping the destiny of the isthmus.

For forty years the Costa Ricans have been enticing foreigners, especially Americans, to come down, convinced their amiability and persuasiveness will acculturate the contemporary intruder to their special way of life. Since the civil war of 1948 the Americans have been responding, most of them retirees who settle in a graceful residential section of Alajuela or San José and then decide to start a business. This is well and good with the Costa Ricans, because it means dollars and employment.

Others have sought sanctuary in the wilderness.[1] In 1951 a band of settlers in this modern invasion of Walker's descendants, forty Quakers from Fairhope, Alabama, established their own town, Monteverde, on three thousand acres in remote pasture and forest land. Alienated by the Cold War militarism then engulfing the United States, they learned of Costa Rica's decision to abolish its military and ventured down. In the beginning Monteverde was a tent village, accessible only by jeep, but it rapidly acquired a reputation as a Shangri-la where nobody carried a gun and peace and pacifism were the ruling civic philosophy. So it has lured an odd mix of Americans escaping the hubbub of city life and leftover "heepies" from the sixties and seventies who are taking their last stand against modernity and its discontents.

But news of Central America's strife concerns Monteverde's citizens, as it does the middle-class Costa Rican businessman three and half hours away from Monteverde's tranquillity. Some years ago several Monteverde residents organized a local Latin American Action Committee, which convenes for discussion about isthmian troubles and even dispatches investigating teams into some of the squalid refugee camps popping up along the border with Costa Rica. It is a troubling sign that not even Shangri-la is immune from the outside world.

Costa Rica's stature among the Central American republics is something of a paradox. In the colonial era, it was probably the most neglected province of the Kingdom of Guatemala that made up Spanish Central America. And its highland towns, where the population clustered, were bitterly divided. Cartago and Heredia were conservative outposts of Spanish imperial rule, fiercely loyal to the crown; but San José and Alajuela were centers of defiance, their peoples attracted to the economic liberalism that eventually undermined Spanish rule in the early nineteenth century. And in its remoteness from the convulsions that swept the rest of the isthmus in the ensuing years, Costa Rica developed a different culture.

In 1821, when Central America declared its independence from Spain, Costa Rica had only sixty thousand people. But it had a crop—coffee—introduced by a liberal Spanish governor who had wanted something that would enhance Spanish tax collection. In the rich volcanic soil of the highlands coffee plants flourished, and by midcentury Costa Rican farmers, granted free land by the government, were shipping their beans over mule trails to the small Pacific port of Puntarenas, now a fashionable resort where *ticos* from the highlands lie in the sun or sip drinks in sidewalk cafes.

Costa Rica had its share of iron men, dictatorial types like Tomás Guardia, but they turned out to be "progressive" in the nineteenth-century sense, which meant that they were more than ready to use the authority of the state to promote economic development. Guardia realized that as long as Costa Rica depended on Puntarenas as its link with the sea, its contact with the European and eastern American market would be limited. The coffee that moved over mountain trails to the Pacific had to be shipped all the way around Cape Horn and then northward to find its customers.

So in the early 1870s Guardia committed the Costa Rican government to an ambitious—and, his critics say, ruthless—American entrepreneur, Minor Keith, nephew of Henry Meiggs (the builder of one of the great engineering achievements of South America, the Peruvian railroad in the Andes Mountains). Keith contracted to link by rail the central highlands—the Meseta Central—with the pestilential Caribbean coast. The commitment was a truly monumental undertaking. Keith had to lay track over terrain that rose from three thousand to five thousand feet, then dropped to sea level in less than a hundred miles. Keith labored with a merciless ferocity. He spent twenty years building the Atlantic route, and in those two decades, it is still remembered, ruled as master over the thousands of workers imported to hack brush and endure fever to build a railroad. In that ordeal six thousand perished, and Keith more than once faced mutiny and bankruptcy. But he prevailed, sometimes forcing his men to work at gunpoint while cajoling his creditors to sustain the payroll.

In 1878, confronted by failure, Keith imported banana trees to the eastern lowlands as a means of providing a ready source of income. Bananas had already appeared in the United States from Jamaica and, though considered an exotic fruit, had attracted public attention and quick profits. Before long Keith realized that in the banana trade lay a rewarding financial future, though not even he could imagine the vastness of empire the banana plant would ultimately sustain. The banana, and the rail lines he built to transport it, would earn him the sobriquet "King of Central America."

Coffee-growing reinforced the power of the old landowning elite, but it made the economy increasingly vulnerable to market fluctuations in the outside world. Bananas meant quicker profits, though with a greater risk, and the rapid spread of banana enterprises along the Caribbean coast, from Bocas del Río to Puerto Barrios, signaled the emergence of foreign economic—and, ultimately, political—power in Central America. Elsewhere the isthmian monocultural economies doomed what social scientists call "pluralist" politics. Heavy American economic and political pressures led to repeated military intervention and crass dictatorship.

The *ticos* escaped none of these afflictions (save American military intervention), yet they weathered the adversities that plagued their neighbors in a different way, and how they have survived economic severity and political adversity in large measure explains why they are different.

For one thing the *ticos* did not make the foreign presence on the coast the scapegoat during hard times. True, Keith imported large numbers of black workers from the English-speaking West Indies, who aroused resentments among jobseekers from the central highlands, but the tax payments the King of Central America and founding father of United Fruit poured into the government treasury (and the restrictions on black migration into the populated regions of the country) placated the *tico* dons. And, more consequentially, a generation of somewhat paternalistic presidents over a fifty-year period from the late nineteenth century to the 1940s broadened the suffrage, encouraged pluralist politics by personal appeal rather than rigid ideological stances, and vigorously promoted literacy. The cumulative impact of these and other traditions allowed the Costa Ricans to survive and learn from tough times.

In 1917 the *ticos* endured their second dictatorship—Guardia, Minor Keith's benefactor, was the first—with the Tinoco brothers, who might have installed a Somoza-like regime in paradise had they not clamped down so severely on cherished Costa Rican political habits and aroused the puritanical fury of Woodrow Wilson. The ruling order learned a political lesson, that its privileged status did not guarantee immunity from the severity of strong-man rule. With the blessing of the United States, it threw out the Tinocos and then promptly expanded civil liberties.

And in the same years, when plummeting coffee prices spelled economic disaster and even hunger, the descendants of the highland dons who had unrepentantly violated Spanish commercial laws with egalitarian abandon changed their thinking about laissez-faire capitalism. A reformist party, its members heavily influenced by progressive elements in the church, appeared, championing social and economic changes and even espousing an anti-imperialism with opprobrious references to United Fruit.

The old liberal elite quickly mobilized to quash the reformers, but in the bleak decade of the thirties it confronted something even more menacing—the communists. In eastern Limón province, hard times had fallen on Keith's domain. Panama disease, which kills young banana plants, swept the coast. Keith wanted to move across the country to the more salubrious Pacific coast, but the upcountry *ticos*, remembering the old prohibitions that limited black residents to the east, would not hear of it. So Keith began curtailing production, dumping hundreds of black and white workers from United's payroll. The communists, many of them disillusioned young sons of the establishment, successfully organized these victims of capitalism's woes and called a strike against the Octopus, as United Fruit was called by its enemies. The harassed *tico* executive was urged by a ruling order terrified of class conflict to suppress the strike with troops, but he refused. In the end the strikers won recognition and a work contract, and the communists got a foothold in the political order.

In the span of a tumultuous decade, the 1940s, two men forged the modern Costa Rican state.[2] The first was a seemingly mild-mannered pediatrician, Rafael Calderón Guardia, virtually hand-picked by the old coffee aristocracy troubled about the political successes of the left in the thirties. Once ensconced in office, Calderón swiftly shifted to the role of champion of a new social order. Exploiting *tico* sentiment against German and Italian families who had migrated into coffee fincas after World War I, he brought Costa Rica into World War II—and began confiscating the finca owners' properties. Allying himself with social progressives in the clergy, he pushed through sweeping legislation for unemployment, old-age, and medical benefits, the minimum wage and eight-hour day, and state backing for the country's fledgling labor unions. By the end of the war Costa Rica had established the welfare state.

When the old order began conspiring against him, Calderón forged an alliance with the communists, whose leader, Manuel Mora, agreed to change the name of the party to the Popular Vanguard to placate those of Calderón's following uncomfortable with a pact with the Communist Party of Costa Rica.

Once the wartime unity of the west with the Soviet Union disintegrated, Calderón's reputation suffered. And he already had another worry in the Costa Rican political spectrum, young idealists who admired his social program but disliked his coziness with the communists and especially chafed over his clericalism. Calderón contended that a truly just social order was not possible unless the state curtailed individual liberty.

His enemies persuasively argued the contrary. Their leader, José Figueres, was himself a coffee baron who got national attention during the war by criticizing the government for tolerating mob attacks on German and Italian residents. For this, and other outbursts, Figueres was declared pro-Nazi and *persona non grata* and fled to Mexico to escape Calderón's wrath. At war's end he returned to a cheering crowd of *ticos* who evidently believed none of Calderón's charges.

Unlike Calderón, who had drifted too far afield of the social and political currents of the postwar era, Figueres correctly sensed the

deep suspicions of leftist solutions to social ills harbored by the
Costa Rican middle class. In 1944 Calderón had installed a puppet
in the presidency. Four years later, as American attitudes toward
the Soviet Union were hardening into ideological rigidity, Calderón
renewed his alliance with the communists and declared for office.
The elite countered with a rightist coalition dedicated to undoing the
offensive social legislation of the past and found an amiable conservative willing to carry their banner.

Figueres went to Guatemala, where only three years before a
revolution had tossed out the dictator Ubico. In the reformist
ambience of Guatemala City, he formed a cadre of mostly alienated
liberals bound by their distaste for Caribbean despots. He returned
to Costa Rica and plunged into a bitter political campaign that
ended with a putative victory for a Conservative enemy of Calderón's
but no ally of Figueres.' But it was a short-lived triumph; Calderón,
charging widespread fraud, managed to get the national assembly to
annul the election.

His action mobilized Figueres, who appealed to his Guatemalan
friends. They responded with two planes laden with guns, ammunition, and military advisers for Figueres' makeshift army. Calderón
rallied the workers from the banana plantations. For six weeks Costa
Rica was convulsed by civil conflict that consumed two thousand
lives. But when it was over Figueres triumphed.

The conservatives who wanted to shift the political timetable
back a decade now had their victory, but for over a year Figueres
refused to relinquish power to them until they pledged that the
reforms of Calderón would not only be retained but broadened and,
in 1949, sustained by a new constitution and state institutions
established to enforce them. Figueres had his revenge against the
man who had run him out of the country, but he embraced his
persecutor's reforms. Then he abolished his army and turned the
presidency over to the Conservatives.

Figueres became the father figure of the modern Costa Rican
state.[3] He recruited kindred spirits, most of them descendants of
the social establishment, into a political party, National Liberation,
which with the begrudging support of its opponents has molded

today's Costa Rica. The social changes generated during the forties have been institutionalized, expanding the role of the state in almost every facet of *tico* life. Predictably the bureaucracy carrying out these diverse functions has become bloated to the point where it encompasses 20 percent of the work force and consumes almost 30 percent of national income.

By the mid-1970s, as Figueres was finishing his second term (which, because of his relationship to Robert Vesco, has gone down as an embarrassment to Figueres' reputation), Costa Rica was already heading for the economic malaise that today plagues the country. After the creation of the Central American Common Market in 1960, the Ticos sensed an opportunity to diversify an economy that still depended, as did the economies of their neighbors, on a few agricultural exports—in Costa Rica's case, coffee and bananas. The government enthusiastically pushed industrial schemes, and American investors, reassured by the security of the only political system in Central America that resembled their own, poured in. Costa Rica had stronger unions and higher wages than its neighbors, but the ambitious *tico* planners believed that new industry and investment could be absorbed without provoking the working class to demand an even greater share of national wealth or disturbing their political hold on the country.

Industrial growth, which American observers have generally exalted as fundamental to any real improvement in the lot of Latin Americans, overwhelmed the Costa Ricans. In 1960 industry accounted for just 4 percent of national exports; in 1978, 30 percent, doubling the industrial work force. Foreign firms got subsidies and generous tax breaks, then dumped shoddy products on the local economy, all the while demanding—and getting— protection from abroad. A managerial class more beholden to foreign economic interests than to the Costa Rican state took form.

Another disturbing consequence is nowadays all too apparent, though its origins go back at least twenty-five years and, some close observers of Costa Rican life would argue, extend to the formative years of the forties, when the *ticos* decided by civil war they would have political democracy *and* social reform. The modern Costa

Rican state, rightly touted as the model of the kind of society we want for the other Central American countries, is virtually broke. In a world where economic diversity is an iron law of prosperity, Costa Rica has created a comparatively impressive state structure to serve a middle-class society that must ultimately depend on coffee and bananas.

Costa Rica is less visibly poor than its neighbors, but it does have its share of poor, and they have become more visible. On my last visit, about forty families had thrown up an overnight shanty town on the banks of the Virilla River between San José and Heredia. Most had been ejected from squalid rentals in *barrios* in Alajuela and Heredia. "Virilla City" is a diminutive version of one of those sprawling *barrios* of unemployed and ill-nourished that ring the other Central American capitals, but, however small, it reminds the *ticos* that all is not well.

The rural poor have experienced the common hardships afflicting the *campesinos* of Honduras or Guatemala or El Salvador or Nicaragua before the revolution—loss of security before the expanding domain of the agro-export empire. (The lot of Nicaragua's rural people is still backward but has dramatically improved with the intensive health and literacy campaign of the Sandinistas.) Peasants who once relied on their small plots to keep their families nourished until the next banana or coffee harvest form a disturbingly large class of landless people. Seventy percent of rural Costa Ricans, it is estimated, own *no* land.

The *ticos* are sensitive on the subject of poverty in their paradise, but they no longer try to deny the existence of a landless peasantry whose increasing demands threaten the fragile political system the ruling order has contrived.[4] In other Central American countries, a vigorously forceful national guard maintains order in the countryside and stands ready to suppress any rural rebellion. When times have gotten hard for Costa Rica's *campesinos* in the past, they have become more militant, like the banana workers in the thirties who formed the country's first communist labor union.

Costa Rica possesses a rural guard, but the *ticos* are reluctant to expand it to wage war against peasants demanding land. Yet the severity of the rural situation in recent years has brought on confrontations with *campesinos* squatting on estates. In March 1984, a group of migratory banana workers settled on an American-owned plantation in the south, and the government dispatched guard reinforcements from San José to eject them.[5] Because their political strength is still considerable, the landowners (even the American immigrant) can resist the kind of massive pressures for agrarian reform that pushes against neighboring governments.

Costa Rica's rural people are as socially conservative as their counterparts elsewhere in Latin America. Their goal is security, which they identify foremost with the possession of land, however small the plot. If land is lost or unobtainable, the *tico* country dweller will look to the higher wage his labor commands or the superior benefits of a socially benevolent government. Rebellion by joining a guerrilla movement is a last resort, something undertaken when all other alternatives are closed.

The economic dilemmas afflicting all Central Americans in the past decade have severely tested Costa Rican democracy. In 1981, when the colón began its rapid plunge in value, the *ticos* knew they were in for a testing, but they had expectations that the crisis would be of relatively short duration. It lasted long enough to return the National Liberation Party, Figueres' creation, to power, but not even the aggressive economic policies of Liberación Nacional have seemed to make much difference. The startling decline in the living standard of middle-class Costa Ricans (and there are proportionately more middle class here than in any other isthmian country) has raised new concerns about the survival of the *tico* "way of life." Domestic articles, clothing, food, and housing costs have approached levels nowadays described as "astronomical." The salary scale established by the bloated state bureaucracy has increased but lags far behind prices. As the director of the national bank observed in early 1984: "Today Costa Ricans are significantly impoverished."

The *ticos* are more tolerant of the left than the people of any other

Central American country—except, of course, Nicaragua—and the "Red *ticos,*" as they are sometimes called by the establishment, have stepped up their criticism. They condemn the austere measures decreed by the International Monetary Fund, brought on by the enormous per capita external debt of the country, for causing the widening hunger and unemployment. They publicize incidents of rural violence as examples of a "police state" determined to prop up the agro-capitalist society, arouse the urban poor to the deficiencies of the welfare state, and have been unrelenting in their castigation of the government for knuckling under to American pressures on the Nicaraguan question.

Since 1981, when the colón began its descent from eight to forty-three to the dollar, the *ticos* have imposed their own version of Reaganomics, and its middle class has adjusted its life-style downward from the optimistic days of ten years ago. There is a palpable bitterness in the ordinarily amiable *tico,* wrought by resentment that the only pro-American country in Central America has been compelled to bear this burden while the United States, measuring its security in essentially military terms, has selected impoverished, backward Honduras as its ally.[6]

9 "Welcome to the Free Republic of Olancho"

In rural Central America, economic progress holds out the promise of a better life for country people but threatens traditional culture and its cohesive social values.

A GENERATION AGO REMOTE PLACES IN CENTRAL America, decrepit country towns with few amenities, began to take on more important roles in the calculations of the economic well-being of the state. The Alliance for Progress emphasized, among other things, rural development as critical to the progress of a society. Obscure villagers long forgotten or not even linked to the outside with much more than a mule path suddenly found themselves the centerpiece of this or that bureaucratic scheme—the graveling of a road to the capital, an irrigation project, the first telephone in town, and so on. There was much attention paid to that sort of activity on the eminently persuasive reasoning that if the Cubans were going to redeem the countryside, or improve the standard of living for country people, then the U.S.-sponsored Alliance for Progress and its Latin American participants could do no less.

Thirty years ago the province of Olancho, which sprawls across east-central Honduras, was among the most isolated mountain domains in all Central America. For most of Honduran history its small towns had been shut off from the rest of the republic. Tegucigalpa and the national district, lying in the adjoining western province of Francisco Morazán, might as well have been located a thousand miles away, given the negligible influence of Honduran governments on Olancho.

Olancho's people are mostly *campesinos,* country folk in every sense of the term. Their lives revolve around the things that most concern Central American rural people—family, religion, and the unchanging daily tasks of seasonal agriculture. They are not unmindful of the grave problems of state or of Central America's future or the ominous American military presence in the country. These things, rather, are much farther down on the agenda than the important matters of maintaining tradition and preserving the proud, independent ways for which Olancho has earned a certain distinction.

It is one of the last of Central America's isolated places to succumb to the reach of the modern state. Olancho's slow but inevitable subjugation to modernity has not been easy, nor have its citizens readily dispelled their old notions of independence, symbolically proclaimed at one time by a legendary sign on the trail leading into the province from the west:

WELCOME TO THE FREE REPUBLIC OF OLANCHO

Honduras may have been a republic in name, but its government ran under a succession of strong men who generally catered to the whims of the banana barons. But in Olancho, *la bananera* did not call the tune.

Santa Cruz de Guayape, meaning the town of Santa Cruz lying near the Guayape River, is one of the last of Central America's isolated places to feel the snares of the expanding state.[1] In the early sixties lumber companies eager to exploit the hardwood forests of Honduras graded a road that ties Santa Cruz to the national highway system. Nowadays the village has a daily bus service, poor even by Honduran standards, but a villager can get out of town if he is willing to get up early enough to catch the bus. Dilapidated trucks haul in such basic amenities of life as canned goods, cheap but serviceable clothing, bottled drinks, and other items. Even the most ubiquitous reminder of the national government's authority, the lottery, has finally made it to Santa Cruz, delivered by a man on a motorcycle. The village has not been turned into a populace of consumers, but at least some of the things available at the teeming Comayagüela market can be bought here.

Santa Cruz has probably 4,500 people living in or around town, most of them tied in one way or another to the soil. For a century or more this has been a place of subsistence agriculture, the ritual of life governed by the May planting of corn and beans (before the rains come) on what seems like every square foot of arable land, divided into minuscule plots among the *campesinos*. To the outsider these are people who cling to primitive farming methods in order to retain a way of life—turning the sod with wooden, steel-tipped plows pulled by oxen, dropping the seeds carefully by hand and covering them by dragging the foot, weeding by hoeing and the omnipresent tool-weapon of every Central American *campesino*, the machete. Women and kids chase birds away from the corn. Bean hills are placed so close together that harvesting is accomplished by yanking the entire plant out of the ground and then threshing the beans out by banging the stalk against a hard object.

Santa Cruz still has few of the amenities of "Tegoose," but remarkable changes have come about there in the past generation, and the village has attracted the attention of the republic's developmental bureaucracy. In the early 1960s an American medical missionary, representing Americas Hand in Hand, came to Santa Cruz with his family. As with most other missionary efforts, he began by offering basic health care to a people most of whom had never seen a doctor. The program was so successful that it has since grown into a regular clinic, serviced by American physicians who volunteer to fly down to Tegoose and then make their way by four-wheel-drive vehicles to remote Santa Cruz and perform even major surgery out in the boondocks.

The missionary who pioneered in Santa Cruz has since shifted emphasis from medical care to the economic problems that prevail in Santa Cruz and hundreds of Central American villages like it. Most of the town's modern troubles have been related to the un-availability of land for sons coming of age. Some had already begun moving away, migrating to the banana plantations on the north coast where they had to compete for jobs with *norteños* and agricultural migrants dispossessed from their lands in neighboring El Salvador.

In a subtle campaign the missionary suggested to the village elders that a vocational school teaching locally usable skills might be the answer. With considerable enthusiasm the villagers of Santa Cruz threw their energies into the project. When, inevitably, they began losing interest, the missionary suggested that he might move to another town up the road. The fear of losing him was sufficient to get people back on the job.

The school finally opened in 1970. Since then, it has made modestly successful improvements in the lives of this essentially agrarian people. Some of the carpentry graduates, discovering there was simply too little demand for their work in Santa Cruz, have packed off to Talanga on the highway to Tegucigalpa. There they have set up shop and formed a small colony from among Santa Cruz' vocational school alumni. The macramé guild, established to sell to tourist shops in the capital, has not fared well because it rapidly became too dependent on outsiders for string and hangings. But the sewing classes initiated by the missionary's wife ultimately pro-vided a way for young women to supplement family income by making clothes for their neighbors.

The farming traditions that the villagers have followed for gen-erations have remained the most resistant to change. The seasonal ritual of planting, cultivating, and harvesting—as inefficient as it may seem to the visitor—is not readily adaptable to modern agri-cultural technology, which calls for farming with machinery on large plots with heavy doses of fertilizer and pesticides. However little the Central American *campesino* produces on his small plot, it is ordinarily enough to feed his family and perhaps have some left over. To change the method of farming requires money these people don't have and running a risk the basically conservative *campesino* is reluctant to take. To plant, cultivate, and harvest as one's father did and *his* father did preserves tradition and family.

Still, as the American missionary soon realized after several seasons in Santa Cruz, such old-fashioned methods were not keeping pace with nutritional requirements that Central American country people must have to ward off the diseases that have plagued them for centuries. Reluctant to disrupt the corn-and-beans system for fear it might be socially harmful, he went to work on finding some way to irrigate river-bottom land during the dry season (from November to April). In hilly Honduras, gravity-flow irrigation is well-nigh impossible. Hand pumps were given a try but soon proved inadequate. A diesel-engine pump provided by CARE burned out when an inattentive worker let the oil run too low.

But the Methodist missionary from the American northwest, whose inland farmers and ranchers continually fret over ways to get more water to their crops, wouldn't admit defeat, especially with a dry season approaching. So he finally prevailed on another American with mechanical aptitude to construct a waterwheel fabricated from an old auto wheel with three-quarters-inch pipe welded on as spokes and crudely attached paddles. After some experimenting with several modifications, the American friend of the missionary assigned production to a Honduran welder.

Students from the vocational school hauled the wheel down to the river in a truck. They rigged a flume to convey the river water lifted out by their wheel to the high point of a garden plot and from there dug trenches to distribute the water to the rows. From late 1977 to early 1979 Santa Cruz endured two harsh dry seasons, but the *campesinos* using the waterwheels fared surprisingly well. The first year thirteen farmers grew a bumper crop of tomatoes, onions, squash, broccoli, cucumbers, lettuce, and various kinds of melons. One man realized a $1,500 profit, in a country where per capita income is still below $1,000 a year.

Another good crop the second season in Santa Cruz caught the attention of Honduran agricultural experts, who began trooping out to remote Olancho to investigate what is, frankly, a simple technology but one remarkably adaptable to Central America's most fundamental problem, how to feed its own people yet preserve their cultural traditions. One outspokenly frank Honduran official called the waterwheel irrigation setup in Santa Cruz the "only project in the country worth a damn."

An American AID official dispatched from Tegoose took one casual look at the operation of the "butterflies," as Honduran *campesinos* call their waterwheels, and dismissed the entire project as woefully inadequate. Probably so for the large-scale farming of the agro-export sector that has been steadily encroaching on peasant landholdings for the past two generations. But little enterprises like the Santa Cruz waterwheel have made the *campesinos* of an isolated village in remote Olancho producers of food for themselves and for others of their countrymen who have had to move to crowded Tegucigalpa to survive.

The missionary's son, a historian who concentrates on the Honduran past, understandably argues that his father had the right idea when it comes to developmental questions in Central America. Santa Cruz' *campesinos* are, by themselves, never going to make much of a difference in the ever-widening gap between the country's nutritional requirements and its rapidly escalating population. Because his approach is so intimately tied to the "small is better" school of agricultural economists, it will never suffice to feed the Honduran people unless it can be widely replicated.

But, quite clearly, such an approach preserves community identity and, equally important, reinforces the notion that it is far better to satisfy social needs by adapting technology to the community than to destroy the community by compelling its members to conform to a uniform technological model. The American missionary might very well have used his influence as a medical missionary to foist off on the suspicious *campesinos* of Santa Cruz methods of farming that would have inevitably destroyed their fragile community. Instead he helped to preserve it. What he accomplished—or, rather, what he inspired the *campesinos* of Santa Cruz to accomplish—will not solve Central America's agrarian dilemmas nor

Honduras,' but has gone far in preserving the identity of that small village, and that is no small triumph.

The planners of Central America's agricultural future cannot count on having very many Santa Cruzes to keep Juan on the farm, growing not only enough food for his family but sufficient cash crops to raise his yearly income significantly. All the trends in rural population and the uses to which the land is being put point in the other direction. For generations the Central American rural economy—even Costa Rica's—has been operated on the prevailing economic wisdom of its ruling social order. Its view of things is that the bigger farms will produce for agricultural export, the minuscule plots (of ten or fifteen acres or even less) for food consumed domestically.

This has understandably made sense to the economic moguls at the top, who have been much more impressed with the profitability of the agro-export market than the well-being of *campesinos* or, for that matter, the preservation of *campesino* culture. Small plots that have fallen into the hands of the bigger producers for increasing the output of coffee, sugar, or cotton or for grazing cattle have also effectively made a generation of migratory rural laborers redundant. They constitute Central America's modern rural proletariat, roaming the countryside looking for seasonal jobs on some landlord's coffee finca, or have headed for the larger towns, especially to the Central American capitals. Their numbers are such that none of the cities can provide the housing, jobs, and social services they demand, because there are so many of these modern rural destitutes. Other than the capitals, already badly overcrowded, Central America has few cities of any size to accommodate them, too few San Pedro Sulas with an industrial base and economic diversity to absorb this steady human flow.

What is happening in Central America's human migration has been going on for a generation and will continue for perhaps another. In 1950, 75 percent of the isthmus' people lived in the countryside; in 2000, an agricultural economist has calculated, only *one-fourth* of them will reside there. Unless some way can be found to alter this ominous statistic, every government in Central America, whether right, left, or center on the political spectrum, is headed for a social and political convulsion in which those at the bottom, fired by the prospect of a better life, will demand more for their children.

None of the above suggests that Central America's governments are indifferent to the plight of country folk. Quite the contrary. Since at least the early sixties most of them have been undertaking economic development programs aimed at encouraging industry, expanding social services, and promoting the agro-export sectors—all aimed ultimately at absorbing the human tide churned up by the modernizing Central American capitalist state.

In 1960, when the Central American Common Market was launched, a vigorous debate ensued between American agencies interested in directing the course of this new regional organization and Central America's ruling elites who liked the idea of promoting industry but feared the consequences of rural reforms. After a few years, when it became clear that the American advisers were interested mainly in modernizing the agro-export sector and less concerned about Central America's corn-and-beans production, the economic magnates fell into line. The isthmian economies diversi-fied, providing employment in import-substitution industries, but the biggest rewards went to those in the agricultural sector who raised crops for export. They expanded and modernized, gearing their enterprises to the demands of a world market.

In the process Central America's ability to feed its people actually declined. Here, the United States, eager to buttress the agro-export sector, was less enthusiastic about having its aid pro-grams sustain domestic food production. Approximately 50 percent of AID programs, for example, are destined for agricultural dis-bursement, but only a small percentage wind up in programs for alleviating hunger. Most of the funds support American efforts to improve the productivity of Central America's agricultural exporters and at the same time to advance the sales of American companies that manufacture pesticides and fertilizer. Even when AID monies eventually wind up in the hands of smaller farmers, their ultimate purpose is to encourage the production of vegetables for export. AID accepts as fundamental doctrine the notion that its funds should not be directed toward reducing food prices for domestic consumers.

"Food is [even used as] a weapon" to widen the market for American grain exporters.[2] While Americans accept as axiomatic that this society should feed itself and that self-sufficiency in food production is absolutely vital to national security, the American government does not follow policies that accord a similar nutritional independence to Central Americans. Our food aid law is PL 480, enacted after World War II to sell or give away American agricultural produce to other countries. In 1982 PL 480 had a $66 million budget for Central America, a sum representing 15 percent of U.S. agricultural exports to the isthmus. Under one provision of the law, the American government sells food to a "friendly" government on long-term credit. The recipient in turn sells the food to its own people and uses the profit to finance other projects. A second feature permits the transfer of food to a private organization (such as CARE), which in turn donates the food to the government with the requirement that it must use any money it receives to promote food production.

Even here PL 480 can have a harmful influence on small farmers. In 1976, an earthquake devastated a broad area in Guatemala, leaving thousands homeless. The quake did not wipe out grain reserves in several villages, yet CARE and Catholic Relief Services, two organizations that contributed much to relief in the aftermath, obtained 27,000 tons of grain and distributed it to victims, driving down the price of locally grown grains and, in effect, discouraging Guatemalan farmers from producing this basic foodstuff. Had CARE and Catholic Relief Services purchased *Guatemalan* grain and then given it away, everybody would have been better off.

PL 480 has a political purpose as well. The Department of State cut off a $10 million wheat shipment to punish the Sandinistas in 1981 and from 1981 to 1983 tripled PL 480 disbursements to El Salvador under Title I, thus giving El Salvador's rulers considerable latitude in their use of the monies derived from selling the food. PL 480 opens up markets for American exporters, mostly the big grain producers. This is an eminently defensible policy for a government that must demonstrate that its foreign economic programs are not giveaways but actually promote the interests of American farmers and, ultimately, the entire country in the third world. It is not so readily acceptable if such policies, by discouraging these countries from growing more of what their people eat, endanger the capability of such countries to meet the nutritional needs of those at the bottom and contribute to the perpetuation of rigidly structured societies whose rural people have little hope for a better life.

Agrarian reform in Central America (and, in fact, throughout Latin America) has never been dealt with as a solely economic question where the most important issues involve the choice of crops that command the highest price or the application of machinery.[3] The debate over how the land is to be divided, who shall own it, and to what degree the state shall interfere in agrarian problems are explosive social and political matters that relate directly to the organization of society, as the debates over the "Land to the Tiller" program in El Salvador have shown. Yet, somehow, the Central American states must confront this problem. Can societies whose export crops earn vital foreign exchange afford to rectify political and social grievances by carving up the countryside into ten- or fifteen-acre plots that grow corn and beans?

The Sandinistas in Nicaragua ran head-on into this dilemma just a few weeks after throwing out the Somozas.[4] Life for country people under the regime had been especially grim. Almost 80 percent of rural Nicaraguans were without any land; they survived on the seasonal work at the plantations or by sending their half-naked children into the cities to sell fruits or flowers or even beg. Revolutionary slogans about turning land back to those who labored on it found a warm reception among Nicaraguan *campesinos*. When Somoza fell they began taking over estates of fleeing Somocistas and threatening large property owners.

Once in charge of Nicaragua's shattered rural economy, the Sandinistas, some of whom had strong convictions about dividing the big estates into small plots, ordered a halt to the seizures. Their reasoning had little to do with ideology but illustrated the harsh economic realities of countries whose dependence on agricultural exports for dollars is high. *Every* Central American country (save, perhaps, Panama and Belize) falls into that category. If the regime, whatever its promises or sympathies with the plight of the rural poor, had allowed the land takeovers to continue, the producers of export crops, anticipating a wave of nationalizations or worse, would have stopped work and perhaps left the country. Had their estates been carved up into tiny plots, sufficient for subsistence agriculture but little more, the minister of agriculture reasoned, Nicaragua would have been worse off.

Still, many angry Nicaraguan *campesinos,* whose demands for land are as strong as those of any of their Central American neighbors, continued with the seizures in defiance of court orders to return land illegally taken. In a few well-publicized instances, they even found an ally in the agrarian institute, which sponsored a mass rally that drew thirty thousand in Managua in February 1980, less than a year after the triumph of the revolution.

What has resulted from these confrontations between angry *campesinos* who want land to grow food and a government that is determined that Nicaragua shall feed its people yet continue earning foreign exchange with agricultural exports like sugar or cotton or beef has been, predictably, a shift by the Sandinistas in favor of the landless.

The Sandinistas know they cannot survive without the support of country folk and they have a much better chance of making their revolution work among rural people who have never gotten much from governments in the past. A month after the noisy march of *campesinos,* the regime declared that seized lands were now considered state property, but unused acres on these estates would be leased out to *campesinos.* This decree caused a scare among private holders, but there were accompanying reassurances that small landowners would be exempt and others, if they could demonstrate they were not Somocistas, would be compensated. Even so, some of the private landowners refused to rent their land and have cooperated only after severe government pressure.

Despite the buffeting from *campesinos* who want land and private owners who fear a Cuban-style agricultural system, the Sandinistas have clung to their belief in a mixed economy. Under their plan for the new Nicaragua, *campesino* associations will farm 40 percent of the land, the state 25 percent, and individual owners, mostly large farmers, the remaining 35 percent. As long as the last are putting their land to "good use" (defined, of course, by the Ministry of Agriculture), as the country's biggest private landowner, who grows half of Nicaragua's sugar cane and produces the Flor de Caña export rum, does, then the regime does not interfere. But land kept out of production for lack of capital or resentment over Managua's agricultural policies is almost certain to be expropriated and transformed into a cooperative. When the agricultural ministry discovered that one defiant property owner was cultivating only three hundred of his twelve hundred acres, it seized the idle nine hundred acres for a cooperative, then provided an irrigation loan to the owner to allow him to increase production on the three hundred acres he retained. Such decisions have profound political implications, of course, but where the survival of the state is concerned, the regime is not going to permit idle land to go unused.

Unlike its neighbors, Nicaragua, according to most assessments, has more than enough land to distribute, in one way or another, for the building of a new order. But from the beginning of the revolution, the Sandinistas had to manage an agricultural economy whose previous directors had allocated 70 percent of production for export and let their people go undernourished or starve. In the year and a half after the overthrow of Somoza, demand for food increased by almost 50 percent. Pledged to abolish hunger and confronted with a decline in corn and bean production, the Sandinistas had no choice but to import these staples of the Central American diet. Yet they still haggled over the issue of turning farmland that earned precious dollars in the agro-export market into food production. In early 1981, forced to a decision by the Reagan administration's denial of a $10 million loan to import wheat, the Sandinistas concluded that Nicaragua could maintain, perhaps even increase, its production of vital export crops like sugar, coffee, and cotton on less acreage if it were farmed more efficiently and that the country could then use the surplus for growing corn and beans. The ultimate goal is self-sufficiency in these basic food crops.

Even in Costa Rica, with its bustling capital and middle-class aspirations for the better life, the benign political chieftains who have shaped the modern state have concluded that agriculture is the mainstay of the republic and likely to remain so for many years. The agro-export market (mostly coffee and bananas) generates the wealth that sustains urban well-being, but there is a growing awareness that something must be done in the countryside. In Costa Rica, as in other Central American states, the larger entrepreneurs have been incorporating the minuscule food-producing plots for a generation.

At one time the Costa Ricans attributed their democratic heritage to the same roots Americans have always claimed, a sturdy, independent yeoman farmer who did not own a great amount of land but remained free of the shackles of a plantation aristocracy. This once-proud symbol of the *tico* countryside has disappeared. In his stead are now the larger landholders who have mechanized and are, by comparison with their counterparts elsewhere, more efficient in production. But they grow mostly for the export market, and they suffer from its fluctuations and cannot easily cover their rising energy costs by doubling or tripling the price of a pound of coffee beans or hand of bananas.

In the process the traditional farm laborer has been losing out, unable to obtain title to a small plot and forced either to squat on land that has been turned into pasture for cattle grazing (a not uncommon practice of the owners of large estates facing government pressures to sell or rent out their land to *campesinos*) or pushed toward the cities of the Meseta Central in search of work. In the sixties and seventies Costa Rican industry (as did fledgling industry elsewhere in Central America) absorbed some of these agricultural migrants, but never in sufficient quantities. They now live precariously in the *barrios* of south San José or in scabrous tin-roofed shantytowns tucked along riverbanks. Here, as in Managua or Tegucigalpa or San Salvador or Guatemala City, they levy demands on a social service bureaucracy unable to accommodate them.

The poverty of country people has persisted. Three-quarters of them own no land and, outside the central valley, often lack the most basic social services. And in Costa Rica the lot of rural folk is better than in the other republics.

This lamentable situation, which lies at the core of Central America's social, political, and economic malaise, is not a recent creation, nor, frankly, are the isthmian governments—right, center, or left in their political leanings—unwilling to deal with it. In some way or another, with varying degrees of commitment, they have been addressing the problems of agriculture for at least a generation. Each of the countries has an agrarian institute, has begun programs to respond to demands for agrarian reform, and has attempted to improve its position in the world's agricultural marketplace.

Yet none has succeeded in fashioning an agrarian policy that has achieved self-sufficiency in food production. Even the Sandinistas, who have undertaken a course in agriculture that American officials consider an assault on private enterprise, have been loath to diminish their enthusiasm for agro-export production in favor of a program that is committed, as its first priority, to a better-fed small landowner who gets the same social benefits as the urban citizen. Central America has the acreage and the capability to feed itself, but it does not have vast, unclaimed public lands that can be given over to pioneers who will first feed themselves, then their countrymen. Most of the land is taken for other things—coffee, sugar, bananas, cattle—because these earn export dollars.

Ultimately the lot of Central America's country people must be improved. The modest accomplishment of central governments to raise their standard of life enhances the work of the missionary at Santa Cruz de Guayape and reinforces the belief that people at the bottom can improve their lives.

The missionary from the American northwest now lives down in Tegoose, but he retains his enthusiasm for the Santa Cruz waterwheel project and believes it can be applied elsewhere. After many years in Honduras, he has yet to relinquish his ingrained Yankee skepticism about the ability of Hispanics to solve problems, a trait he attributes not to laziness or intellectual deficiency but to a fear of losing status in the community if one tries something different and fails. In a small but revolutionary way the missionary confronted that seemingly unalterable characteristic of village culture when he first gently pushed the residents of Santa Cruz to experiment with the waterwheels and grow food year-round.

Not every revolutionary in Central America carries a gun.

10 Panzós

P ANZÓS IS A VILLAGE IN THE GUATEMALAN DEPART-
ment of Alta Verapaz.[1] There, on May 29,
1978, regular Guatemalan troops and armed
landowners from the surrounding countryside machine-gunned
more than a hundred Indian *campesinos* in the town square and
chased the fleeing and wounded into the mountains. Amnesty
International, which monitors human-rights violations around the
world, declared the Panzós massacre the most reprehensible out-
burst of official violence against a people in that year until the
savage Iranian counterrevolution of the summer.

What happened at Panzós bespoke much about the condition
Guatemalan society had reached from thirty years before. Then a
reformist government was enthusiastically undertaking programs to
bring neglected places like Panzós into the national scheme,
through social services and promotion of rural labor organization,
yet preserve its Indian identity. The '54 revolution frustrated such
plans, of course, but in the next decade Panzós became important to
Guatemala's rightist government because it lay along a broad strip of
the country, stretching from Huehuetenango in the western highlands to tropical Izabal province in the east, where the National
Agrarian Transformation Institute would resettle landless *campesinos* from the crowded western region and boost Guatemalan grain

production. The Maryknoll Order of the Catholic Church, which has been active in Guatemala for the past thirty years, moved some sixteen hundred peasant families to cooperatives in the region.

In addition to the shifting of a large number of people from the more heavily populated Indian towns of the west, these plans meant profound social and economic changes for places like Panzós. The Agrarian Institute anticipated that as many as 75,000 families can be settled in the "Strip," and with AID assistance, the government has undertaken the construction of a highway from Barillas, Huehuetenango, across northern Quiché and Alta Verapaz, to Modesto Méndez on the Río Sarstún, which in its course to the sea forms the southern Belize boundary. There have emerged ambitious plans for a trans-Guatemala pipeline to move Alaskan oil from the Pacific port of Champerico to Puerto Barrios on the Caribbean side for ultimate shipment to the U.S. east coast. Not satisfied with its short Caribbean shoreline and port facilities, Guatemala has renewed its territorial pressures on newly independent Belize with unsubtle suggestions that Guatemala might be willing to relinquish its old claims to all Belize in exchange for concessions in the south. "It's only your backyard," say the Guatemalans: "No," respond the Beliceans, "you want our front yard."

In the past fifteen years or so, the Strip has become an active region for oil exploration and nickel mining, which has brought large numbers of industrial workers to an old agricultural region. Land that was once dominated by coffee plantations and carried modest value has very rapidly escalated in price because of its mineral resources. The surge in the number of mining laborers has brought increased union activity, strikes, and the inevitable confrontation with law-and-order regimes in Guatemala City.

The Panzós massacre had its immediate origin in a conflict between Indian *campesinos* who have moved onto vacant lands and large landowners who realized the quick profits that can be derived by exploiting natural resources and who determined to run the Indians off the land. Officials in Guatemala City concluded that the Indian land occupation around Panzós was another maneuver by leftist enemies to challenge its authority in the countryside, an episode in the thirty-year struggle against communism, with the landless Indians portrayed as dupes of Marxist terrorists trained at the University of San Carlos. The severity of the government's response—the shooting of such large numbers of people in broad daylight, a deviation from the government's usual routine of simply whisking away suspected guerrilla organizers in the middle of the night—was interpreted as a gruesome example of the lengths to which the government would go to quash the Indian demand for land.

Panzós symbolizes more than the fierce determination of a besieged right-wing government to get tough with its domestic enemies. The massacre that occurred there in 1978—at a time when Guatemala already stood condemned by the United States for its human-rights violations—was a grisly act in a drama that has been going on for four centuries. The "dirty war" in Guatemala, which by the left's indictment began with the right's retaliation after the overthrow of Jacobo Arbenz in 1954, represents something beyond the classic conflict between capitalists bent on exploiting the rich Guatemalan interior and Indian *campesinos* mobilized by Marxist organizers and guerrillas. Guatemala's war is a war of antagonistic cultures.

"Guatemala," reads a slick pamphlet issued by the national tourist agency, "the land of six million smiles." It is an outdated blurb. This most populous country of Central America has more than eight million people. By century's end, when Central America's numbers are expected to reach a dense 40 million (from just over 23 million in 1984), Guatemala will have one-third of them.

Fifty percent of Guatemala's inhabitants are Indian. To be classified as "Indian" here means much more than racial heritage. It denotes the way you dress, the language you speak, the social ceremonies you honor, and your philosophy of life. In the past and still today to be Indian in Guatemala means you must defer to authority, for those who rule this country retain a firm conviction, inherited from the Spanish conquerors, that the power they wield must not be jeopardized. Few Americans who have rediscovered "native" American culture in the past quarter-century can understand the severity of Guatemala's ruling order toward its "natives." General Custer would have.

Though the progeny of Indian-Spanish union, the *ladino* inheritors of Spanish authority are no less severe in their estimation of Indian culture. They may live among Indians, extol Indian culture as a tourist attraction, and find Indian dress and custom appealingly exotic, but for all comparative purposes the Indian is regarded as inferior. An Indian who picks up a smattering of Spanish or begins wearing *ladino* dress is "improving" himself, but if he clings to the ancient religious practices or drinks too much on fiesta day he is "stubborn." As far as the *ladino* is concerned, it is the Indian who must cross the cultural dividing line to civilization and the white man's way. If necessary, the *ladino* will make him.

If the Indian is docile, then he is treated with paternalistic affection, as a child who is to be guided and to whom the ladino has a certain historical obligation—up to a point.[2] *Ladinos* who can afford servants or landlords with tenants will treat the Indian with avuncular charity, referring to them as *indito* ("little Indian") or *muchacho* ("boy") or *chico* ("little one") even if the person is full-grown. The *ladino* rarely addresses an Indian with *don* or *señor* but by his given name or with the familiar personal pronoun *tú*, normally reserved for family members or close friends, rather than *usted*, which is used in polite conversation between equals. Working-class *ladinos* may be less paternalistic because their economic status is not much higher than the Indian's, but they still expect the Indian to be subservient, especially when he is in the *ladino*'s world. They may publicly rebuke an Indian for some minor grievance or snicker at the Indian's misuse of the Spanish idiom. And the Indian's reluctance to bathe is universally regarded as evidence of his backwardness.

But even if you don't bathe the government expects a smile.

The smiling face of Indian Guatemala touted by the *ladino* overlords has become big business in Antigua, the old capital twenty miles over the mountains from Guatemala City, in a beguiling, tranquil setting that contrasts sharply with the boom-town atmosphere of the republic's seat of government. Antigua is more Spanish. It has narrow streets with houses and buildings set close to the street, leading from the four directions to the central square. There the American or German or Japanese tourist can prepare for the flight up to Tikal in the Petén by haggling with dwarfish Indian women plopped on the stone street with their handiwork—scarves, tablecloths, shawls, colorfully clad dolls. Most of these items are mass-produced in weaving mini-factories in town. The visitor tires more readily at this elevation—Antigua is a thousand feet higher than mile-high Guatemala City—but the Guatemalan business class and a few American associates hereabouts have provided resting places for the weary in comfortable restaurants with shrub-decorated patios and friendly shops that sell Indian craftwork or jade. The most visible reminder of the remote past is an enormous stucco structure, fractured by the battering of earthquakes, where in the sixteenth century the Spanish chronicler Bernal Díaz del Castillo composed his "True History" of the conquest.

Here the Indian is servant to Hispanic culture, and it is difficult to imagine that Antigua, seat of the Spanish kingdom of Guatemala, lies on the frontier of what a thousand years ago was one of the great civilizations of the western hemisphere. Its destruction began systematically within a generation of the first Spanish invasion. Mayan society was an intricately complex organization, a state, that the conquerors dismantled and replaced with their own contrivance for the political, economic, and spiritual well-being of the conquered. Once-proud Mayans became ordinary commoners, their dress a makeshift amalgam of Spanish and Indian garb, their daily routine carefully monitored by an elaborate code that prohibited such privileges as owning a horse or carrying a weapon.

Some of the deposed Mayan nobility joined their conquerors by migrating to the cities, adopting Spanish as their tongue, and using the surprisingly flexible imperial code to acquire land, slaves, and the perquisites of rank. But in the ancient Mayan communities the Mayan lords and priests soon became Indian "citizens" living among peasants forcibly reminded that their new masters were Spaniards. Spanish priests, artisans, merchants, and the like moved in to perform the role of the once-venerated Mayan upper crust. Predictably, the Mayans resisted, and, it is recorded, the Spanish required a century and a half to subdue them. In 1697, the last significant Mayan rebellion collapsed, and the Spanish conquerors, who believed the countryside must serve the city, distributed the conquered throughout a network of agricultural communes, covering an area of six and a half square miles. Over the years the peasant, using a blend of Indian custom and Spanish tolerance, transformed these communes into Indian communities. Little of the ancient Mayan greatness could be restored, of course, because the Mayan (and the other fifteen or so identifiable Mayan subgroups in Guatemala) was a subject. But through social custom and the ingrained belief that one must work with others and not control them, Indian culture has persevered over the centuries.

And with the persistence of Indian culture has been the recurring fear of successive generations of Guatemalan leaders that the spell of their authority might somehow dissolve or that the *ladino* view of "progress" or "development" might wither before Indian stoicism. The Indian's role in the national economy, symbolized by the women peddlers of tapestries and tablecloths in the Antigua square or during festive market days in the highland villages, has been described as "penny capitalism." But the Indian has a fundamentally different approach to economic realities than the vigorous *ladino* street hustlers of Guatemala City or the yelling vendors packed into downtown San Salvador. He is not acquiring capital for some bigger or more profitable venture but enough money to buy food. When that need is satisfied he will use whatever is left over to pay his obligation to the community or enhance his social status among his fellow Indians. A hatmaker or potter works individually, giving the observer the impression he is the singularly minded craftsman, but is in fact fulfilling a communal obligation. Greed, envy, competitiveness—the generating human forces vital to the survival of the capitalist tradition—have no lofty place in the Indian's value system.

But even in a passive way the Indian has constituted a perceived threat to the prevailing order. The removal of Spanish imperial rule, which at least had provided some legal (if paternalistic) safeguards to Indian survival, meant that Indians throughout Latin America (as they were in the United States) were left to the mercies of republican governments dominated by men even less disposed to see much value in Indian culture. Throughout the rest of Central America, except for a neglected tropical lowland stretching from eastern Honduras to Costa Rica—the Mosquitía—three centuries of the Spanish presence had absorbed the Indian population. But Guatemala remained numerically Indian country, and its leaders, particularly those who exalted liberal, progressive philosophies, saw in the Indian a menace to their culture but a necessary source of labor for the expanding capitalist state. By the early twentieth century the status of the Guatemalan Indian had been reduced to the level of a Russian serf, lower than his ancestors at the height of the Spanish empire.

When the United States entered World War II to free Europe from fascist enslavement, Guatemala, then in the firm grip of its last old-style strong man, Jorge Ubico, dutifully followed. But Ubico's Indian subjects were as thoroughly ensnared to the economic system as any slave laborer in the German empire. By law Indian peasants, whether they owned a few acres or no land, owed their labor for as many as 150 days a year on the coffee fincas, at a daily wage of from five to twenty cents. In addition the peasant stood obligated to serve the government with three weeks' labor on the public roads at no reimbursement. When Ubico's government, using as pretext the declaration of war against Germany, seized coffee plantations owned by German immigrants, the country's Indians gained no respite from their obligation.

Today foreign companies proliferate in Guatemala, but fifty years ago three American concerns—United Fruit, International Railways of Central American (IRCA), and Electric Bond and Share—greatly benefited from Ubico's largesse. United and IRCA controlled ports and rail, Electric Bond 80 percent of the republic's electricity. So great was their combined influence that even after Ubico's overthrow in 1944, his successor, Juan José Arévalo, determined to extend the sway of the government over these enterprises, had to grant special concessions virtually exempting them from Guatemala's new labor laws and significantly reducing their tax burden.

Arévalo's six years brought a revolution to the countryside. Taking as model the rhetoric (if not the practice) of the Mexican revolutionaries, Guatemala's new leftist leaders declared subsoil wealth state property and began expropriating the largest plantations. Rural as well as urban workers now had the right to strike, and foreign companies were required to employ 90 percent Guatemalans in their labor forces. For a few years Guatemala's Indians, who had suffered four centuries of servitude, found a special place in the society with a commitment from the government to integrate the Indian into the new Guatemala yet preserve Indian culture.

Nowadays, American officials survey the latest statistics of government repression in the countryside and wish they had another Arévalo in Guatemala City. For all the reforms generated in his six years of office, Arévalo did not disturb the basic land tenure system in the country, nor did his reforms seriously erode the power of American companies. These tasks Arévalo bequeathed to his unlucky successor, Jacobo Arbenz.

This still-controversial Guatemalan executive came into office just as Washington was converting to militantly anticommunist credos. Nineteen fifty was the year of the National Security Council's Memorandum 68, America's anticommunist manifesto, followed in the summer by the Korean War, demonstrable proof of Soviet perfidy. Besieged by rightist critics who disliked Arévalo's labor laws and the Indianization program, Arbenz relied more and more on the powerful communist-dominated labor unions that had sprung up since Ubico's ouster. Communists in government, an explosive issue in American politics in the late forties and early fifties, had Central American reverberations. All the republics, tuned to Washington's militancy, took the hard line—except Guatemala. There the government witnessed so many defections from the center and assaults by the right that its only firm domestic allies were those on the left.

Then Arbenz made a mistake. Hoping to unify dissenting Guatemalans on a presumably unifying issue, he took on the big American multinationals, singling out United, the most visible and most powerful foreign presence, with a decree expropriating more than 400,000 acres of United holdings on the Pacific and Atlantic coasts. Arbenz argued that United had only fifty thousand acres, or 10 percent of its lands, under cultivation, and that the compensation of $600,000 was a figure derived from the company's own tax assessments.

United wanted $15 million for its 250,000 acres on the Pacific. In the United States it launched a bitter propaganda campaign about the Red menace in Guatemala. It had friends in high places. John Foster Dulles, the new American secretary of state, had served as a partner at the New York firm of Sullivan and Cromwell, legal counsel for United. Other members of Eisenhower's administration had close connections with the Boston financiers of the company. Since other Central American governments were pressing United and other American companies for revisions of contracts, Arbenz' reform program was viewed as a menace to American interests throughout the region. And Guatemalan landowners correctly perceived in Washington's determination to deal with Arbenz an opportunity for them to reverse the reformist tide in the countryside.

In March 1954 the tenth inter-American conference convened in Caracas. At the ninth meeting the United States had promoted hemispheric solidarity against external menace; now, a half-dozen years later, it was calling for unity in its crusade against the internal menace, communism in Guatemala. Dulles himself argued the American case, putting off importuning Latin American delegates who wanted an economic commitment from Washington to deal with their domestic problems. In the end Dulles got his declaration that communism was incompatible with western hemispheric tradition. Then he flew home, leaving the astonished Latin American delegates with virtually empty promises. Argentina and Mexico, historically sensitive to outside interference in their own affairs, had abstained. Only lowly Guatemala, represented by its fiery foreign minister, Guillermo Toriello, defied the American goliath.

Within a month the American government, reacting positively to United's press campaign to present itself as the victim of international communism in the heart of the Americas, was championing the company's claims. Within two months the American government, charging that Guatemala menaced its neighbors by getting arms from eastern European states, had reinforced its military ties with Honduras and Nicaragua. Within three months, using a CIA plan that was refreshingly inexpensive, it subsidized a revolutionary movement operating out of Honduras that ousted Arbenz and his putative fellow travelers.

In Washington Dulles declared that Guatemala's destiny now lay in the hands of Guatemala's people, and Americans congratulated themselves that communism had been purged from the isthmus.[3] In Guatemala the war moved back into the countryside, and it has been going on there ever since.

The Panzós massacre terrified the Indians of Alta Verapaz. To the west, in Quiché province, Indian organizations, which for years had been sending delegations to the capital to rectify land titles and obtain protection from the harassment of local landlords, now suffered a similarly harsh retaliation from Guatemala's military government. The army established a center for its counterinsurgency in an Indian cooperative in Chajul. Not satisfied, apparently, that its presence in Chajul was enough to intimidate Indian leaders, the soldiers began bombing nearby settlements, killing *campesino* animals and ruining their crops. They broke into houses, wrecking the insides and taking away suspected *campesino* organizers. Many were later found dead along country roads, their bodies showing the marks of brutal torture.

The survivors realized they had to publicize what was going on in remote Quiché in the rest of the country. They dispatched a group to the capital to deliver an appeal before the National Congress, but after they got inside the building government security forces drove them out. The delegation returned to Quiché, and the persecution continued. Still, the Indians did not give up. In early 1980, 130 of them headed for Guatemala City. On this pilgrimage the *campesinos* avoided the national government and instead took their case to the press, but local newspapers refused to carry the story. So they commandeered a couple of radio stations and broadcast their grievances to Guatemala City's *ladino* citizens, many of whom seemed oblivious to the persecution of Indians in Quiché. They even took over the offices of the Organization of American States.

Government spokesmen went on national radio and television and called them communist subversives.

The *campesino* representatives became more desperate. Having failed to arouse much sympathy among their countrymen in Guatemala City, they concluded their only recourse lay in bringing their story to the world's attention. They decided to occupy the Spanish embassy, naively believing that not even the fierce President Lucas García dared violate diplomatic immunity. On January 31, 1980, twenty-nine of them entered the embassy and politely informed the ambassador why they had chosen his government's embassy in which to make their protest. When the interior minister, charged with the security of the capital, learned of the takeover, he sent four hundred soldiers to surround the building.

The minister, respecting the embassy's immunity, decided to wait things out. But General Lucas García would not hear of such foolishness.[4] When the incident dragged on, he summoned the minister to his office and told him to resolve the matter. The minister babbled something about international law, but Lucas brushed this aside with an unequivocal command for action.

Security forces blasted their way inside, tossing grenades randomly, unmindful, it appeared, that the occupants of the building included not only the Spanish ambassador but a former Guatemalan vice-president, a former foreign minister, and half a dozen embassy staff. When the police broke in, they and the *campesinos* took refuge in the ambassador's office on the top floor. From there the ambassador, Máximo Cajal, began making frantic phone calls to government offices to call off the raid, but these went unheeded.

Miraculously the ambassador managed to escape. In the presidential palace, General Lucas now gave the final order for resolving the crisis. The police locked the ambassador's office door and began tossing fire bombs through the windows. Outside a large crowd stood horrified, listening to the cries of thirty-nine people burning to death.

One *campesino* survived. He was taken to a local hospital but was later spirited away and killed. The Spanish ambassador condemned the Lucas government for its brutality and left for Mexico. His recollection of the terrible event diverged sharply from the official version that a guerrilla had accidently started the fire with a Molotov cocktail.

But the *campesinos* had finally managed to publicize their cause. Throughout the western world the story of the takeover and horrible aftermath spread. In Guatemala City, thousands of *ladinos* joined a funeral march for the victims of the embassy. But their comrades returned to Quiché knowing that despite the publicity the government's war against them would continue.

The war not only went on, but also picked up with murderous ferocity. General Lucas left no doubt to Guatemalans or the rest of the hemisphere about how he intended to deal with "subversives." In 1981, Amnesty International, in a painstakingly detailed report on conditions in Guatemala, announced that since 1978, when Lucas came to power, almost five thousand Guatemalans had fallen victim to the regime's counterinsurgency program. Bodies showed up in ravines, at roadsides, and in hurriedly dug mass graves. In the three years covered by the report, security officials had picked up more than six hundred people who were never heard from again. In early 1980 a former vice-president of the republic, in an unusually candid statement on the situation, declared: "There are no political prisoners in Guatemala, only political murders." Needless to say, he left that country shortly afterward.

Guatemala City's *ladinos* might have lived with this repression uncomplainingly as long as the midnight arrests and murders involved only illiterate Indians in faraway Alta Verapaz or Quiché, but when their neighbors and kin began disappearing, they started to voice their concerns. Too many young *ladinos*, well educated and from good families, started appearing in the newspapers, their photographs carrying the caption "Disappeared," accompanied by poignant appeals from the family to spare the son's or daughter's life. In an instance of gruesome institutional persecution, in 1980 the government singled out the University of San Carlos for unpatriotic activities. Since then a dozen of its law professors and fifteen administrators have been killed. Seventy-one students detained for questioning have disappeared, and more than fifty university teachers dispatched into the countryside have died violently.

Where disappearances are followed by demands for money—kidnapping of rich children and adults is a highly favored way of raising funds by Latin American guerrillas—the government can always blame terrorists. But when the government itself stands accused, General Lucas (and his successors) have generally indicted either the death squad (Escuadrón de la Muerte), which disposes of "criminals," or the Secret Anticommunist Army (Ejército Secreto Anticommunista), which presumably takes care of the "subversives." Occasionally, in its zeal to attribute killings to these organizations (over which, Guatemalan officials claim, they have no control), the government will publish figures actually *higher* than independent agencies such as Amnesty International put out.

Whatever the amount of these atrocities attributable to moonlighting right-wing assassins, there can be little doubt about the Guatemalan government's rather elaborate bureaucracy for preserving its authority. The president has under his command a special presidential agency which serves as a communications headquarters for the regional police, who carry out security operations throughout the capital. In 1978 an ex-mayor of Guatemala City accused the regional police of being the country's biggest death squad. Several months later an assassin killed him in the civic center.

Security forces in the capital often dress in plainclothes and travel about in unmarked cars. Out in the country villages, where most of the residents are Indians, the countersubversive campaign.

generally shielded from the scrutiny of outsiders, is conducted more openly. There uniformed soldiers of the regular army break into houses, arrest and interrogate suspects, and then execute them. There have been instances where the invaders began their operation by first digging a mass grave and then dispatching squads to round up victims to fill it. For assistance the army relies on the mobile military police, who function in town and country; civilian agents in every hamlet who provide recruits and information; the National Police, headed by an army officer, with a special division, the National Police Detective Corps; and (as in El Salvador but having a less notorious reputation) the Treasury Police. Plainly, the Guatemalan government is prepared for any threat to its security.[5]

For its excesses against its own people the United States rightly condemns Guatemala's leaders. But our moral and political disapprobation, which, incidentally, has alienated the Guatemalan right and, predictably, failed to convert the left, has produced negligible results in "humanizing" the thirty-year war in that country. Guatemala is determined to wage its dirty war in the countryside. If it cannot get arms from the Americans it will get them from Israel or some other country sympathetic to its problems with terrorists. If the United States chastises its leaders about police-state tactics against the Indians, the Guatemalan right will continue, as it has for thirty years, to congratulate itself for adopting the tough anticommunist methods that we championed a generation ago. Just because we've become more sophisticated about dealing with the communists doesn't mean our former disciples have.

What is happening in Guatemala—what occurred at Panzós and the Spanish embassy—is an unpleasant reminder that our ability to direct the anticommunist crusade at home is not readily transferable to other societies, even if they are small, presumably manipulable countries like Guatemala. In America the radical left has been rendered virtually impotent, with no chance for power, because the discontented can be placated by philanthropic gestures, by programs, by slicing the pie in a more agreeable way. American calculations of progress are not disturbed by a population that is 50 percent Indian and does not value ambition, material possessions, and individuality.

But in Guatemala the existence of a society that is half-Indian is a threat. It matters little to Guatemala's ruling order, which promotes the republic's Indian heritage as a priceless tourist attraction, that Indian culture poses no realistic peril to its authority. Because of their numbers the Indians of Guatemala are perceived much in the same way as the Spanish conquerors regarded them four hundred years ago, as a potential menace that must be continuously monitored. We cannot understand the gruesome logic that dictates Guatemalan policy toward half its own people, but Americans of a century ago would have.

Part II

11 My Brother's Keeper

A MERICANS LOOKING AT THE STRIFE OF CENTRAL America see their security threatened and their borders overrun with refugees. The number of Central Americans escaping to this country has escalated sharply in the past five years, but the hardships of this new wave of immigrants pale by comparison with the suffering of those escaping a civil war who cannot make it to the United States. The isthmian refugee in this country forms part of the larger pool of illegal entries from the western hemisphere, mostly from Mexico, but the Central American fleeing his home to a neighboring country represents the vast human suffering, largely undocumented and unreported, of a people at war with themselves.

The most anguished of isthmian refugees, their torment largely unknown to the outside world, are terrified bands of Guatemalan Indians fleeing the slash-and-burn military tactics of their own government. By mid-1982, a Roman Catholic bishops' report estimated, the ferocious counterinsurgency in the Guatemalan highlands had dislocated a million people. Two hundred thousand had sought sanctuary in neighboring countries.

Most have trekked north to the border with Mexico, a 565-mile line, marked by isolated customs and patrol posts, that rises from Ocós on the Pacific over the mountains and then follows the Usumacinta River into the dense jungle of the Petén. It has always been more or less open to travelers and migrants from both sides, but in recent years the numbers have increased sharply, as Indians from the highlands, unable to escape the vengeance of a government that considers them allies of the guerrillas, have sought refuge in the valleys of southern Chiapas state in Mexico.

The Guatemalan refugees constitute a visible embarrassment to authorities in Guatemala City. Their position is, predictably, that the nature of a counterinsurgency is such that ordinary soldiers cannot often distinguish between guerrilla and civilian, so inevitably innocent people suffer. The people run away, the government contends, because they simply don't want to be around when there's fighting going on or, frankly, leave on the advice of guerrilla organizers. It should be added that the guerrillas have admitted executing people they consider government informants, so a few of the refugees may indeed be persons who fear retaliation from the left.

The refugees themselves tell a different story, of repression, flight, and death.[1] In one grisly episode of their continuing ordeal in early 1982, near the border town of Ciudad Cuauhtémoc, Mexico, a Mexican farm worker heard the roar of a Guatemalan military helicopter. It swooped down on some trees just south of the line and opened up with its machine guns. The Mexican laborer who witnessed the terrifying events that followed told of dozens of panicked men, women, and children scurrying from the inadequate cover of a tree canopy to the Mexican side. Some of the fleeing Guatemalans carried infants and thrust them into the hands of dumbfounded Mexican onlookers. Miraculously, none of the Guatemalans died in that escape, but when the pursuing helicopter had finally left, almost three hundred had joined the two thousand Guatemalan refugees then heading each week into Mexico.

Theirs was a not uncommon story of an army raid on two villages that left more than thirty of their families dead and the survivors in flight northward. The helicopter squad, circling the hills, had spied them just south of the border. Taking no chances, the soldiers had presumed they were guerrillas and opened fire.

Behind them, in the highlands that have been their homes for generations, the refugees say, there are scores of villages and hamlets lying burned and deserted because of the Guatemalan government's intense counterinsurgency maneuvers. The Indians speak in frightened tones of soldiers, whom they pejoratively refer to as *pintos* (the "spotted ones," a reference to the soldiers' American-style combat fatigues), who methodically hack their victims to death with machetes, starting by lobbing off the ears and then the nose, because they want to conserve their ammunition. Or the soldiers will exterminate entire families by blocking the doors of their huts and incinerating those inside with gasoline.

Figures on the number of Guatemalans huddled in border encampments range from 50,000 to 200,000 depending on whose statistics one believes. But whatever the numbers, their suffering has attracted Catholic and international relief organizations and, of course, the United Nations Commission on Refugees, which are attentive to their predicament but limited in their ability to do much about it.

The refugees place a far greater strain on the resources of the border towns, which lie in an already impoverished region of a country that is exporting a third of its rural displaced to the north. (The other two-thirds are going into the cities, mostly to Mexico City, which is on the verge of becoming the largest city in the world.) Mexicans who argue that the nation cannot take care of its own have brought considerable pressure on the government to deport the Guatemalans. When in summer 1981 officials responded by sending eighteen hundred Guatemalans back across the border, the U.N. commissioner for refugees and leftist Mexican political groups sharply criticized the move. There were disturbing reports that Guatemalan soldiers executed some of those returned in the deportation.

For Mexico, its economy already depressed, the Guatemalan refugees constitute a social and political problem as well. In the early 1980s, when the refugee issue in the south became more acute, the government decided to prevent the growth of refugee camps along the border on the understandable argument that they would be rapidly transformed into breeding grounds for the guerrillas. Mexico's relations with Guatemala were already strained because of border disputes. So officials have tried to disperse the stream of refugees into villages and farms in the Chiapas interior, the southern Mexican state that abuts all but the straight-line northeastern boundary of Guatemala.

The Mexicans' dilemma has been made more acute by the large numbers of Guatemalans they must somehow deal with and the sprouting of almost a hundred refugee camps in Chiapas in the past five years. In Mexico City there is heightened concern about the security of the south, which lies perilously close to Mexico's oil fields. The Mexicans don't want a Guatemalan "Palestine" in Chiapas, a region once hotly disputed between the two governments, so they are trying to induce the Indians to move northeast into Campeche, toward the remote Yucatán peninsula.

But the Guatemalans have resisted. Among the most determined to stay are the 2,500 residents of La Gloria, a refugee camp in southern Chiapas. One of them, a farmer who had spent the past three years in five different camps, has explained simply: "We don't want to forget our language, customs, or the feelings in our hearts."

Mexican officials are publicly sympathetic, saying they won't make any refugee move to Campeche or back to Guatemala, then privately admit they must do something. The U.N. commissioner for refugees pays a considerable portion of the refugees' upkeep, but the Mexican government, historically sensitive on the subject of social welfare from the outside, distributes the aid through its own relief agency, COMAR. In July 1984, COMAR announced that it was shutting off aid to La Gloria. The agency's local representative announced: "We have to follow guidelines from higher up."[2]

La Gloria's entrenched residents have subsisted on emergency donations from Catholic relief agencies. They appear determined to resist another move. They can understand why the government does not want any more settlements so close to the border, knowing about the isolated but highly publicized raids of the Guatemalan military on several of the camps. The Guatemalan government, quite frankly, stands to gain if the Indians are resettled in Campeche, for its troops can then wage their war in the highlands without the embarrassment of refugees clustered along the Mexican border. But for the Indians, the move to the northeast means more than another trek. Campeche is too far from the protective embrace of Mayan culture, and this consideration, in their minds, far outweighs any diplomatic or geopolitical dispute between two governments.

Just as compelling is the plight of refugees from another conflict, the civil war that has raged in El Salvador since 1979. Americans are mostly familiar with the story of Salvadorans who have escaped to the United States. Those who have come to this country, the Immigration and Naturalization Service (INS) argues, do so for economic reasons, not fear of political repression, which would qualify them for asylum. Yet too often the INS does not go very deeply into the background of these people. By far the largest percentage of them are from the cities. They tend to be people whose daily activities can be closely monitored, and who are associated (sometimes only vaguely) with political organizations that the government suspects. Or they may have been seen once too often at a union meeting or a street demonstration. Their names get on police reports or come to the attention of the subsecretary of the government's security agency. Fearing apprehension, interrogation, torture, or worse, they sneak out of the country, paying a "coyote" several hundred dollars or sometimes much more for smuggling them northward. For those who can afford it, the passage can be a nocturnal flight with the proper documents in a Lear jet rather than a long journey across Mexico and the cramped quarters of a car trunk or a produce truck at the border. Guatemalan newspapers advertise in columns about services providing easy access into the United States.

It's easy to see why the INS requires a more stringent test for political asylum. If it did not, many more thousands who quite justifiably fear reprisal in their own country would qualify. But if most of the Central American refugees arriving (legally and illegally) in this country are from urban areas, then it is a safe presumption that isthmian refugees who migrate from Guatemala into southern Mexico or from El Salvador into Honduras are rural people.

The ordeal of the Salvadoran *campesino* fleeing across the mountains into Honduras is as harrowing as that of the highland Guatemalan Indians escaping their government's fierce counterinsurgency campaign. The Salvadorans' migration began even before the turn of the century, when illiterate but proud *campesinos* tied their worldly goods in dingy sheets and headed with their families along one of the numerous mountain trails into Honduras. In those days there were no border markings or guards to deter them. The Honduran government did not try to stop them; it was more interested in placating the demands for workers by the banana companies then emerging on the north coast. All a man needed was two strong arms and a machete.

Some went into the mining districts of central Honduras, as did the father of Fidel Sánchez Hernández, the Salvadoran leader who waged the one-hundred-day war on Honduras in the summer of 1969 yet often expressed his admiration for the country that offered his father sanctuary. The encouragement Honduras offered to Salvadoran immigrants in those years represented more than a need to expand the labor supply. It offered symbolic evidence of the building of a more unified Central America on the foundation of shared labor, a persistent dream of Honduran president Dr. Policarpo Bonilla. Unfortunately, Bonilla linked his cause too closely to the ambitious schemes of José Santos Zelaya, and his goals perished with the Nicaraguan chieftain and enemy of the big powers.

Still, the Salvadorans kept coming, after the bloody *matanza* in 1932, when the prospect of survival and perhaps even prosperity in the unoccupied lands of Honduran valleys lured a generation of *campesinos*. They came, persisted in the face of growing Honduran animosity in the fifties and sixties, and suffered the vengeful wrath of war-crazed Honduran persecutors in the Salvadoran–Honduran war of 1969.

And since the outbreak of the Salvadoran civil war of 1979 they have once again begun packing their few belongings and heading for the mountainous sanctuaries across the Honduran border. Up and down a line that a generation ago remained largely unpatrolled, Salvadoran military units on one side and Honduran military units on the other now continually monitor, looking for Salvadoran *campe-sinos* and suspected guerrillas trying to cross. Almost thirty thousand have made it, establishing temporary lodgings in a string of isolated refugee camps that have sprung up on the Honduran side.

A few, precious few, of them are survivors of a fierce military campaign in the first half of 1980, when the junta of reform/repression began a savage counterinsurgency in Chalatenango province, north of the Salvadoran capital.[3] On the hastily created agrarian cooperatives set up under the government's new reform laws, soldiers rounded up organizers and systematically shot them. Peasants fearful of military reprisal sneaked out of their shabby villages and headed for the Sumpul River, which forms a part of the twisting border with Honduras. At Las Aradas, a remote border village of some fifteen hundred, the fleeing *campesinos* found temporary lodging and care from people who had only slightly more than themselves. Las Aradas' citizens lacked the conveniences of city life, but they believed their isolation protected them from the war, and they willingly succored their countrymen and helped them across the border.

The desperate Salvadorans and their benefactors had no way of knowing that the two governments, technically still at war, had agreed to cooperate in patrolling the Sumpul to prevent guerrillas from crossing the river. On the Honduran side, soldiers spent their waiting hours carrying stones from the riverbed and building a low-slung rock fortification. As they worked, Salvadoran guardsmen waited in the nearby hills. For this "cleaning operation," as government spokesmen called such incidents, they had two helicopter gunships. The respective Honduran and Salvadoran commanders had already worked out details of the military plan during a meeting at another border town thirteen miles from Las Aradas. Both, evidently, believed that their respective countries' national interest in curtailing guerrilla movements along the border justified what turned out to be a murderously efficient "cleaning operation."

On May 14 the Salvadoran troops closed off Las Aradas and began their siege, from the ground and the air. Survivors later told of machine-gun fire so intense that gaping holes were blasted in the walls of huts. Terrified by the fusillade of the machine guns and the insistent roar of the circling helicopters, people began running toward the river. As they fled, the Salvadoran soldiers raced behind them, firing low so as not to hit any of the waiting Hondurans on the opposite bank.

The desperate *campesinos* who managed to thrash across the river were forced back into the Sumpul to confront their pursuers. Back on the Salvadoran side, their hands were bound and they were forced to lie face down on the riverbank. Then began the frenzied interrogation of the survivors, with incessant questions about guns and guerrillas and muted denials. The guardsmen smashed their rifle butts on backs and heads and legs. Assisted by ORDEN (Nationalist Democratic Organization, the Salvadoran paramilitary group) enforcers, identifiable in their black shirts and skull-and-crossbones insignia, the soldiers herded entire groups off into the bush and machine-gunned them. Survivors later swore that they flipped children in the air and hacked them to pieces with machetes. A soldier told one horrified mother of an infant victim: "We're killing the children of subversion."

Miraculously, through chance and unexpected acts of mercy, the Sumpul River massacre left a few survivors. A man racing from the carnage left his baby son in a small ditch and watched, believing Salvadoran troops would kill him. Instead they carried the child away to one of the children's settlements that have sprung up since the war commenced. A young woman, fifteen bullet wounds in her body, made it through the night, lying in the blood-saturated Sumpul. Throughout she listened to the milling soldiers on the bank chatter about the day's work. Two of her three children died in the shooting, one quickly with a bullet in the chest. The other slowly bled to death from a wound in the crotch. During her watery ordeal she felt portions of bodies graze against her as they floated downstream, yet she remained in the river, trying to comfort her last child, a three-year-old boy. Next morning, after the Salvadoran soldiers had moved away, four Hondurans saw the boy move and crossed the river to get them.

A Honduran fisherman later reported that he snared the bodies of three children in his fish net. The Salvadoran government stated that no massacre occurred at Las Aradas. In Tegucigalpa, the president of Honduras concurred, but to his consternation his military commander in the western area declared that the shooting had taken place but no Honduran soldiers had participated. Still, the Salvadoran officials might have been able to sustain their official position, given the isolation of Las Aradas, but on the day after the massacre a Brooklyn-reared Capuchin priest working in Honduras had climbed the hills and looked down on a ghastly sight. The banks of the river were dotted with milling black specks. Getting closer, the priest saw voracious buzzards gorging on the corpses of the Sumpul River victims. An ORDEN patrol kept him from crossing over, but he did return to his house, picked up a tape recorder and camera, and went to a nearby village, where survivors of the killings at the Sumpul on the day before told him their harrowing stories.

His fellow priests in Santa Rosa de Copán published his report, which blamed both the Salvadoran and the Honduran soldiers. For his action the authorities in Tegoose threatened his expulsion from the country, and Radio El Salvador broadcast death threats against him. Yet the priest managed to get his damning report to Washington. Senator Edward Kennedy inserted it in the *Congressional Record*.

In early 1981, when the guerrillas' call for a general uprising in the cities failed, the government launched another retaliatory campaign in the mountains. And, once more, the "feet people" caught in the middle paid a tragic price for their efforts to escape the war.[4] In most instances of military or paramilitary violence against civilians in the Salvadoran war in the countryside, there are no witnesses because the attackers leave no one alive. But on March 17, 1981, in a flight tragically similar to the Sumpul River crossing of the previous May, a few Salvadoran *campesinos* managed to avoid machine-gun and rocket fire of helicopters and cross the Río Lempa to sanctuary. Father Earl Gallegher, the same American priest who had documented the atrocities on the Sumpul ten months before, and a Fort Wayne, Indiana, woman assisting refugees in

Honduras helped the Salvadorans. The children held on to Father Gallegher's beard as he ferried them across the Lempa. The Indiana woman tied infants close to her body with her brassiere straps and pulled them to safety. Despite their heroic efforts, more than two hundred disappeared.

The survivors of these tragedies and their countrymen who have fled the war in El Salvador have established new lives in makeshift camps along the rugged Salvadoran–Honduran border. As did the Indians fleeing the Guatemalan insurgency, they told of military sweeps by security forces in the Salvadoran interior to deprive the guerrillas of a base of operations in Chalatenango province. One tactic has been to run the villagers out of their small hamlets and away from their garden plot and cut off the rebels' food supply. As one Salvadoran commander explained: "If the guerrillas are the fish and the people are the ocean, then we will dry up the ocean so we can catch the fish."[5] What this has meant, in less metaphorical terms, is a war of machine guns and helicopters against simple people who possess only hoes and machetes.

Most of the Salvadoran refugee camps in Honduras were set up in 1980 and 1981, and almost from the start they have attracted the attention of international relief agencies, Catholic social services, and, surprisingly, the United States Congress. Motivated partly by opposition to Reagan's military emphasis in administration policy toward Central America and by genuine sympathy for the plight of the refugees, several congressmen have undertaken fact-finding missions to the isolated region of western Honduras to interview the Salvadorans. An umbrella relief agency that includes, among other organizations, Doctors Without Frontiers and World Vision, has also made a major effort to attend to (and publicize) the problems the Salvadorans have faced.

At two of the most important settlements, La Virtud and Colomancagua, Salvadorans arrived exhausted, malnourished, and still terrified. They told of planes swooping down on their villages and dropping incendiary bombs. During the first weeks, some arrived in such poor shape that despite medical attention they succumbed to the intestinal maladies that afflict the undernourished. The survivors have tried to make a new life for themselves, despite their confinement by Honduran military patrols. They have set up tiny shops to make shoes or hammocks or pottery and have begun raising a few crops and chickens. Still, their lives have remained restricted. Only with difficulty can they go from one camp to another, and with each successive military commander has come a new set of petty rules. At La Virtud, conditions are better. Most of the refugees in this area depend on Honduran families, who are desperately poor themselves but benefit from international relief activities by their willingness to help the Salvadorans.

Yet, even in the presumably safe environment of the camps, the refugees have not found immunity from the war a few miles away over the mountains. Residents at La Virtud and at the other camps have complained of harassment from Honduran soldiers and mysterious nighttime raids across the border by paramilitary units from El Salvador. Their presence on the Honduran side, various congressional witnesses testified in 1981, offered incontrovertible proof of secret cooperation between the militaries of the two countries.

Since then the Honduran government has succumbed to American pressure to allow United States military operations deep inside Honduran territory. The refugee camps along the border fall within a war zone, and the Salvadorans have faced persistent threats and blatant acts of intimidation to compel them to move farther into the interior. Critics of American policy argue that neither the Honduran government nor the Department of Defense wants the inevitable scrutiny of international relief agencies in the area interfering with their efforts to create a more secure military zone along the border.

Most of La Virtud's residents have resisted relocation farther inside Honduras, even for what an American might consider a relatively short distance (thirty-five miles). Their reluctance to move has frankly baffled the U.N. commissioner for refugees and other representatives of international relief agencies interested in their well-being. But in their feelings about their former homes La Virtud's citizens are no different from the Indians in La Gloria, Mexico. While they would doubtless be safer another thirty-five miles from the border, they don't want to lose sight of the Salvadoran mountains. And they have heard disquieting news that villages in the Honduran interior don't really want to accommodate 25,000 to 35,000 displaced Salvadorans. The Salvadorans remember what happened to their countrymen in 1969.

Amnesty International, which in the past has singled out Guatemala and El Salvador for human-rights abuses, has increasingly turned its attention to Honduras. In 1981, in an investigation of the Honduran political situation, Amnesty International concluded that the majority of human-rights violations in that country involved Salvadoran refugees. They have fallen victim to harassment and even death by Honduran military squads and Salvadoran units permitted entry into the country. Even in presumably safe Tegoose, Salvadorans have become, to use the Spanish participle with its ominous connotation, *desaparecidos*, "disappeared persons."

Like their distant fellow victims of war in southern Mexico, the Salvadorans in Colomancagua and La Virtud have fallen into that category of war's refuse known in 1945 as "displaced persons." As long as Central America's civil wars persist and the antagonisms between the isthmian states remain, their future is uncertain. They lack the means or the craftiness of the middle-class Salvadoran (introduced in the next chapter) to escape to Miami or New Orleans or Los Angeles. The residents of La Gloria and La Virtud are country people, refugees from the bottom level of society trying to survive among those also at the bottom but in a safer situation. They are rapidly becoming Central America's largest class of stateless persons, without the basic rights of citizens and dependent on the generosity of distant agencies and the tolerance of immediate authority. They are the Ixil Indian from Guatemala in Chiapas, the Chalatenango *campesino* in Honduras, the Nicaraguan *ladino* in Costa Rica, the Miskito Indian in the remote jungle of eastern Honduras.

They are more than refugees fleeing a war. They are the largely innocent victims of the fractured and tormented isthmian governments more interested in their own perpetuation than in the well-being and security of a generation of rural people uprooted by conflict.

The placid campus reminds a visitor of a small-town junior college in Iowa or Pennsylvania. Nothing about it suggested that not forty miles away guerrillas were dictating the rules of daily life in another Salvadoran town or that Salvadoran troops were at that moment fighting in hills only a thirty-minute drive distant. Salvadorans, observers are sometimes surprised to discover, have managed to accommodate the rhythm of their daily lives to the beat of a civil war. In his own way the pleasant chap at the technical school had adjusted quite well.

"If things get much worse," he casually informed me, "I'll take my family north."

"To Honduras?" I queried.

"No," he said, "to Houston."

Here was a man with an option, a plan of escape for him and his, and he will probably become (if he has not already) one of the statistical by-products of the Central American travail—a refugee.

The Salvadoran diaspora extends as far north as Canada and southeast into Costa Rica, where penniless Salvadoran migrants have signed on as gardeners or maids to sympathetic *tico* families who are troubled with thoughts about their country becoming the next Lebanon. In Miami and San Francisco uppercrust Salvadorans have established themselves in style; their less fortunate countrymen may find sanctuary in a midwestern church, living in daily fear of discovery by the *migra,* the U.S. Immigration and Naturalization Service, whose agents will doubtless, as under present law they must, decide they are economic and not political refugees and send them back to Central America.

But all of them, rich or poor, whether they've traveled ten miles across the border into Honduras or a thousand miles by walking or by plane to the United States, are refugees, and, in one way or another, we have an unbreakable link with them.

One place of refuge for the Central American expatriate, whether from the right, left, or middle, or of no consequential political affiliation, is New Orleans.[1] Central Americans have been coming to New Orleans for more than a century. In 1984 the city boasted a world's fair; in 1884 it promoted a stylish exhibition at which Central American leaders enthusiastically advertised their countries as a promising domain for American entrepreneurs. Over the decades Central Americans, particularly those on the torrid Caribbean coast, looked to New Orleans, not the remote mountainous capitals of the isthmian states, as their "capital." Alienated politicians and conspiring generals would show up on St. Charles Street or in the Vieux Carré looking for guns, men, and, while they were in town, a good time in the Storyville red-light district. In 1909, when rival armies in Nicaragua were shooting it out for control of the republic's treasury, their respective emissaries were holed up in fashionable New Orleans hotels buying arms and recruiting good old southern boys for the cause.

But nowadays Miami has supplanted the Crescent City as Central America's capital. New Orleans still gets its isthmian refugee, but he is less likely to be the disaffected political aspirant or the cashiered general trying for a comeback than the ordinary down-and-out citizen fleeing the war and looking for a better life. Seventy-five years ago the Central American expatriate in New Orleans was something of a celebrity, his presence duly noted in the local press, biding his time for a glorious return to his country, like General Manuel Bonilla plotting his revolution in a New Orleans brothel with Lee Christmas, the American mercenary. The Central American escapee today is fleeing not just a hostile political climate or adverse economic fortunes—he is quite likely a *permanent* refugee.

An ineradicable stigma attaches to the person who must sneak into this country to survive. Carlos, a Guatemalan illegally in New Orleans, is not atypical. He left Guatemala in 1979 as a stowaway on a cargo ship. His reasons were eminently understandable to the fifty or so Central American friends he has made in the New Orleans area but not to the American Immigration and Naturalization Service. Once he worked quietly in a small Guatemalan town. Then one day he made a mistake; he opposed General Romero Lucas García's takeover in July 1978. A relative of Carlos' ran for a local office on an opposition party ticket. A few days after the election somebody discovered his bullet-riddled corpse in a ditch. Other family members were arrested—usually for the rather common, and usually reliable, assumption that anything your brother or cousin is mixed up in must involve you as well—and died mysteriously by gunshot while being transported to interior jails. Always the explanation was the same: killed in a guerrilla attack, a modern variation of the old *ley de fuga*, shot while trying to escape. Carlos was disbelieving. None of the guards traveling with his arrested family members had perished.

Carlos' real problem lay in the tendency of Guatemala's ruling order to interpret one's civic activities as evidence of dangerous political convictions. From the age of fourteen—the median age of Central Americans—he had been part of a workers' youth organization, the National Liberation Movement. To support himself and his family he got a job as a dockworker. From there he moved up to a position in the town courthouse. For his aspiration in local politics somebody shot him. He survived, but the bullet left him with a weakened arm.

After recuperating he got another job on the docks, but by now the government was cracking down on union activists, and the company, subservient to government wishes, was requiring its workers to list party affiliation on their identification cards. Lucas García set up a military base in the small town so that his soldiers could keep an eye on dockworker organizations. Again, Carlos fell prey to the system, this time to the heavyhanded recruiting methods of the Guatemalan military, which routinely makes sweeps of small villages looking for recruits. His captors beat him but finally let him go when it was obvious he had too little strength in his arm to carry a weapon. After this, Carlos and two friends decided to head north. Carlos had a friend in New Orleans.

Their plan was simple enough. They worked on the docks, and it was easy to leave one of the huge cargo containers open for hiding out. That night they slipped in, carrying two bottles of water and some pills to quell their appetite during the journey. For almost four days the container was their sanctuary. When their water ran out, they sneaked out at night to replenish it. After the ship docked at the

Industrial Canal in New Orleans, they waited for the immigration inspection, then casually walked off the ship. Their first stop in the United States was at one of the ubiquitous quick-stop groceries, where they ordered "Cokes," the universally understood word for one of this country's best-known symbols.

Within a week they had jobs, working at a car wash for $2.90 an hour. Carlos fell prey to an alert *migra* but kept jabbering that he was an anti-Sandinista refugee (thus making him eligible for political refugee status) and needed to get his papers. He ran out and lost the pursuing immigration officer after a block's chase. Later he got a job in a restaurant, went to another car wash, then wound up in yet a second restaurant. In the process he was able to get a social security card by copying another and changing two digits. Bogus cards are available for people in Carlos' predicament for fifty dollars.

His English is still far from passable, and he has often missed his homeland, but even when Lucas García fell and the evangelical Efraín Ríos Montt (who has since been toppled) took over, Carlos expressed little interest in returning to Guatemala. He likes the United States, though he fears the *legal* Hispanic residents, who sense their future is jeopardized by this new generation of illegals. Even so, Carlos does not want to go back to Guatemala. If captured and deported, he would try to find a way back north toward home. On his personal recommendation almost two dozen of his Guatemalan friends have slipped into New Orleans. His is a modern refrain of Goethe's *Amerika, du hast es besser* chanted to a Hispanic accent.

It would be infuriatingly difficult for a disinterested person to decide if Carlos is an economic or a political refugee.

Except for the commonality of a Spanish tongue and their status as victims of the modern Central American ordeal, the new wave of refugees in New Orleans remains as bitterly divided on political issues as their countrymen back in the isthmus. Carlos and his comrades have found momentary refuge from the persecutions of the Guatemalan right, but they have not found peace. Political dissidents from Sandinista Nicaragua have discovered sanctuary here as well. There is a Nicaraguan Democratic Force (NDF), intensely supportive of the Reagan plan for destabilizing what the President calls the "Soviet-Cuban lackeys" in Managua. NDF has a military subsidiary, the Nicaraguan Freedom Fighters. Their spokesman is a seventy-year-old former Conservative Party opponent of the Somozas, Sergio Baltodano.

Señor Baltodano agrees with Reagan on the Soviet menace in Central America. He may be sympathetic to the plight of Carlos and the other victims of Guatemala's thirty years of repressive politics, but his priority lies in recovering lost political status in *his* country, just as Carlos' manifest concern is his future in a society where he will probably always be an alien, if not a fugitive, because in *his* country the ruling order refuses to bend. Political tolerance in Central America, with the possible exception of Costa Rica, is a virtue of neither left nor right.

Miami's Hispanics are fanatically anticommunist, for obvious reasons—Miami has been for two decades and more the homing base for the entire spectrum of Cuban dissidents who agree on little save their visceral hatred of the Cuban *líder máximo*. But New Orleans' Hispanic political character is, and always has been, different, offering a receptive atmosphere to those on both sides of Central America's burning issues. This sometimes questionable mark of urban distinction may have something to do with the city's reputation as the one American metropolis equally committed to the spiritual and material values of humankind. Whatever the reason, the Central American left has found a niche here that would be well-nigh impossible to carve out in any other American City.

New Orleans has always boasted rambunctious urban politics, incomprehensible to the straitlaced upstate Protestants. The intensely competitive refugee politics here merely follow in that tradition. Alpha 66, the militant anti-Castro organization, which plants bombs in unoccupied buildings, has a solid base in New Orleans, as does CISPES, an acronym for the Committee in Solidarity with the People of El Salvador, one of the infuriatingly numerous action committees loosely associated with NONSO, the New Orleans Nicaragua Solidarity Organization, a subsidiary of NNSNP, the National Network in Solidarity with the Nicaraguan People.

Those refugees who fall in a "political" category, whether from the isthmian left or right, have a much better time of it in this country than those who are simply fleeing the hard times that have befallen Central Americans. The former, at least, can more readily obtain a sympathetic, if not always successful, hearing from the Immigration and Naturalization Service. But the so-called economic outcasts must of necessity lead a furtive life, depending on the generosity of friends already here or, increasingly, a network of religious organizations to succor them in their American experience or spirit them to safety through God's underground van service to Canada.

New Orleans has such a support group, the Ecumenical Immigration Services (EIS), subsidized by the Lutheran, Catholic, and Baptist churches, an unlikely doctrinal triad bound by a common mission to do something about the plight of terrified Central Americans, most of them Salvadorans, who have come within EIS' charge. The most visible members of this organization are a Lutheran minister and his wife, both Salvadoran, who have shielded as many as sixteen refugees at a time in their modest home while trying to find church families to parcel them out to or get political refugee status for them from the INS.

Catholic priests in the New Orleans Ecumenical Immigration Services, several of them affiliated with the Maryknoll Order, long active in Central American rural communities, are more militant. Unlike the Protestants, whose missionaries in the isthmus rarely directly suffer from government persecution, the Maryknolls have had a long and often bitter experience with the Central American established order. The assault on three of their missionaries and a Catholic layworker in El Salvador, in which the four women were tortured, raped, and then killed, was one of the more publicized incidents of the suffering of this order in Central America, but there have been numerous other instances of violence against the Maryknolls in recent years. Their agony has spilled over into the debate over sanctuary among Catholics in this country.

In hundreds of congregations in the United States, Protestant and Catholic, the church is caught up in the Central American crisis in a personal, direct way. These congregations form part of the sanctuary movement, which, together with the network of private organizations, not only provides shelter to Central American refugees but shields them from American authorities. Unlike the INS, which often demands virtually unattainable proof of immediate danger to one's life because of political activities before granting political refugee status to a Guatemalan or Salvadoran immigrant, member churches of the sanctuary movement generally indict the rightist governments of Central America as the cause of their charges' plight. They are willing to shield the illegal in the service of a higher law.

The practice of sanctuary is rooted in the Judeo-Christian experience. It has been recognized in English common law. Modern churches that have adopted Salvadoran or Guatemalan refugee families are not easily dissuaded by arguments they are breaking the law. In their view, the separation of church and state does not mean the church yields to the state's total jurisdiction over the terrified victims of the Central American agony who have managed to make it to this country. Some ministers are even defiant: Sixty of them in the sanctuary movement have officially informed INS officials they intend to harbor Central American aliens illegally in this country. Uniformly their justification rests on sanctuary as an ancient, and thus sanctified, custom. Catholic, Baptist, Presbyterian, Quaker, United Church of Christ, Methodist, Lutheran, Unitarian, and Mennonite churches have joined in the movement. Several prominent Catholic archbishops have publicly condoned it.

God's disciples are a powerful opposition for the government. For the INS, already overworked before the Salvadoran civil war with illegal entries from Mexico, the role of American Christendom as a pious scofflaw of American immigration statutes (which call for a $5,000 fine or two-year jail sentence for harboring *each* illegal alien) has become more than an irritation. Yet no administration, quite frankly, wants to collide head-on with a church that is shielding illegal aliens. The INS prefers to intercept them at Brownsville or some other spot on the border and send them back to San Salvador or Guatemala City before a church van whisks them north for safekeeping.

INS authorities are more callous but harshly precise about Salvadoran and Guatemalan illegals: "They are not political refugees fleeing persecution," a prominent immigration official has announced, "but [escapees] from high unemployment and food shortages brought on by years of unrest."[2] Once in Mexico, this argument continues, the isthmian refugee is safe from political persecution, so his continuing journey to the United States must be economically motivated. There is not much acceptance by the INS of the manifestly recognizable truth that one's economic condition is generally determined by one's political situation.

Since 1959, the year Fidel Castro triumphantly entered Havana and inaugurated the revolution that has transformed Cuba into a socialist state, the United States has received about one million Cuban refugees, approximately one-tenth of the island's population. They are, for reasons understandable to any American official of the past generation, "political" refugees. Christianity and its tradition of protecting the downtrodden have had little to do with their safekeeping in this country. They have come to our shores because for the United States government their complaint about living in a Soviet-style economy is a valid passport into this society.

Central Americans do not enjoy this special designation. Their flight is often a secretive one, a harrowing passage across Mexico, followed by a nighttime crossing of the two-thousand-mile border, a porous boundary for most of that distance, between the United Mexican States and the United States of America. Once on this side, they gravitate to the familiar Hispanic-American landscape.

Since the outbreak of the Salvadoran civil war in 1979, it is estimated, $5 billion has left Central American banks to secret Swiss accounts, Miami banks, the New York financial district, and points north. The human migration numbers far fewer, but the size of this migration in just five years, as compared with twenty-five for the Cubans, is having as consequential, if not so dramatic, an impact.

Many of the Central Americans, once inside our borders, have headed instinctively for southern California.[3] Juan Francisco (his surname is omitted) is Guatemalan, one of this generation of feet people. In October 1983 he slipped across the Sonoran border into Arizona with a young wife and infant. There he paid his last dollars for bus tickets to Los Angeles. His first contact was a Roman Catholic church. Within a few hours of their arrival, Juan and his family were members of the greater Los Angeles Central America refugee community, a network of houses, health clinics, and shelters that have sprouted up to accommodate Salvadoran and Guatemalan victims in our midst.

Like so many other Central American migrants, Juan Francisco professes little interest in politics, thus making his claim to refugee status immediately suspect to the INS. But he is nonetheless a political victim, as he sees it, for wanting to leave a country where there are so many killings. He has found sanctuary with El Rescate, a subsidiary of the southern California Ecumenical Council with the specific mission of aiding Central American refugees. El Rescate has been able to place Juan and his family within the protective shield of the Santana Chirino Amaya Refugee Committee, which will give them sufficient assistance over the months until they are absorbed into the vast Hispanic community of southern California.

The largest concentration of Salvadorans anywhere is, of course, San Salvador. But Los Angeles has at least 200,000, possibly as many as 300,000, Salvadorans, making it the second-largest Salvadoran city in the world. San Francisco, it is generally acknowledged, is third. In the United States the number of Salvadorans is said to reach half a million, 10 percent of that country's population.

They keep coming, says a Salvadoran engineering student who fled his country when the military closed the university in 1979, because the "coyotes" (those who smuggle refugees across the border for sometimes hefty fees) show them advertisements and tell them they will be free of political persecution. But once arrived they soon discover the realities of life in a country where the newcomer, especially if from the bottom of society, winds up on the bottom in the promised land.

But then, starting out on the bottom has generally always been the lot of the newcomer to this country. The illegal refugee does not believe he will remain on the bottom.

The sharp increase of illegal migrants traceable to Central America's crisis has occurred just as the American government has undertaken a comprehensive review of its immigration policies. This reassessment, largely the work of a special commission, has in the process raised some fundamental and occasionally troubling issues about the role of America's immigration policy in a world of three billion poor and a million waiting for legal entry into the country.

More precisely, the current squabble over what to do about Central American refugees has sharpened the larger debate over the social, economic, and political impact of Spanish-speaking persons in the United States. This debate, according to students of our historic immigration policy, has become increasingly strident, arousing nativist sentiments of a half-century ago, when our national immigration law rested frankly on the notion that some nationalities were far preferable to others, and creating uneasy feelings among those who have come since 1965, when the old law succumbed to a more humane approach, that reforms will bring on new forms of discrimination. Mexico, for example, claims a special relationship, based on geography, history, and economic ties, to this country. A tightening-up of U.S. immigration laws—even though one widely publicized proposal would actually increase *legal* immigration from Mexico—is feared both by government officials in Mexico and their countrymen in the United States because of what such a law might lead to, not what its framers intend.

The Central American refugees have, quite unintentionally, stimulated not only a debate over our immigration policy over the last generation but just as consequentially a reconsideration of our relationship to the Spanish-speaking populations of this hemisphere. The 1965 law (and its subsequent amendments) rid the country of a patently racist immigration policy. Since then, the national makeup of immigration has greatly diversified, but because we are now getting, legally and illegally, the largest number of immigrants from the western hemisphere, the linguistic component is mostly Spanish-speaking.

Thus what is happening, several critics have pointed out, is that we are rapidly moving from a nation of immigrants whose native tongues survive only in the old ethnic neighborhoods to a society whose newest arrivals represent many nationalities but one tongue that in some regions of the country is more commonly used than English. Liberals who decry the racist tones of labor leaders who want to keep out the "floods of illegals taking jobs away from Americans" are themselves insistent on linguistic homogenization.[4] This is an English-speaking country, they say, and must remain so, citing the case of Canada, where a concentrated French-speaking minority has had, principally because of the perseverance of its language, a powerful impact on Canadian politics. Working-class Americans, many of them descendants of early-twentieth-century eastern and southern European stock, then considered strange and not easily assimilable, express occasionally virulent racist antipathies toward the Hispanic newcomer and doubts about the loyalty of American citizens of Hispanic descent.

Thus the debate over immigration goes far beyond the question of how many enter legally or illegally, what impact they are having on the American economy, or how readily they will be absorbed into the mainstream of American society. It has to do not only with the place of Hispanics in this country but with our relationship to Latin America.

13 "We Lost the War, but We Won the Game"

I T WAS A WAR OF SHORT DURATION, ONE HUNDRED hours; an invasion that saw a Salvadoran army plunge quickly into Honduras only to halt dead in its tracks, then shamefacedly withdraw to its own territory; an air strike that embarrassingly aborted when the Salvadoran leader could not locate his target, an international airport; frenzied radio broadcasts and incendiary editorials from rival capitals; thousands of displaced Salvadorans fleeing from vengeful Honduran mobs roused to patriotic fury to save their homeland from squatters; and, not the least, a soccer match. [1]

Among foreign observers of Central Americans there is a conventional wisdom that holds they will fight for the most inconsequential or trivial reason. In the first decade of this century, Theodore Roosevelt, commenting on Hispanic political violence, called Latin American wars an inevitable by-product of the "revolutionary frame of mind," and when combative isthmian executives began a round of gruesome little conflicts in 1906, he vowed to put a stop to them. After all, he argued, the Central Americans might very well believe that they were settling legitimate quarrels as the "civilized nations" of Europe did—by slugging it out on the battlefield—but this was specious reasoning when weighed against the far more persuasive American argument that such bloody confrontations could not very well be tolerated by the American policeman on the isthmian block. So in 1907, when a Nicaraguan army overwhelmed a combined Salvadoran-Honduran force at the small Honduran village of Namasigüe, where the use of machine guns for the first time in Central American wars wreaked such a devastating toll that Namasigüe became a metaphor for the bloodiest battle in history in terms of casualties per minute, Roosevelt dismissed the affray as just another annoying event among people with the "revolutionary frame of mind."

Yet in our time minor border skirmishes are exaggerated by the American government as dangerous provocations meriting the most serious response. A leftist government with combative instincts in Managua is portrayed as an immediate menace to its neighbor, while its neighbor maneuvers its soldiers along a tense border that neither effectively controls. But Central Americans have the unenviable reputation of getting serious about their wars only when the issues are trivial—a family that can somehow avoid coming apart over the big issues of life but disintegrates into profanity and fistfights over the little things.

That's the martial fate of Central Americans. Nobody but they believe they've ever fought for a noble or just cause. Anybody even remotely familiar with the American Civil War *knows* that Abraham Lincoln had something bigger in mind than collecting federal customs duties in Charleston when he dispatched a rescue mission to Fort Sumter, yet Central Americans have never been able to convey to the outside world that their wars have represented much more than one country pushing its neighbor(s) around, or two republics ganging up on one, or some other trivial *casus belli*. The Middle Eastern hostilities at least have the ultimately credible justification of religious commitment as their *raison d'être*, but the isthmian countries (save Belize) are preponderantly Catholic, so there is no great sectarian zeal to explain their wars.

Germany and the Soviet Union, whose armies have twice in this century devastated Europe, have as excuses intensively competitive ideologies and a manifest need to dominate the plains lying between them; Britain and France warred in two one-hundred-year wars as rivals for world empire. Analysts of global conflict rarely suggest Central Americans may have fought their conflicts for similarly credible reasons. No sensible person would argue that the German performance in the 1936 Berlin Olympics so infuriated Hitler that he was determined to prove Aryan supremacy by waging war, yet eminently mature American observers believe that in 1969 Honduras and El Salvador warred over a soccer match.

The truth of the matter is that the Honduran-Salvadoran war of 1969 had very little to do with a series of intensely fought soccer games, though there was certainly considerable public commotion over the contests. Its origin is initially traceable to migration into Honduras from early in the twentieth century, when Salvadoran peasants joined thousands of immigrants from the rest of Central America and the Caribbean islands to work on the banana plantations on the Honduran north coast. Over the years successive Honduran governments shut down the flow from most sources, but the Salvadorans, encouraged by authorities in Tegucigalpa to open new agricultural lands in then relatively underpopulated Honduras, kept coming. They were welcomed as energetic, skilled additions to the Honduran economy.

In time, naturally, resentments against the Salvadorans grew as their numbers steadily mounted. Along the banana-strip towns of the north, it was estimated, Salvadorans made up almost 50 percent of the population. In the thirties and forties, Tiburcio Carías Andino, the legendary strong man of the Hondurans, aroused these latent hatreds among his countrymen by making much of Salvadoran domination of the national grain trade. The "32 peasants" revolt in El Salvador brought a new wave of agricultural settlers escaping the harsh realities of Salvadoran country life. But the first widespread hostility against Salvadorans occurred in the fifties, after a banana workers' strike on the north coast in 1954 that focused attention on the large numbers of Salvadorans in the country. In 1959, a decade before the soccer war, harassment became so bad that three hundred Salvadoran families packed up and moved back across the border into their own country. Paradoxically, the troubles of Salvadorans in Honduras multiplied in years when a liberal, civilian president, Ramón Villeda Morales, held power in Tegucigalpa. Villeda pushed through an extensive agrarian reform law that dispensed land to Hondurans and, as long as he was in office, evicted Salvadorans. The military officers who tossed him out in 1963 actually tried to improve things, pledging they would not apply this odious discriminatory provision, but the political returns of whipping up antiforeign feelings were not lost on them.

And there were other troubling elements in the relations between the two countries in the sixties. Both had subscribed to the Central American Common Market treaty of 1960, but within a few years the Salvadoran advancement in industrial development, Hondurans argued, had given its citizens unfair advantage in the Honduran economy. Again, the rabble-rouser of xenophobia was yet another civilian, the patron saint of Honduran liberalism, Modesto Rodas Alvarado. Out in the countryside a vigilante group, the Mancha Brava, stepped up its random intimidation of Salvadoran farmers. The two respective oligarchies in El Salvador and Honduras now fashioned a war of words, intended mostly to quell demands for agrarian reform among their own *campesinos*—Salvadoran landowners resisting claims for reform by their own people in El Salvador yet vigorously championing their cause in Honduras, and vice versa. Along the then weakly patrolled border, where bandits raided villages on the other side, the random atrocities they often casually committed escalated into accounts of savagery when reported in the national press of both capitals.

There occurred a serious clash in 1967, when a Salvadoran national guard patrol raided a Honduran ranch house where, allegedly, the murderer of a Salvadoran bordertown mayor had hidden. The guardsmen kidnapped the suspect and spirited him across the border to the town of his crime, where he was tried, found guilty, and sentenced to jail. A few days later another squad of Salvadoran guardsmen returned and torched the ranch house. This was followed by a comical incident in June when four Salvadoran military trucks crossed the frontier and penetrated five miles, stopping finally in Nueva Ocotepeque's square, where, disbelieving they had entered Honduras, the Salvadorans surrendered. At the investigation the commanding officers of the invaders swore they had fallen asleep, a ridiculous explanation that earned them the nickname "Sleeping Beauties." Tensions eased somewhat with the involvement of the Organization of Central American States and a timely goodwill visit of President Lyndon Johnson to San Salvador. The two Salvadorans languishing in a Honduran jail got to go home, and the kidnapped Honduran was released. He returned to a thunderous reception at the Tegoose airport.

To foreign observers of Central America these seemingly minor confrontations were the substance of most isthmian quarrels, not very serious incidents that two countries had foolishly permitted to cause a momentary rupture in an otherwise apparently peaceful relationship. In actuality these border troubles diverted attention from something far more consequential for the Central American family—the discordant, out-of-sync political and economic development of the isthmian states.

El Salvador had tried to diversify its economy in the sixties and counted on an agricultural frontier in Honduras to absorb its landless peasantry because they could not be accommodated in El Salvador. But it was doing so just as the retarded Honduran economy offered hope for Hondurans through land reform pledges by a vigorous agrarian institute. The institute's director, confronted with the choice of taking land from the big Honduran landowners and the banana magnates of the north coast *or* dispossessing Salvadoran squatters, expediently chose the latter course.

The dispossessed Salvadorans, many of whom had tilled Honduran soil for years, not only had to leave the country but, in numerous instances, lost all their possessions and suffered physical abuse from bands of Honduran vigilantes. The Honduran press, sometimes compared in its editorial flavor with American tabloids, championed the expulsions as a great patriotic victory. An especially vitriolic journalist laid down the basic considerations every loyal Honduran manifestly supported, describing the Salvadorans as "criminals unworthy of basic human rights who should at least have the decency to get out of Honduras." The appearance in Tegucigalpa of Nelson Rockefeller during this troubled period, dispatched by

President Richard Nixon to assess the western hemispheric condition, apparently convinced his hosts that somehow the United States stood responsible for dumping the Salvadorans in their country, and this conviction and Rockefeller's visit provoked a riot.

But as far as the rest of the world was concerned, the war that ensued a few weeks later occurred mainly because of the riotous atmosphere surrounding the soccer matches. The first game was played in Tegucigalpa. In a less than sporting spirit, Honduran fans camped outside the hotel where the Salvadoran team was lodged and partied all night before the big game. The next day, predictably, Honduras won. When the Honduran team arrived in San Salvador for the second game, the Salvadoran fans reciprocated by keeping the Honduran players awake for *two* nights. A sizable number of Honduran nationals came over to San Salvador for the match. Most had the good sense to watch the game on hotel television, but the Hondurans who showed up at the stadium suffered verbal abuse and, if singled out, were pelted with stones and urine-filled plastic bags. (Central Americans often take their soft drinks in plastic bags tied at the top around a straw.) In Honduras these incidents were reported as savage assaults on defenseless Hondurans. There were, inevitably, stories about Salvadoran gang rapes of Honduran women on the streets of San Salvador. And, later, an OAS investigating committee determined that Salvadoran authorities had indeed allowed their countrymen to commit "brutal aggressions" against the visiting Hondurans. The final game, moved to Mexico City's Aztec Stadium because of all the unrest, ended with a Salvadoran victory.

But in Honduras the vengeful mobs had already turned out in the cities to ransack Salvadoran businesses. Some of the Salvadorans fled to escape physical harm; others stayed put and did not suffer a scratch. Indubitably, as sworn testimonies attest, there were cases of severe physical suffering, a few involving women whose breasts had been hacked off.

The number of Salvadorans trudging across the border began escalating rapidly in late June and early July, continuing even after the Salvadoran invasion of midmonth, reaching, one chronicler has calculated, as many as 300,000. Most told stories of hardship, of losing their land and possessions, and, though not personally having suffered physical maltreatment, of knowing about compatriots who did.

In San Salvador these rumors, tinged with bitter memories of the trouble between the two countries over the preceding decade, were enough to move the Salvadoran assembly to demand justice. The Salvadoran leader, a tough-minded military man, General Fidel Sánchez Hernández, now apparently concluded that he could negotiate and run the risk of losing face among his own people, or send his vengeful troops across the border and be a national hero. He chose what for the soldier is the heroic course.

Even the moderate civilian personalities in El Salvador's rightist-weighted political spectrum found themselves swept along in a war fervor. There were few voices—not even that of José Napoleón Duarte, then mayor of San Salvador—expressing much concern that a war with Honduras might very well undermine the resurgent economy by destroying the Central American Common Market, which greatly benefited El Salvador, and complicate the situation in an overcrowded countryside. For the abused Salvadoran in exile, the military clique in San Salvador now portrayed itself as an avenging force, ready to strike at its enemy with a sudden air and ground attack.

This was to be a war of revenge, aimed at compelling the bullheaded Hondurans to modify their agrarian policies, not a war of territorial conquest. By adopting such a strategy the Salvadorans had what was for them a reliable model—the intense ferocity of the Israeli military in the June 1967 Six-Day War. Salvadorans have long taken foreign models for their national character. In assessing their own work ethic and grand economic ambitions, they often characterize themselves as the "Germans" of Central America (and in this description, of course, the Hondurans are portrayed as the happy-go-lucky "Italians" of the isthmus). In their posture toward their neighbors the Israeli analogue is a convenient one. Not only has Israel become a major supplier of arms to right-wing governments in Central America, but the Israelis sent significant amounts of weapons to Somoza in the seventies. And the symbol of the diminutive Jewish state holding its more populous Arab neighbors at bay has much appeal to the Salvadoran top brass. The fact that the two countries are in sharply different situations and have diametrically opposite political and social values has little to do with the appeal to the Salvadorans of regarding their country as the "Israel of the isthmus."

But the Salvadoran military in the soccer war, lamentably, lacked the tactical sophistication in war of its faraway model. Nor does the rugged Central American landscape offer an inviting terrain for tank warfare. When the Salvadoran generals decided in mid-July 1969 to escalate from a series of minor border skirmishes to a full-fledged assault, they gathered an imposing ground strike force in the east, where the Pan American Highway passes into Honduras, and in the northwest, near the Honduran border, for an assault on the town of Nueva Ocotepeque. Their intention was a coordinated strike into southern Honduras, where the Honduran portion of the Pan American Highway connects with the road to Tegucigalpa, and a drive from Nueva Ocotepeque on San Pedro Sula, cutting off the north coast from the capital. The plan vaguely resembled the kind of ground strategy the Israelis employed to divide their enemies. But the Israelis usually do not have to scale mountains to wage their wars.

The Salvadorans had another ambitious martial tactic, an air strike on Tegucigalpa, designed not so much to do physical damage but to scare the bewildered Hondurans into tossing out their unpopular (and presumably inept) leaders and begging for a settlement. The Salvadoran air force then consisted of eleven planes, of World War II vintage, as against almost two dozen Honduran military planes. It possessed only one usable field, Ilopango, the military and international airport of the entire country. Realizing they were outnumbered and probably outclassed in the air, the Salvadorans elected to strike quickly with a late-afternoon assault on Toncontin, airport of the Honduran capital, and several other fields. Even though the Salvadoran bombers were lumbering DC3s, the time of day chosen for the run meant that darkness would prevent the Hondurans from responding.

Murphy's law now played havoc with the Salvadoran plan. Two of the attacking planes, taxiing for position on an Ilopango strip, hit each other. The rest of the squadron made it off the ground, came over Tegucigalpa at a fortuitous moment for a strike without much fear of intercepting fighters, but could not find Toncontin airport. Frustrated, the lead Salvadoran pilot flew away; he got separated from his comrades, but did manage to find an airport, La Aurora in Guatemala City, where he could put down.

The following day the superior Honduran air force, its pilots bent on revenge for the aborted Toncontin raid, headed for Ilopango. There they were able to blow a few holes in the runway, then got in a dogfight with several Salvadoran fighters. At Acajutla, El Salvador's main port, the Hondurans blew up oil storage tanks.

But on the ground the war was not so comical. The Salvadoran strike forces, better equipped and more ably commanded than the smaller Honduran defenses, plunged into Honduras at the designated points of attack. They quickly seized Nueva Ocotepeque and dispatched a force east to cut off the north Honduran coast from Tegucigalpa. But a few miles out of Nueva Ocotepeque the Salvadorans stalled in one of the innumerable valleys of the Honduran countryside, where the Hondurans had taken a stand. A Salvadoran flanking unit, sent to cut off the Hondurans from the rear, got lost. And in the east, where the roads were better, the invaders thrust easily into the Honduran peninsula at four places. Then, despite their superior weaponry and the suddenness of their assault, the Salvadorans, their soldiers rapidly running low on ammunition, slowed and finally stopped short of Nacaome, their principal objective.

Further complicating matters, the Salvadoran command soon faced another problem, the diplomatic weight of the Organization of American States and the moral condemnation generally visited on the attacker, whatever the justness of his cause. Sánchez Hernández, the Salvadoran president, had become an instant hero to his people; but his Honduran counterpart, Oswaldo López Arellano, who had demonstrated such an ineptness in handling the Salvadoran immigration issue that he was on the verge of being tossed out when the Salvadorans attacked, won political redemption in this war. As bad as it was, the Honduran military had defended the *patria* and given its people a momentary national unity that history and geography have so often conspired to deny them.

In two resolutions the OAS castigated the Salvadorans for the invasion but in a third pledged that if El Salvador would pull back to its own territory its citizens in Honduras would be protected. It offered at least a reluctant acknowledgment of El Salvador's *raison de guerre*, and Sánchez Hernández acquiesced.

Two weeks after their initial plunge into Honduras, the Salvadoran troops returned to a thunderous reception in the national capital, 200,000 of their countrymen still in enemy territory.

What really had brought on this bitter little war that cost two thousand lives in four days and left 100,000 homeless?[2]

In the early years of this century, the United States government usually assumed that the interstate clashes of Central America had to do with the rival political ambitions of Nicaragua and Guatemala. After José Santos Zelaya came to power in Managua in 1893 and Manuel Estrada Cabrera in Guatemala City seven years later, these two dictators, through a shifting pattern of intrigue with their protégés in Honduras and El Salvador, threw the isthmus into a series of bloody wars that lasted off and on for more than a decade. Observing this disruption, the American government, determined to have a pacified Central America for a secure neighbor to the future isthmian canal and a safe environment for banana investors, plunged into Central America's troubles. Its military intervention destroyed Zelaya's grip on Nicaragua and in the act Nicaragua's ambition to bring two of the states—Honduras and El Salvador—and ultimately the rest of Central America under its influence. In fracturing what was at that time a movement to achieve isthmian political union, the United States not only misinterpreted the causes of these wars but by its involvement severely retarded the historic driving forces of Central American nationhood. Despite the severity of his rule Zelaya was molding a unified Nicaragua and, had the Americans not brought him down, a united Central America.

By a similar process of oversimplication we have misread the soccer war of 1969. The initial analysis, of course, completely rejected the spontaneous outbursts surrounding the soccer matches of that summer as the precipitating event and looked deeper into the preceding decades for war's origin, to the rapid increases in El Salvador's population and the large migration of Salvadorans into the comparatively sparsely populated Honduras. Soon after the '69 war, the doomsday economists who warn of inevitable conflicts among rapidly expanding populations characterized the soccer war as gruesome proof of Thomas Malthus' grim prediction that the supply of food cannot keep up with the pressure of population. El Salvador, one of the most densely packed countries in the world, had begun exporting its people in order to survive, and the growing resentment over the Salvadorans in Honduras had finally erupted in riot, explusion, and war.

Yet, as in so many of Central America's problems, the reasons these countries wage war may appear deceptively simple—ambitious political rivalries or, in the case of the soccer war, El Salvador's overpopulation. But in deciphering the often hidden origins of this conflict, one uncovers causes more complex and less amenable to outside solution than an international police force or population controls can provide. The real issue in the soccer war was not so much the surge of agricultural population but the diminishing amount of land available to them, in both densely populated El Salvador *and* in sparsely inhabited Honduras.

For the past century there has been a steady change in both countries from very small holdings, tilled primarily for food, to consolidated farmlands, used to grow cotton, coffee, or bananas or to graze cattle. The agricultural economies of not only El Salvador and Honduras but, in varying degrees, all the Central American states have moved closer in the past fifty years into the agro-export world market. This has been, in the calculations of gross national products of these countries, undeniably beneficial. But it has left a cruel legacy—the squeezing out of the agricultural peasant, who in the past could grow enough corn or maize on ten acres or so to feed his family *and* perhaps two or three others in the city. In modern times the peasant's holding has been reduced to two or four acres or he has been thrown off the land altogether to make room for vigorously expanding coffee or cattle barons.

Despite its surging population in the past generation, Central America has enough arable land to feed itself. In this country there is more than enough land to feed the American people and have sizable quantities left over for the export market. But Central America has organized its agricultural economies to reap the rewards of the world market. In doing so, it has reduced the holdings of its agricultural peasantry, sentencing these people to a life of poverty, subsistence, or migration. The rapacious Salvadoran army that struck Honduras in summer 1969 was thus defending, not their countrymen suffering abuse at the hands of outraged Hondurans, but the large landowners of El Salvador whose acquisitive practices had forced the Salvadoran peasants into exile.

In the past, Central America's wars had to do largely with the intensely rivalrous politics of the region—an ambitious Nicaraguan chieftain like Zelaya trying to bring the other governments under his sway early in this century or, in modern times, the Costa Ricans providing sanctuary first to the Sandinistas and then to their enemies. But the soccer war added an unsettling dimension to Central America's age-old conflicts. It was a conflict waged between frankly militaristic governments on behalf of their respective peoples, ill-treated by their neighbors, unwilling to resolve the legitimate social and economic grievances of their own countrymen. The war unleashed powerful animosities and much physical abuse, but it also reinforced latent feelings of solidarity among people at the bottom. It reminded Honduran country folk that the Salvadoran *campesino*, dispossessed of his plot of ground, may seek justice from his neighbor across the border rather than from his own government, just as modern Salvadoran refugees, believing they will be shielded, have clustered in camps on the Honduran side. The troubles of a neighbor become one's troubles.

Late in the Nicaraguan civil war, when it was clear he was losing, Somoza dispatched his air force to pulverize the Sandinista-controlled towns of northern Nicaragua. From hills in southern Honduras people who presumably had no stake in the outcome of this bloody conflict to the south looked on as screaming Nicaraguans fled the devastation. A Honduran *campesino,* watching this human travail, turned to an American sitting nearby. "We feel," he said solemnly, "what they are suffering."

14 The Miskito King

C ENTRAL AMERICA HAS PROBABLY 4.5 MILLION Indians, most of them in Guatemala, but the broad swath of jungle lowlands and dense forests that form eastern Nicaragua is the domain of another Indian people, the Miskitos. They have historically resisted authority from the interior. The Spanish tried fitfully to subdue them, then gave up, and since Central American independence in the 1820s successive Nicaraguan governments have gradually extended the sway of national authority over the Mosquitía, as this region is called, but Managua has yet to break the fierce independence of its Indian minority. It is not only geographic isolation but cultural and religious differences that galvanize the resistance of the Miskitos.

In the seventeenth century, Englishmen from Jamaica and other West Indian islands began landing on the Caribbean coastline, using the sheltered coves as bases to raid interior Spanish towns and, later on, establishing crude villages to exploit the lumber of the vast forests that blanket the Mosquitía. The Miskitos had early contacts with the enemies of Spain, and they readily assumed a special importance in the eyes of the English. They lived off the sea, trading their catch to the Europeans for weapons and accepting the protection the English shrewdly proffered.

So strong was the Miskito attachment to the English presence in

Central America in the nineteenth century that royal emissaries made agreements with Miskito chieftains. In 1848, when the Americans began trooping across the isthmus on the way to the California goldfields, an arrogant English diplomat even mobilized an Anglo-Miskito army and seized the Nicaraguan port of San Juan del Norte, renaming it Greytown. To the northwest the English held sway over the Bay Islands off Honduras and of course over what is today Belize. But the Miskitos, not much more than a few thousand people in those days, were the presumably loyal allies of her majesty against the Nicaraguans. English cartographers drew their maps of Central America showing the Mosquitía as a protectorate, and Queen Victoria's rather proper agents even recognized a Miskito king. His was not much of a kingdom, and he was not much of a king, but the gesture reinforced the Miskitos' will to resist Nicaraguan authority.

Predictably, since the Americans and English were rivals in Central America, the Nicaraguans had a champion for their claim to the Mosquitía in the United States, whose successive administrations in the nineteenth century viewed Miskito nationalism as farcical and the English protectorate as nothing more than the administration of "crowns, Christianity, and Jamaica rum" to a few thousand "savages."[1] When in 1860 the English recognized Nicaraguan claims to the region and in the 1890s finally dismantled their protectorate, Washington cheered the fiery Nicaraguans. The emergence of the nationalist Zelaya changed American attitudes about Mosquitía.

Today, Washington champions the Miskitos' defiance of Managua. The Miskitos have become, with the triumph of the Sandinistas, a people whose fate is suddenly of dramatic import in Washington. A long-standing historical grievance is presently at stake in eastern Nicaragua. How the "Miskito question" is finally resolved will say a great deal about the strength of the Sandinistas as well as the survival of an Indian culture on a collision course with a revolution.

The Miskitos are a people skilled in adaptation and survival. When the English, before the turn of the century, finally relin-

quished any pretense of protecting them, they readily accommodated the growing numbers of foreign, mostly American, lumbering
and banana companies that soon dominated Central America's
eastern coast. By tradition the Miskito economy was essentially one
of barter; with the lumber and banana businesses came the foreigners' wage-labor system. Miskito men began leaving their villages for months at a time, often for a year, to work in logging
operations or hack banana stalks. But they did not forswear the old
ways, when Miskito fishermen had labored in a subsistence economy, using their fish and turtle catches to trade for food and
enhance their position in village society. Just like the highland
Guatemalan Indians, the Miskitos have never fully been incorporated into the monied economy.

Panama disease and other blights decimated the Nicaraguan
banana kingdom almost fifty years ago, consigning the empire of
green and gold to Nicaragua's neighbors. Lumbering and mining
continued, with the result that vast areas of the tropical rain forest
have fallen before the saw. There are regions of eastern Nicaragua
that exemplify ecological disaster. The once vast pine stands of the
northeast are gone, as is much of the cedar and mahogany. The
Miskitos, once a seagoing people, are now largely confined to a
network of agricultural villages, linked by religious and linguistic
bonds.

But the outside again threatens their culture, only now the
menace to their independence springs from a century-old determination of Spanish, Catholic Nicaragua to consolidate the nation
by incorporating the Protestant Miskitos into the new order. The
enemies of the Sandinistas are championing the cause of the Miskitos with the zeal that only the exploitation of religious conflict
fueled by political and cultural animosities can generate.

Whether the Miskitos are ready for the Sandinista program for
Nicaragua remains an uncertainty. The Somozas, who ran Nicaragua with a noticeably heavy hand, got the reputation of tolerating
Miskito separateness, though this policy of neglect really meant that
the regime never did much for the Miskitos either. The Sandinistas
can ill afford to adopt this attitude, and they know it. For one thing,

their enemies have exploited latent Miskito fears about the exercise of political authority from Managua for any reason. And, more seriously, the Miskitos have found themselves the pawns of a war that rages off and on between the Sandinistas and the rebel armies operating along the Honduran border.

In their enthusiasm to disseminate the blessings of revolution and, of course, to advance their political cause among the neglected Miskitos, the Sandinistas dispatched militias and Cuban doctors and teachers into Mosquitía's villages and schools. When the Cuban teachers tried to change instruction from local dialects to Spanish, the Miskitos protested. In February 1982 the Sandinista militia, suspecting that former Somocistas were behind the Miskito resistance to their revolution, raided a Moravian church in Prinzapolca looking for ex-guardsmen. An exchange of shots left four Indians and four Sandinista soldiers dead. A Sandinista squad later arrested several Miskito preachers, accusing them of counterrevolutionary activities.

But the Sandinistas, unlike their predecessors in Managua, have shown no sign they intend to retreat back across the forests and mountains and leave the Miskitos to their own devices. Along the Río Coco, which forms the boundary between northeastern Nicaragua and Honduras, the Sandinistas have moved some eight thousand Miskitos forty or fifty miles into the interior, then burned down their villages and destroyed their crops.

One who escaped a Sandinista raid told of a harrowing ordeal. He and his brothers were roused from their house and ordered outside to a place where they were forced to watch as a Sandinista firing squad machine-gunned seven recalcitrant Miskito miners. Their bodies were dumped into freshly dug graves. That night, when the Sandinista guards marched them down to the river to what they believed was certain death, the Miskitos plunged into the water. The guards opened up with their machine guns, spraying the water as the Indians swam furiously for the Honduran shore. Only one of the four made it. He was hit several times but managed to crawl ashore, where a searching Honduran patrol found him the next morning. The Hondurans patched his wounds and took him to a refugee camp.

Almost ten thousand Miskitos have fled Sandinista Nicaragua to a sprawling refugee camp in Mocorón, Honduras, twenty miles north of the Río Coco.[2] The camp is a project of World Relief, associated with the National Association of Evangelicals, and by far the most ambitious relief effort for displaced Miskitos from eastern Nicaragua. They occupy small villages in what is still a remote area of Honduras. There are no roads connecting this province (Gracias a Dios) with the mountainous interior of the country, and the average *hondureño* has only a sketchy knowledge of the presence of so many Nicaraguan refugees in his country. Funds for their upkeep, of course, come not from Tegucigalpa, which can ill afford to sustain these people, but from a variety of international relief agencies— the United Nations High Commission for Refugees, the Peace Corps, CARE, and even a few Swedish and Swiss agencies.

Mocorón is an international relief undertaking, and its existence underscores the wide concern the ordeal of the Miskitos has attracted. The director of the camp, son of missionaries in Honduras and a onetime athlete, runs Mocorón like a compassionate military field commander. Several days a week a truck chugs down the narrow road to pick up weary Miskitos, their only possessions tied in dirty bundles, and take them to Mocorón. There some twenty or thirty, mostly cousins or brothers of an extended family, live in tents until they can put up more permanent wood shelters. The camp director provides food and clothing until the refugees are able to raise their own crops.

It is not an idyllic place. It has far fewer amenities than the squalid Nicaraguan villages the Miskitos have fled, but here, at least, they have little concern about the interference of the Honduran state. Tegoose might as well be ten thousand miles away. So the Miskitos have tried to reestablish their daily lives without the harassment of Spanish-speaking authorities from the interior. They have built their one-room bamboo-and-plank huts for entire families. For drinking water, bathing, and washing, the refugees must rely on a nearby stream. Their diet consists of the Central American basics—rice, beans, tortillas. With little meat, fish, or eggs and no ready supply of potable drinking water, malnutrition and sickness are a perpetual menace. Some in Mocorón despair of ever returning to Nicaragua, but others, trying to keep spirits high, have even organized a local band for nightly entertainment.

Half of Mocorón's population is under the age of thirteen. Theirs is an uncertain future, but everyone, from the old people on down to those with only a fleeting awareness of their predicament, wants to go home.

The Miskito cause has a champion who has connections in Washington, a modern "king" with the very un-Hispanic name Stedman Fagoth Müller, chief of MISURASATA, an organization representing the Miskitos (175,000) and two less numerous Indian groups of eastern Nicaragua, the Sumo (15,000) and the Rama (1,500) in 256 communities.[3] Mr. Fagoth bears a personal grievance against the Sandinistas, and he has carried his case all the way to the United States Senate. In July 1982, he maintains, a Sandinista army squad raided the Miskito village of San Esquipulas, storming the house of Fagoth's father, who died shortly afterward, although apparently not at the hand of the Sandinistas. The Sandinistas would not permit a "Christian burial," Fagoth continued, and when the Miskito leader later interred his father in a proper ceremony they returned and blew up the grave with dynamite. Today's Miskito "king" is less regal and no longer enjoys a special relationship to the British crown, but he is no less beholden to modern imperial forces. Mr. Fagoth has found a warm reception for his cause among hard-liners in the United States, particularly former secretary of state Alexander Haig, the American Security Council, a conservative political organization, and *contras* operating in Honduras and Miami. The Sandinistas dismiss him as a CIA agent. Ironically, in their zeal to promote national unity in the early days of the revolution, the Sandinistas themselves were enthusiastic promoters of MISURASATA. When the eastern question surfaced, the government coordinator, Daniel Ortega, and the poet-priest minister of culture, Ernesto Cardenal, generally accepted the notion that the country's Indians deserved a special place in "Nicaragua Libre." They already had a representative organization (ALPROMISU), loosely associated with the Canadian-based World Council of Indigenous Peoples. ALPROMISU's directors shifted to positions similar to MISURASTA's, and Fagoth took a place on the Council of State, Nicaragua's governing body. Another Indian leader, Armstrong Wiggins, joined the Government House as Miskito representative. For about a year relations between Managua and Zelaya department, where most of Nicaragua's Indians live, went fairly smoothly. But from the start the Sandinistas were determined to incorporate the Indians into their national program. They established a separate ministerial post for the Atlantic Coast, agreed to respect Indian property titles, and, in general, publicized the special problems of the east to the much more populous western region of Nicaragua.

But in Nicaragua, as elsewhere, governments determined to mold a new order yet respect the cultural and ethnic differences of its people often discover that minorities are reluctant to give up the old ways for the uncertain promise of a new life in the larger society. MISURASATA flourished as a means of expressing traditional Indian causes, while the appeal of *Sandinsimo* waned noticeably among a people who in fact had played only a minor role in the overthrow of the Somoza regime. The central authorities in Managua soon became suspicious that the Miskito king intended to follow his predecessors down the separatist path.

Fagoth's complaint runs deeper than an understandable anger over the way the Sandinistas treated his dead father. He has charged them with forcibly imposing Marxist-Leninist doctrine on a people long accustomed to running their own affairs. But the doctrines of Marx and Lenin have little to do with explaining what the Sandinistas are doing: they are attempting to implant the authority of the Nicaraguan state in a region where, historically, it has never taken root. More specifically, the Sandinistas have cracked down on the Miskito lumber operations and taken their much-publicized literacy campaign into the virtually autonomous Miskito educational system. MISURASATA also indicts the Managua regime for murdering a Miskito leader, Lyster Aythers, in September 1979 and then, when confronted with the charge by a band of outraged Miskitos, refusing to abide by a promise to return his body.

The antagonism between MISURASATA and the Sandinistas goes far beyond Indian resistance to the literacy campaign, which rejects teaching in Miskito, Sumo, and Criolla dialects in favor of, naturally, Spanish, or the predictable hostility between a heavily Catholic Nicaragua and a determined Moravian Protestant minority. Fagoth is convinced the Sandinistas, who have thus far respected private property in western Nicaragua, look upon the community-owned holdings of the east as fertile ground for nationalization schemes. In early 1980 the Nicaraguan government expropriated several Indian communal holdings around Puerto Cabezas.

When the Indians protested, the foreign ministry of the Sandinista government actually signed an agreement with MITSURASATA stating that the literacy campaign in the east would employ Indian dialects and that 80 percent of the value of Mosquitía's resources would be returned to the Miskitos. Fagoth argues that the Sandinistas have never lived up to their part of the bargain and, in fall 1980, began a repressive campaign in eastern Nicaragua aimed at eliminating Miskito leaders and preparing for the eventual transfer of Indian communal property to the state. Fagoth himself was arrested and thrown into a Managua jail, and he was released only when he promised to go to the Soviet Union for educational training. He agreed, then fled to Honduras.

The Nicaraguan church, an early supporter of the Sandinista cause, has been an increasingly voluble critic of the government's treatment of the Miskitos since 1982. In a letter dated February 10, 1982, signed by Archibishop Obando y Bravo, the bishops of Nicaragua (Catholic and Episcopal), while recognizing the legitimate security interests of the Sandinista army in relocating Indians living along the Honduran border, condemned their policies as a violation of human rights. Archbishop Obando, who from 1979 has shifted from enthusiastic champion of the Sandinistas to sometimes outspoken opponent of their authoritarian ways, has presented the Sandinistas with a difficult choice. Because the archbishop adopts the government's argument that it has an obligation to defend the *patria*, the national domain, he is reluctant to approve the arguably severe measures the Sandinistas have taken in the east. If the government announced as a first priority the "preservation of human rights" in the Mosquitía, it would be virtually bound by the Miskitos' meaning of this imprecise term—the Sandinistas would have to pull out of the east and, as its predecessors have done, leave the Indians to their own ways. If, on the other hand, the Sandinistas hold fast to their plan to exert national authority over the Mosquitía, which constitutes one-third of the landmass of the country, MITSURASA-TA and the Miskito king would have to bend.

The determination of the Sandinistas to extend their control over the Miskitos necessarily takes precedence over those gestures to designed to placate international critics. If preserving state security means arbitrary arrests of Miskito leaders or forced removal of entire villages from the border into the interior, where the inhabitants will be less inclined to lend their support to rebel armies just across the border, then the Sandinistas are quite prepared to undertake such measures. They have prevented curious outsiders from investigating the plight of the Indians by the simple expedient of forbidding foreigners to visit the Mosquitía. They have continued to insist that their policies of relocation are essentially military decisions, justified by the presence of armed enemies on each border who intend to exploit Miskito grievances against *any* Nicaraguan government.

The Sandinistas have passionately defended their Miskito program. They have proclaimed to the world that the charges of mistreatment of the Indians are not only untrue but are a *gran mentira*, a big lie.[4] The Miskitos number, the Sandinistas say, only sixty thousand. Fagoth and Brooklyn Rivera, their putative leaders, are, the Sandinistas charge, former Somoza henchmen who now are on the payroll of the Central Intelligence Agency. The Miskito refugees who have fled to Honduras live in squalor, while those relocated by the Sandinistas into the Nicaraguan interior (to what the government calls Tierra Libre, "Free Land") are living in agricultural villages with adequate housing, health care, and education facilities.

Eager to seize any opportunity to embarrass the Sandinistas, the American government has discovered the Miskito cause. For the first time since the 1840s, when the British protectorate over the Mosquitía aroused American wrath, "human rights" has become the catchword of American policy toward eastern Nicaragua. But it is not so much the suffering of the Miskitos that attracts Washington's attention as the prospect that the Sandinista revolution, weakened in the western part of the country by its political and economic problems with the bourgeosie, might come to grief because of its social goals in the east. Quite understandably, Señor Fagoth and his associates believe they have found a natural ally in the Americans.

In fact, the Miskito cause has less to do with the appeal of human rights than with the problem of a gradually eroding culture that has little in common with the rest of Nicaraguan society. The prospect for some kind of American-approved solution to the Miskito question is not likely, even if the Sandinistas lost out in Managua and a less zealous crowd of Nicaraguan bureaucrats charted national policy for the east. Managua's determination to settle the Miskito question reaches back well into the nineteenth century and is sustained by nationalistic impulses few of the big powers, including the United States, attribute to small countries.

Some benign observers, mostly anthropologists with a special concern for indigenous cultures threatened by the expanding state, have suggested a compromise roughly similar to that worked out between the Panamanian government and the San Blas Indians. By its provisions, the San Blas are pretty much left alone by the government. The Miskitos, naturally, are favorably disposed toward such a generous agreement in their dealings with the Nicaraguan government. But the amount of territory the San Blas control is relatively small, whereas the Mosquitía constitutes a third of Nicaragua's landmass, containing the most extensive forests in all Central America. No regime in Managua can afford to tolerate a virtually independent Mosquitía nor a Miskito king. The historic tide in Central America is running against once-isolated people like the

Miskitos, and the American government is in a poor position to change it.

Following a rather severe report on the plight of the Miskitos, the Sandinistas have been more agreeable to negotiating with their alienated subjects. Though the atmosphere remained tense on the eastern coast during the recent political campaign, some Miskitos have responded. Brooklyn Rivera has broken with Fagoth and virtually taken MISURASATA away from him. In retaliation the Miskito "king" has created MISURA for his loyal subjects and delivered its services to the *contras* in Honduras. To them, Indian or Nicaraguan, the Sandinistas extend only their defiance.

15 Señor Lone Ranger

Y
EARS BEFORE, WHEN HE HAD LED DARING
attacks on Somocista outposts or brazenly
assaulted the dictator's stooge assembly, he
went by the *nom de guerre* Comandante Cero, "Major Zero."

Edén Pastora is, at least to the outside world, the most heroic
figure of the Sandinistas' struggle against the Family. In victory he
was a celebrity among celebrities, a superhero among heroes, like
Castro come down from the mountains to the triumphant parades in
the capital. But unlike Fidel, Comandante Cero never became *el
líder máximo,* the charismatic figure able to project his personality
over a revolutionary bureaucracy. Pastora has not been able to
survive the revolution within the revolution. And unlike Ernesto
"Che" Guevara, the ideologue of the Cuban revolution, Pastora was
never able to fuse his revolutionary dynamism with acceptable
practice once the revolution had triumphed. In victory he lost
purpose.

But then, in his struggle against the Somozas, his goal was not
power but the triumph of his ideals, a democratic Nicaragua. Three
years after the Sandinista victory, he was again at war, camped in an
enclave just over the border in northwestern Costa Rica. Once the
Nicaraguan guerrilla's guerrilla, he was no longer honored with that
accolade by his old comrades in Managua. To them Comandante

Cero had become simply a "traitor" to the Sandinista rebellion, to the legend of Sandino, to the people. But to his journalist followers who applaud his stand for the "pluralist social order" in Sandinist Nicaragua and his indignant condemnation of the *contras* in Honduras, Pastora has become a *nica*-style "Lone Ranger."

Once clean-shaven, in his Costa Rican lair he began sporting a full set of whiskers, reminiscent, some say, of the *barbudos* of Castro's soldiers in the fifties. A decade ago, when his singular purpose was getting rid of the Somozas, he received ample moral support from the Costa Ricans. After Pastora quit the Sandinistas, the worried *ticos* provided him sanctuary, although they gave it begrudgingly. His former Sandinista comrades alleged that Pastora was getting at least a portion of the CIA money that was going to the anti-Sandinistas operating out of Honduras.

His professed goal is the removal of the Sandinistas who have betrayed the revolution. For this reason Pastora is doubly dangerous to those who still rule in Managua. They can readily appeal to nationalist sentiments when rousing the public against the *contras* to the north, but Pastora was once one of them. He requires special vilification. The *contras* are merely against the revolution; Pastora is a defector. His is a more damnable sin.

Less than a year before they tossed the dictator out, the Sandinistas were actually worrying that the growing middle-class opposition to the regime would persuade Somoza to make a deal, cheating the Sandinistas of victory and an opportunity to create a new order. They needed a happening, something so daring that it would immediately galvanize attention on the armed struggle. Bernard Diederich, *Time*'s bureau chief in the Caribbean, author of biographies of the Carribean tyrants François "Papa Doc" Duvalier of Haiti, Rafael Trujillo of the Dominican Republic, and several years later of Somoza himself, sensed the Sandinistas' frustration during a party for one of their leaders in Panama City. The man had been in the custody of Honduran authorities, who were on the verge of turning him over to Somoza when the Panamanian strong man Omar

Torrijos agreed to take him in. Diederich and novelist Graham Greene went to meet the Sandinista chieftain. While the others danced to Nicaraguan music and ate cake, the recently freed guerrilla spoke passionately about the need for something daring to sustain the cause.

It was Pastora who provided it. Actually, Comandante Cero had been planning a dramatic raid for eight years.

Pastora had first visited the national palace, one of the few structures in downtown Managua to survive the 1972 earthquake, as a boy with his mother to pay her taxes. Like so many other modern Central American rebels—indeed, like Fidel himself—Pastora had not suffered a childhood of grinding poverty and in maturing had come to revile the crassness of Somoza's Nicaragua. A sometime medical student, a businessman, and certainly not a Marxist, he had been an early convert to the Sandinista cause. In 1970, when the struggle against the dictator had seemed decades away from success, he had begun planning a raid on the assembly. In the shifting strategies of the Sandinista leadership, his proposal usually got shunted aside to await more favorable circumstances.

In August 1978 the Sandinistas finally sanctioned the plan, and Pastora and two dozen guerrillas, all quite ready to die in what most doubtless thought was a mad scheme, gathered secretly in homes in Managua to plot the last details of the "assault on the house of the swine," as they contemptuously referred to Somoza's rump congress. They chose a day when the building would be full of assemblymen and various functionaries discussing the latest economic aid package from the United States. Wearing the familiar uniforms of infantry cadets, they brazenly drove up in front of the palace in two military trucks in broad daylight. Cero and "Dos," commanding a second squad, led the way, yelling that Somoza was coming. The disbelieving guards opened fire. Dos' men cut them down. Pastora raced upstairs to the main assembly hall, stuck his head in the door, and authoritatively ordered everybody to the floor. Despite the ubiquity of pistols in the crowd, Nicaragua's legislators compliantly obeyed. The entire operation required less than three minutes.

For Tacho II, who was stuffing himself with lunch when news of the attack came, the incident at the assembly was something far more serious than an isolated battle between the dictator's guardsmen and some crazy Sandinistas sacrificing themselves to the cause. His first impulse was to call for a full-fledged retaliation, and in anger he sent helicopters to strafe the building. But Comandante Cero had his men well placed for just such an eventuality. When Pastora ordered some Somocista deputies to stand vulnerably at the windows, Tacho called off his counterattack. Two of the deputies even got on the phone and begged Somoza to save them. Very quickly Comandante Cero became more than a nuisance to Tacho II.

Pastora laid down his demands: stop the shooting or the Somocista assemblymen would die, one by one.[1] Many of those huddling on the floor really believed they were doomed. But Somoza hesitated, something that infuriated his guard commanders, who believed their leader should exhibit no weakness in this standoff, even if a shootout meant the sacrifice of some loyal Somocistas. After all, why shouldn't they be willing to die for the dynasty?

When Somoza vacillated, Pastora upped his demands. He wanted, and got, Nicaragua's Catholic archbishop to convey his new proposals—$20 million, release of almost sixty political prisoners languishing in the dictator's notorious jails, a two-hour-long Sandinista propaganda piece to be aired over the government radio station, and a Mexican, Venezuelan, or Panamanian escort out of the country. As Tacho contemplated, his cronies in the national assembly sweated it out, urinating in trash cans because the few rest rooms in the building could not accommodate them, and resigning themselves to certain death if the Man got tough and retaliated.

Miraculously three hundred of the captives managed to escape by pushing out a window air conditioner and leaping to safety, but Pastora and his minuscule force still had a thousand hostages. As Somoza and his coterie soon learned, much to their displeasure, many of the captives expressed sympathy with their kidnappers, a not unusual occurrence in such situations, but the news did Somoza's cause no good. Some of the assemblymen, discussing their predicament with a reporter who had been permitted inside the palace, told the press that Comandante Dos, a woman, was quite pretty and that Comandante Cero was an impressive hombre, just like Che Guevara.

In the end Pastora made the head of the dynasty submit, though an American newsman who managed to get Cero on the phone learned that Tacho had talked the Sandinistas down from their $20 million demand to $1 million. As required, the government radio blared out the Sandinista diatribe against the rich and privileged in leftist tones that embarrassed the middle-class Nicaraguans who had been increasingly critical of Somoza and now had some reason to worry about what *might* come if the Sandinistas triumphed.

Their unease was of no concern to Comandante Cero. He was now at center stage, the triumphant moment for the committed avenger against the forces of evil. The Costa Rican and Panamanian ambassadors, representing two neighboring countries that had condemned the dictatorship, escorted Pastora and his comrades out of the building and into a waiting bus for the ride to the airport. Pastora played his role to perfection. "We'll be back in two months," he yelled to an enthusiastic crowd of young Nicaraguans watching the spectacle.

At the airport he was the last to board the plane for the flight out of Somozaland, turning to wave a triumphant two-armed salute. The Sandinistas were soon displaying photos of Comandante Cero's dramatic farewell on their posters. An American mercenary, a former Green Beret, commenting on Pastora's flamboyant behavior at the airport, said contemptuously, "That guy is a punk who has been watching John Wayne movies."

For his daring raid on the national palace (and the money it brought the Sandinistas) the victors readily installed Comandante Cero in their new government, naming him deputy defense minister. It was not an unimportant post, and from the start Pastora watched approvingly as the Sandinistas enthusiastically undertook their much-heralded economic and social reforms. Though not doctrinaire in his political philosophy, he nonetheless applauded the nationalization of the banks, the creation of the People's Property Area (composed of the vast former holdings of the Somoza family), and especially the literacy campaign.

But with the literacy crusade came the Cubans, and with the Cubans, inevitably, the East Europeans and Russian advisers with their rigid notions about how to survive the ordeal every postwar society must endure. This meant cracking down on the opposition, most notably *La Prensa,* a rather ordinary paper by American standards but one that had gained considerable hemispheric attention before Somoza's fall because of its criticism of the regime. The assassination of Pedro Joaquín Chamorro, its publisher, in early 1978 had probably done more than anything to galvanize the Nicaraguan middle class against Somoza. And after the Sandinista victory *La Prensa* was the first to express doubts about the course the revolution was taking, and, especially, grave concerns about the links the Sandinistas were forging with the Cubans and the Soviets.

Agreeing on the need to get rid of Somoza, the Sandinistas in power have been able to agree on little more. And the circumstances in which they found themselves during the first years of power, an economy in a shambles and a society with profound social divisions, required leaders who could translate the powerful commitments that had sustained the victory into a credible program for the postwar state. In Nicaragua this has meant, largely, the emergence of the ideologue, the victorious revolutionary whose central purpose is survival, and if survival means suppressing dissent or condemning the opposition as treasonous, then such practices, considered a legitimate reason for rebellion when carried out by the preceding government, are manifestly acceptable under the new order.

Pastora (and his kindred spirits), who fought against the Somoza dictatorship, struggled for a Nicaragua free of the political corruption the Family symbolized. But the ideologues of the new Nicaragua waged a war for a restructured society. For Pastora, freedom of the press and a "pluralist" society were not just ideals to be strived for in the distant future but easily realizable goals once the dictatorship fell.

Pastora in power was still the guerrilla who makes war for the triumph of conviction, for the ideals of statecraft and governance the "liberal," rational, compassionate person holds dear. Somewhere along the way he forgot that for the creators of a new order the fundamental criterion for determining loyalty is not commitment to ideals but support for the cause.

With the radicalization of the Nicaraguan revolution—or, as its most intransigent critics say, its Sovietization—have come two armed threats to the regime. One, calling itself the National Democratic Front (FDN), which the Sandinistas call the *contras*, is composed of former guardsmen, political hacks, and malcontents, and a smattering of abused and alienated Miskito Indians and small farmers. Its strength lies mostly to the north, in remote sanctuaries along the Honduran border, and its funding depends heavily on the American government. The other armed faction, ARDE, the Democratic Revolutionary Alliance, once led by Pastora, represents the frustrations of early supporters of the Sandinista revolution who were disgusted with its turn to the left. When Pastora quit the Sandinistas and surfaced in Costa Rica, proclaiming his dismay over the course his former comrades were taking, he made respectable the voicing of opposition within Nicaragua from those who want to "save" the revolution but who do not want to be lumped with the *contras*, who, for all intents, are dedicated to overthrowing it. But to the Sandinistas Pastora is still the "traitor."

In the relatively tolerant political atmosphere of Costa Rica, Pastora and his comrades established their base, far from the protective shield of the American military establishment in Honduras, close to the worried *ticos*, who continually fretted over their predicament in professing their neutrality on the one hand and providing sanctuary for the Sandinistas' most famous defector.

In San José the Democratic Revolutionary Alliance established its headquarters in a nondescript office, jammed with tables, desks, and typewriters clacking amid the jabbering of voices in Spanish and English.[2] The Costa Ricans were soon calling the place the "house of the Nicaraguans." Its representative faces were well known: Pastora himself, the Miskito Indian leader Brooklyn Rivera, and Alfonso Robelo, who, like Pastora, once had belonged to the Sandinista ruling junta but left in a huff. The *alianza* continually bragged that it would compel the Sandinistas to obey the ideals of the revolution "at gunpoint," swearing that 2.5 million Nicaraguans were in agreement. In Managua the Sandinistas responded with vilifications and distributed more weapons to their legion of adolescent followers.

Robelo made it big in the cooking-oil business during the Somoza era but wound up supporting the Sandinistas and even served a stint in the government as representative of Nicaraguan business interests. His link with the National Democratic Movement (MDN), with its conspicuous numbers of ex-guardsmen and opportunists, drew Pastora ever closer to anti-Sandinista elements whose aim is, quite openly, the subversion of the revolution, not its purification. When Pastora and Robelo set up a joint political operation in the Costa Rican capital in September 1983, Comandante Cero signaled that he was rapidly losing hope for any kind of political reconciliation with his old comrades in Managua. Within six months Pastora's bands on the northern Costa Rican frontier, their arms freshly replenished, were carrying out raids across the border. For a few days they even managed to seize the old port of San Juan del Norte, on the southeastern Nicaraguan coast.

The Sandinistas beat them off, but the mystique of Pastora remained. ARDE's radio station broadcasts into Nicaragua every night, though the hard-pressed and disgruntled citizenry of the populated west coast listen only in small numbers. But on the sparsely settled Atlantic littoral the number of listeners is reputedly far higher. It is no surprise: both ARDE and MDN enjoy their most solid support in the Mosquitía, where the heavy hand of the Sandinistas, particularly forceful in their efforts to create a more secure border, has alienated a large majority of the population.

Señor "Lone Ranger's" basic problem was that he was touting his cause of pluralism and freedom of the press from a foreign country, so that even his putative allies still in the Sandinistas' shadow—the Council on Private Enterprise and other disaffected groups—were hesitant to voice solidarity with Pastora's cause. In Managua the lottery vendors yelled out the number "zero" with fear, and even the more outspoken political groups still functioning in

Nicaragua, such as the Social Christians, were reluctant to voice any support of ARDE. One of them comments: "There's a lot of discontent here, if Pastora would just take advantage of it instead of sitting in Costa Rica." On the east coast, rumors went, the Miskitos and other abused groups would rise in a moment if only Edén would show up to lead them.

The essential problem is that Pastora must deal as much with his putative allies, the ex-Somocistas who want to reverse much of the Sandinista reform program, as anyone else. He can ill afford to lose his credibility among the disaffected Sandinistas like himself who still believe the old ideals of the revolution can be preserved without cracking down on dissidents and malcontents. Señor Lone Ranger boasts that 5,000 of the 160,000 armed Nicaraguans would desert to his cause once he invaded the homeland. Pastora has even won some illustrious defections from the Sandinista ranks, notably two Nicaraguan ministers to the United States. And he has been able to get widespread attention for his cause among western European socialists.

Pastora's stay in Costa Rica was a troubled one. ARDE established its military camps close to the Nicaraguan frontier, and the frequent raids across the border roused the Sandinistas into retaliation and brought more pressure on the Costa Rican government to end its sanctuary for Pastora and his followers. The *ticos* are professedly neutral in Nicaragua's internal struggle, but as a practical matter they saw fit to harbor Pastora on the grounds that his assessment of the Sandinista revolution—betrayal of its ideals— accorded with their own views.

Pastora is a man of action, and his assaults on his former comrades brought the Costa Ricans into bitter internal debates. Costa Rica's special relationship to the Sandinista revolution is not fully appreciated outside Central America. The *ticos* were lifelong enemies of the Somoza regime; they harbored the dictator's enemies and worked for his downfall. Despite the souring of relations between the two countries since the Sandinista triumph, Nicaragua, its economy stifled by American pressures on its ports and rebel activities on both frontiers, desperately needs its southern connection.

But by spring 1984, Pastora had angered an important segment of the Costa Rican press by his border raids. Several prominent *tico* editorialists, angered by Pastora's sarcastic comments on the reliability of Costa Rica's commitment to his anticommunist cause, began calling on him to take his revolution someplace else.

A few weeks later, as Pastora held a news conference at his military headquarters just inside Nicaraguan territory, a thunderous blast demolished the building, killing several journalists and injuring others. Pastora, the intended victim of the assault, was severely hurt but survived. The Costa Rican president politely waited a few days, then expelled him to Panama. Moved to a hospital in Caracas, he learned that a majority of ARDE's directorate, believing that a much closer association with FDN made for sound military calculation, asked Pastora to leave the organization.

His ouster was a signal that the Sandinistas' strategy of reminding the Costa Ricans of the precariousness of their neutrality had worked.

When ARDE's directors requested Pastora's resignation, Señor Lone Ranger became philosophical about his predicament.

"To have the ability and moral authority to democratize the Sandinista government," he told reporters gathered around his hospital bed, where he lay recuperating from the blast that nearly claimed his life, "we must first democratize the opposition."[3]

In rejecting the Sandinista plan for a new Nicaraguan order and later in rebuking the *contras* for harboring too many Somocista thugs, Pastora once again assumed his role as the loner. His old comrades in ARDE, who still retain their faith in the rectitude of his cause, are sufficiently realistic to know that they probably can't get back into power unless they have American money, and the only significant amounts of American funding are going to the *contras*, the Nicaraguan Democratic Force. ARDE's chieftains are going through the old wrenching political torment of warriors trying to forge an alliance with people whose politics they abominate.

Señor Lone Ranger has thus far refused to bend, to admit that the enemies of his enemy are his friends. After his recuperation in Venezuela he began talking more and more about entering the Nicaraguan political campaign by pressing the Sandinistas to accommodate the "plural democracy" touted by the regime's enemies and move away from so much reliance on the Cubans and the Soviets. Pastora has always believed that the Sandinistas are not a tightly knit faction but are divided over not only tactics but about what Sandinismo really means. The Ortega brothers (Daniel, a presidential candidate, and Humberto, minister of defense) and Jaime Wheelock (minister of agriculture) are moderates. (Lamentably, the most doctrinaire of the hardliners, Tomás Borge, minister of the interior, happens to control the Sandinista police.)

Pastora has maintained that the Ortega brothers and several others strategically placed in the Nicaraguan government are sufficiently flexible on the touchy subject of Pastora's conditions for negotiations. Agreement with them, stalwarts of a bureaucracy that officially labels him a traitor, would be preferable to a misalliance with the old Somocistas in FDN. Pastora's explanation is worth quoting:

"We are Sandinistas. We s)port revolutionary changes. We support the gains already made ʋy the Nicaraguan revolution. We are not interested in overthrowing the government in Managua for the sake of overthrowing it. We want rather to democratize the Sandinista revolution.

"Managua," he continued in yet another of his dramatic interviews, "should look for a solution within Nicaragua with us, the Nicaraguans. But the problem is that there is a wing of the opposition [the old Somocista guardsmen fighting out of Honduras] that wants to destroy the revolution. These groups are helped by the Reagan administration, while on the other hand Moscow manipulates radical elements in Managua.

"If there is a united democratic opposition, I think that an arrangement [for an end to the war] can be reached. If there is no democratic opposition, the revolution will radicalize. Who will be guilty if this happens? The rigidity and inflexibility of extremists in

both Washington and those in Managua, who have godfathers in
Moscow and Havana."[4]

Central American guerrilla heroes are not of predictable ideological persuasion. They rise to command, ordinarily, because of
personal qualities—bravery, commitment, derring-do—rather than
a well-fashioned political and economic program for governance.
They are at their best as determined opponents to the regime in
power, forsaking the comfortable life for the hardships of struggle in
the bush, pushing themselves and those who follow until the final
victory over the despised leader and his army of hirelings. But once
victory is theirs they must make the transition from guerrilla to
governor, from warrior to administrator.

The guerrilla who fights a corrupt, dictatorial regime that jails
its enemies or worse, stifles political liberties, and gorges itself at
the public trough wages a noble cause. But in the aftermath of a
devastating civil war, the goals for which he has fought cannot be
easily realized just because the tyrant has been dethroned. In
opposition a crusade can rest firmly on moral principle and sense of
justice; in victory it must survive on guile, necessity, and expediency. Commanding his squads of dedicated *muchachos* in the war
against Somoza, Comandante Cero proved himself the noble warrior. Sitting behind a desk in the Sandinista bureaucracy, he could
never accommodate himself to his comrades' revolutionary logic
that even though the tyrant was gone, the enemies of the revolution
were still conspiring.

For all his charisma, Pastora remains a secondary consideration
in the ranking of the Sandinista regime's enemies. First are the
ex-guardsmen and FDN military units lodged along the Honduran
border. Because they enjoy the favor of the American government,
the Sandinistas correctly believe, they pose the more immediate
danger to the revolution. ARDE is a threat of less immediate
consequence. If the FDN fails, then the Americans will shift their
attention to Pastora, believing that the Nicaraguan Lone Ranger will
return and bring to war-weary Nicaraguans a measure of moderation
and decency and, above all, will mitigate the virulent anti-

Americanism that permeates Nicaraguan life. It is a fairly certain presumption in Washington that Pastora will kick the Cubans and Soviets out of Nicaragua if he ever gets power.

If Edén Pastora can sustain his revolutionary zeal without the anti-American rhetoric that is central to Nicaraguan nationalism, he may eventually triumph, but if he is victorious only by the intervention of American arms, he will forever remain in the minds of Nicaraguan nationalists a betrayer of the cause he professes to serve.

His is the agony of the guerrilla committed to ideals. The cost of making deals along the way to power may be too high a price to pay. The original Lone Ranger, it is well to remember, never stayed around to enjoy the fruits of victory, only to ensure the victory.

16 God Is on Everybody's Side

T HEY LOOKED THE ARCHETYPAL YOUNG AMERICAN family, this athletic missionary, his reserved wife, and the infant daughter I met in the parking lot of Toncontin airport in Tegucigalpa. We were soon bouncing along in a ponderous American station wagon, through the winding streets, up the hill, and past the bowllike soccer stadium, headed for the La Ronda hotel.

The man had been in Tegoose several years before to help start a Protestant mission in the Valley of the Angels, twenty miles or so to the north and light-years away from modernity. He worried about his faltering Spanish, a language not commonly spoken in his native Michigan. His religious endeavors interested me. I had been follow-ing accounts of the impressive numbers of converts to the Protestant sects, in the cities and in the countryside, a topic receiving much publicity when General Efraín Ríos Montt, a member of the Church of the Word, took power in Guatemala. In the span of a year or so the evangelicals had spread like the proverbial wildfire in Central America. Some well-known American evangelical television stars, notably Jimmy Swaggart, built an impressive following.

"You're still waging an uphill battle in Central America if you're a Protestant," I said, a comment reinforced later by a sign I spied on a house in Cartago: "We Don't Admit Protestant Propaganda."

At the La Ronda the polite missionary couple and their now exhausted child repaired to their room. I sought the comfort of the Rondinella, the La Ronda's bar/restaurant. The only customers were Americans—certainly not missionaries, so probably military—dancing with pretty *hondureñas* to the lonesome twang of an American country singer. But next morning, in the lobby, the missionary entourage gathered, ready for the Valley of the Angels, believing, doubtless, God was on its side.

In Central America, as in the rest of Latin America, the statement that most people are Catholics generally holds as true nowadays as it did twenty-five, a hundred, or even three hundred years ago. When the Spanish conquerors moved into the isthmus from their strongholds in Mexico and Panama, the proselytizing clerics were not far behind. As much the disciples of the Spanish crown as of the Pope at Rome, they served state and church, forcibly converting native peoples from their Indian gods and destroying their icons. A sizable amount of Mayan calligraphy, priceless to generations of archaeologists, was lost forever because a zealous Spanish bishop decided it represented a heathen faith and must be destroyed. Yet when the Spanish empire confronted one of its first divisive issues, the question of forced Indian labor, a brutal system that had virtually killed off the native population of the West Indies, a Dominican friar stepped forward to condemn the practice. The Indians remained a servile race, but at least the church had extended some measure of religious protection over them.

Over the centuries the church ordinarily came down on the side of the Spanish rulers, and after they had passed from the Latin American scene, it stood as religious bulwark behind their republican successors. In a few countries, notably Mexico and Colombia, the inherited privileges of the clergy in landholding and education, to say nothing of its domination in all matters spiritual, provided an enormous power and provoked retaliation from liberal reformers. But, ironically, in depriving the church of its landowning role, they opened the way for expanding agricultural entrepreneurs to move in on Indian communal lands. Where the Roman Catholic Church lost its status as the established state church or was stripped of its monopoly on education, it retained influence in society. For the military regimes that sprang up in the twentieth century the church has played a role as crucial as the one it carried out for the Spanish kings. By telling the harassed subjects of these repressive governments they must suffer the authority of their masters, the agents of God appear as condoners of dictatorship.

Until the past twenty years or so, then, the church in Latin America stood as spiritual reinforcement to the status quo.[1] And it offered a powerful reassurance to an American government that, after World War II, grew increasingly alarmed over the inroads Marxist thought and international communism could make in a troubled continent. From rich to poor, Latin Americans were Catholic, and, it was naively presumed, since the American Catholic family was rabidly anticommunist, the rest of the hemisphere was safe from the Red menace.

Now in Central America religious preference is no longer a reliable indicator of political belief. Catholic priests serve in the Sandinista government in Nicaragua, and a Catholic archbishop in El Salvador adjures soldiers not to fire on unarmed peasants and is assassinated in his own church while saying mass. His fellow prelates in El Salvador and other isthmian countries implore their flocks to respect "proper authority." In the countryside priests organize peasant cooperatives, and Catholic laymen in the social aristocracy condemn them as traitors and communists. Protestant missionaries implore the Guatemalan Indians to accept Jesus as their personal savior and obey a government that for thirty years has been abusing them. Their sectarian comrades from the United States make pilgrimages to Managua to reassure the Sandinistas that not all Americans consider them godless communists. A prominent Sandinista, decked out in military fatigues, declares that Marxism and Christianity are compatible, but in a triumphant tour of beleaguered Central America in 1983 (an event touchingly commemorated by Guatemalan schoolchildren a year later), the Pope chastised Catholic priests for taking on temporal authority in a government with Marxist overtones. Then the Holy Father declared, "Neither capitalism nor collectivism must imprison mankind."[2]

In the infuriatingly complex world that is Central America today, of guerrillas in power and out of power, of priests inciting their flocks to organize for their rights while their brothers bless the helicopters that will machine-gun them, or of Marxist intellectuals who cite the Scripture more than the bearded philosopher, just about everybody claims God for a comrade. He is ally to conservative and liberal Catholic theologian, the former citing the dangerous leftist doctrines emanating from Vatican II, which brought long-sought reforms in the church, the latter exulting in the triumph of social activism, the theology of liberation as a proper, even necessary, role for priests in the deliberations of the Medellín (Colombia) conference of 1968. Since then, the division within Latin American Catholicism has been deep and bitter, and even a pope like John Paul II has not been able to heal this wound.

Initially, in those South American countries that were returning to military rule in the sixties and seventies, then in Central America, governments responded harshly toward these upstart clerical champions of the oppressed. Priests who for years had labored in shantytowns ringing the cities or nurtured their flocks of illiterate Indian *campesinos* in the countryside, telling them of a better place in the afterlife, now had an official mandate for action. They became more critical of government repression and systematic denials of human rights. When authorities reproached them for "misleading" their parishioners, the priests merely intensified their attacks. For some, this meant taking on the burden of social outcast.

Governments that perceived a threat to state authority from these "Red priests," as they were commonly labeled, might readily stifle labor agitators or student protestors, but going up against the almighty church was another matter. A tough anticommunist colonel might have few qualms about ordering his men to bash in the heads of yelling Marxist students from the universities, where it was commonly assumed that just about everyone from the dean on down to the janitor was a Red, but as a practicing Catholic he was expected to show proper restraint in cracking down on Christ's disciples. For some officers or agents entrusted with that expandable mission of preserving national security there was the ready presumption that a priest (or a bishop) who espoused doctrines of social activism must by definition be a fellow traveler. In this case it naturally followed that the offending cleric had debased his Christian teaching and no longer enjoyed the protection of his collar. By such grim logic the assassin of Archbishop Romero in San Salvador doubtless considered himself a true patriot and good Christian. "Be a patriot, kill a priest" has become the Salvadoran nationalist's motto.[3] The archbishop, not his murderer, had violated his faith by his unholy teaching.

But, as Churchill told Stalin after the generalissimo sarcastically inquired how many divisions the Pope had, God's disciples may not carry guns but the church has its legions. And in Latin America the church can exert an influence as potent as any government for the simple reason that 90 percent of Latin Americans are baptized Catholics. None of the other organizations that have endured state repression can defy governments with the collective strength the church can muster. And their oppressors may curse the left-wing priests, but they are not likely to convert to one of the Protestant sects just because the priest dispensing the communion wafer and wine happens to be a caustic critic of their behavior.

One unexpected impact of Medellín, as noticeable in Central America as anyplace else in Christendom, was the revival of the old Christian creed of brotherhood (and sisterhood) as preferable to the rigid hierarchical structure the church had encumbered itself with over the centuries. Archbishops, bishops, and priests and nuns remain as designation of rank, but after Medellín the idea that all of them were warriors in God's community and thus stood obligated not only to minister to the people but work with them and fight alongside them enjoyed broader acceptance. In the urban *colonías* lacking even the basic municipal services or in the wretched agricultural villages without church or school, these clerical zealots began conveying more than God's reassuring words. They carried out their religious task and later, and with equal vigor, undertook the role of social organizer, getting funds for a school in a community long neglected by the state or keeping the conscriptive hand of the military off the neck of a sixteen-year-old boy.

But if in the past the church projected at least a semblance of opposition to the most dictatorial regimes, its role in Central America has in the past decade posed considerable problems for the military regimes that hold sway. The philosophy of opposition, the moral rebuke of political leaders when they abuse the people, has been transmuted into the theology of liberation. The more committed Catholic theologians justify this change on the grounds that it represents a necessary and inevitable liberation of theology. Whichever phrase is invoked, this movement in the church has provided a powerful ideological stimulus to attacks on capitalism because, the liberationists contend, it is an inadequate economic system for the large majority of impoverished Central Americans. At the same time, liberation theology holds that only the socially activist church offers a truly humane alternative to the godless communist state. Predictably the masters of Central America's regimes see these religious crusaders and their community supporters in rural areas as unwitting tools of international communism.

One sympathetic student of the church's rapidly changing posture has chronicled its transformation in villages in Nicaragua, El Salvador, and Guatemala.[4] In the old days the agricultural laborers in these places, devout Catholics, lived in one-room thatched huts, working three or four months of the year. The mother endured and survived her pregnancies without proper medical care, the father barely provided subsistence for his family, the children grew up without schooling. The village had a church, but only irregularly did a priest appear to give the sacraments. When one did show up, he monotonously advised these illiterate peasants to accept their lot. God was on their side, but His reward for their suffering would come in the afterlife.

Another priest arrives, but he remains. His message is different, liberal quotation from the third chapter of Exodus and reminders to his stoic parishioners that God delivered the oppressed Israelites from captivity in Egypt. His listeners know the priest cannot lead them across the border into the promised land of

Honduras, but his message—that the church will deliver them from their oppressors—is not lost on them. And unlike his indifferent predecessor, this priest is no itinerant. He follows up his sermons with visitations to family huts and organizes Bible-study groups.

The isolated parishioners now come around to the belief that sin is more than their personal failure in God's eyes, something that has been ingrained in them for centuries, and that the wretchedness of their lives is the work of institutional sin, the sin of the indifferent and oppressive state, which the church, as God's agent, condemns for its failure to provide them with work or adequate housing. By now, of course, the local priest has already attracted the disapproving gaze of the commandant of the provincial *guardia* or perhaps even that of the president of the country. There follow discreet inquiries to the bishop or archbishop about the "potentially harmful" activities of this or that priest in some isolated village up in the highlands. The bishop, if one of the disgruntled conservatives whose view of the church's role lost out at Medellín, might very well shift the priest to a *barrio* in Tegucigalpa or a more sedate parish in Santa Ana. But if himself a convert to liberation theology he could very well deliver a stern warning to the government that the lot of the poor on this earth is very much God's business. The Sermon on the Mount, after all, is a profound social message, and Christ occasionally plunged into essentially secular affairs and brought "good news" to the synagogue at Nazareth "to set free the oppressed."

Christians in this country, Protestant and Catholic, are understandably befuddled about this dangerous political role the church is taking in Central America. (Jews express little concern, apparently, that Israel is an important arms supplier to Central American governments, defending the sales as necessary to the worldwide war on terrorism.) Liberal Catholics see in it an inevitable broadening of the social gospel among the down-and-out; conservatives see in it a dangerous departure from the historical role of the church, going far beyond the Biblical injunctions of helping thy neighbor. A great many Americans are frankly alarmed that the politically active church is harming its religious mission. To them, such an expanded involvement of the church in people's daily lives is not only unwarranted but dangerous because it makes the church the enemy of the state. A half-century ago American Catholics were deeply split on the question of American support to the republican government in Spain, which had communist support, and the anti-democratic fascists, who proclaimed themselves God's warriors.

We are too often inclined to refer to our own history of church–state relations in trying to explain this religious phenomenon in Central America. This society rests on the solid bedrock of communities, which because of colonial isolation and the indifference of faraway central authority developed an almost passionate conviction that only cooperation between neighbors could meet local needs—schools, meetinghouses, water supplies, police protection; in short, the range of basic social services. The churches and synagogues provided the community with its spiritual needs and, in a limited way, economic assistance to its families if a church member's house burned down or his family encountered high medical bills. But most basic social services in the American community have historically been carried out by the secular authority. Americans are great organizers; they demonstrate an ethos that manifests itself in school boards and city councils, and even in such mundane things as neighborhood improvement associations. We developed out of necessity an almost religious faith in creating these local institutions to serve local needs. America was built from bottom to top; early on in its history it created a sense of community. That more than anything (certainly more than our material wealth) captures the admiration of Latin Americans.

In large measure, it can be argued, Latin America was built from top to bottom. We created the city to serve the country, an old bromide goes, but the Spanish created the country to serve the city, and their inheritors of power, despite their indifference to the needs of country dwellers, have rarely encouraged "local" initiative in providing community needs. And one historical legacy of this approach to civilization-building (and Latin America, despite our patronizing assessments, *is* a civilization) is that isolated villages like the ones described earlier have not only had less than the cities but much less. They have entered the modern age without the minimal social services every community must have.

The secular state, even in the most rigidly authoritarian Central American country, has undertaken some fitful efforts to expand social services in these isolated places, but its efforts have often been curtailed by its suspicions that community-directed efforts to raise the standard of living are really threats to its authority. Even the best-intentioned leaders are overwhelmed by the magnitude of the undertaking necessary to bring remote areas into the twentieth century. Not twelve miles outside San Salvador, high on a mountainside, is the village of Panchimalco. It has an overpowering church, its walls fractured by earthquakes over four centuries; cobblestone streets; a collection of dingy huts, the homes of *campesinos* who work on the estates down in the fertile valley; and a *single* telephone, a concrete-block pay station erected by ANTEL, the national phone company. Without that phone, Panchimalco is not much different in 1984 than it was in 1884.

In communities in this country, it is true, the churches have satisfied more than the spiritual needs of the community, but they didn't have to provide potable water or pave streets. In Panchimalco and places like it, the church must provide the driving zeal to community self-help because governments cannot or will not.

Thus the Christian Base Communities, as they are called, with their pockets of influence scattered across Central America, are looked on by right-wing governments as subversive. It is frustrating, doubtless, for a solidly Catholic general or president who has been nurtured on the dogma that the church is, if anything, anticommunist to witness the growth of cells of hostility in which priests command not only the spiritual but the political loyalties of the populace. Little wonder, then, that the plotters of Archbishop Romero's murder in El Salvador convinced themselves that by his reprobation of their acts and values he was not only a traitor to the republic but a traitor to God. By a similarly twisted logic, Christian agents in the service of their governments have been disrupting the base communities, first by threats and intimidation, followed by physical punishment—castration, rape—and murder, by methods ranging from gassing priests in ovens to tossing them out of cargo planes over the ocean. The organizers of base communities, their persecutors argue, are communists; if they are not professed Marxists, then by their activities they mock God and are not entitled to the protection of their frocks or habits.

Solentiname is (or was) a village on an island in the southern extremity of Lake Nicaragua, which with the smaller Lake Managua and several imposing volcanoes dominates the landscape of western Nicaragua. In the mid-1960s, with the Somozas still entrenched in Managua, a Nicaraguan cleric, Ernesto Cardenal, fresh from a Trappist seminary in Kentucky, settled here. Over the years he organized the islanders into an agricultural and artistic community that attracted considerable attention in the rest of the country. A decade after its founding, Solentiname was a Sandinista stronghold, its residents convinced that church doctrine dictated opposition to the Somoza regime. When the war against the dictator erupted, Solentiname's faithful assaulted a national guard outpost in San Carlos, near the Costa Rican border. They were victorious, but their Christian compassion kept them from finishing off Somoza's guardsmen. Somoza had no such compunction; he dispatched a raiding unit to burn Solentiname to the ground. Most of its inhabitants fled. Cardenal, the town's spiritual and political driving force, joined the rebellion and is now cultural minister of Nicaragua.

In Suchitoto, an agricultural area thirty miles north of San Salvador, the go-getting organizer of the base community was Padre José Alas, who arrived in 1968. A year later he had founded thirty communities and had begun to dispatch organizers in the surrounding countryside. Five years into his mission Father Alas had his disciples immersed in the study of economics—Marxist, socialist, capitalist. Then he began taking on the developers, speculators who had bought a few farms in the late sixties and later, in the next wave of land reform, tripled and even sextupled their asking price for the properties. When the peasants who wanted to buy the land could not persuade the owners to lower their price, they marched on the capital and pried a law out of the assembly establishing a 100-percent profit limit on resale of lands. In early 1970, when the government sponsored a national forum on agrarian issues, Father Alas spoke eloquently for reform. Shortly afterward, he was picked up in front of the national palace. He reappeared—a naked, tortured wreck—only after the auxiliary bishop of San Salvador camped in the office of the defense minister to demand his release.

But Alas, despite his beating, was not done. When the government built a huge hydroelectric dam on the Lempa River, flooding lands around Suchitoto, he organized a political forum, the United Popular Action Front, a secular pressure group springing from a religious cell. By now, of course, Alas was "the Red priest," a public enemy less than a decade after his arrival in Suchitoto. After two of his fellow priests were shot, Alas went into exile; the person who convinced him he must leave El Salvador was Archbishop Romero.

In El Quiché, in the Guatemalan highlands, the story is different but the outcome lamentably the same, persecution and death. There, three decades ago in the aftermath of the '54 revolution, a conservative movement, Catholic Action, established Bible-study groups in Indian villages. After the 1968 Medellín conference, Quiché's bishops began pushing base communities among the Ixil Indians, one of the most abused of Guatemala's indigenous peoples. In the late seventies Guatemalan authorities, convinced these Ixil communities were dangerous subversive cells, inaugurated a repressive campaign that threatened the entire Ixil community. The organizers concluded that they must formally shut down the Ixil operation if they were to show the world the horrors of Guatemalan repression. El Quiché's progressive bishop and his associates departed the country to found the Guatemalan Church in Exile. Those who stayed behind went into hiding in the mountains or established havens in the capital, where they receive priests who have slipped down from the hills and after a few months return with the consecrated bread.

But there is no unity in the church. The higher one goes in the Catholic hierarchy in Central America, the more controversial is the role of a militant clergy in the estimation of the vigilant cadre of bishops and archbishops that collectively shapes the destiny of Catholicism. In the past year the Pope has become more critical of the theology of liberation and the priests who espouse that doctrine. The bishop who combines Marxist sociology with the traditional Christian doctrine of ministering to the poor runs the risk of alienating his superiors, to say nothing of arousing the suspicions of a high-ranking military official infuriated by the activities of priests out in the country.

The Protestant sects, by contrast, have less of a problem. Their missionaries must ultimately answer, not to a resident bishop or archbishop in the capital, but to a sponsoring council or an individual church far away in the United States. And generally, though not exclusively, the Protestant missionaries tend to come down on the side of those who rule, sometimes in a very publicized manner. When General Efraín Ríos Montt, a born-again Christian and member of El Verbo, the Church of the Word, a California-based sect, took over in Guatemala, he opened the country to this militantly anticommunist religious sect. In the Guatemalan highlands General Ríos Montt's soldiers began cracking down with the zeal of crusaders come to rescue the Holy Land from the infidel, and his helicopters ferried El Verbo's proselytizers into remote villages to wean illiterate Indians from the pernicious doctrines of the Red priests.

Even so, the Protestant sects, whose members ordinarily subscribe to the Biblical injunction of rendering unto Caesar that which is Caesar's, sometimes wind up on the other side. In Nicaragua, some twenty Protestant groups mobilized a vast aid program after the devastating '72 earthquake. Repulsed by the abusively fraudulent manner in which Somoza handled the assistance that flowed into the country, some of them began openly supporting the Sandinistas a few years later.

Now that the Sandinistas are in power the Protestant evangelicals are having second thoughts. Some interpret the government's program in the Mosquitía as a crusade against Protestantism. The Sandinistas are not openly seeking to extend the realm of Catholicism over the Protestant Miskitos. Rather, theirs is a strategy to consolidate their revolution throughout the republic. In order to accomplish this heavy obligation, they are waging what to many of the Protestant evangelicals is a religious war in the east. When I arrived in San José in March 1984, the papers were carrying a story about a Protestant evangelist who had a confrontation with the Sandinista soldiers in Puerto Atlanta, Nicaragua, one of whom had cut off the minister's left ear. The Sandinistas are not likely to persuade the Miskitos by such acts that despite their Marxist professions God approves the policies they are taking, that He is on their side.

Yet the Sandinistas' controversial plan for the Protestant Miskito east coast is rapidly proving to be less a problem than the bitter schism among Nicaragua's Catholics. Pope John Paul II got an earful of Sandinista rhetoric when he visited Managua on his 1983 visit to Central America. Aware of the Pope's disapprobation of the Sandinistas' symbiotic union of Marxism and Christian doctrine, the government used the occasion of the Holy Father's appearance to stage a noisy demonstration of popular support for the revolution. And, as if to throw down the gauntlet, junta leader Daniel Ortega condemned the Pope, wrote a Honduran editoralist, as if he were a "proconsul of the United States." Still, the Pope managed to get the attention of all Christendom by his obvious reprimand of Father Ernesto Cardenal, one of several Catholic priests serving in the Nicaraguan government.

What is happening in heavily Catholic Nicaragua is alarming to traditionalists, who argue, with convincing historical evidence, that Christ's disciples cannot serve two masters.[5] Since the Pope's visit, the archbishop of Managua, Miguel Obando y Bravo, a critic of the Somozas, has become somewhat of a folk hero to the Nicaraguan Catholics with his acerbic comments on the frailties of the new regime. The Sandinistas are holding firm. They continue to promote the "popular churches" of the base communities. Parishioners often voice their displeasure with the "unpatriotic" utterances of the church hierarchy, and the government has expelled several "offensive" non-Nicaraguan clerics from the country. Yet the church insists on playing more than a religious part in the new Nicaragua.

That's the troubling feature of the religious character of the Central American convulsion. God is indeed on everybody's side. Judging from the sometimes gruesome practices of the warring elements, though, it is not so clear who is on God's side.

Part III

17 The Real Stakes

T HE HOTEL INTERCONTINENTAL, A CURIOUSLY
modern edifice shaped vaguely like a Mayan
pyramid, rises midway up a hill overlooking
the grassy lots and damaged buildings that represent what is left of
downtown Managua, Nicaragua. Next door stands the imposing
headquarters of the Interior Department, a massive structure that is
the nerve center of the Sandinista police, guardians of the new
order.

The Intercontinental, foreigners swear, is the only decent place
to stay in the country, and despite its image as a Somoza showcase,
the Nicaraguan government prefers foreign visitors to put up at the
Intercontinental. Here they must pay for their rooms in the dollars
the Sandinistas desperately need to fund their revolution. At its
sumptuous (and modestly priced) buffet, which has given the Intercontinental a high culinary reputation in recent years, the Nicaraguans can play the cordial host. Their country is at the vortex of the
cold war in Central America, so the Intercontinental has an international guest list. There are stories about the Russians and the
Cubans taking over the top floor (at the behest, of course, of the
Sandinistas), segregating the modern benefactors of a still bitterly
divided Nicaragua from everybody else.

But in the tropical ambience of the Intercontinental bar, where I
sat with a Canadian trying to improve his Spanish and two voluble

Libyans (both of whom had just struck out with an American teeny-bopper who had ventured down from California "to experience the revolution"), the nationalities are not segregated. After I had finished explaining to the good-looking and likable Libyans that "Hey, baby, you want to get with it?" is not the most propitious introductory remark one makes to a woman (to which the Libyans replied, "Yes, but she smiled at us"), the conversation shifted to politics, *nica*-style. The Libyans were, I gathered, consultants, representative of the international technical experts (including Americans) the Sandinistas have been importing to advise them.

Lubricated by successive rounds of Victoria, the beer of the revolution, our conversation became more liberated. We were soon distracted by a more serious reference to Nicaragua's place in Cold War politics. At the other end of the gently curved bar, a man whose inebriated slur could not disguise an East European or Russian accent sat lurching to and fro, trying to get some response from an American at center stage. The Russian had been downing one Flor de Caña rum after another, while the American, dressed comfortably in a leisure suit, was trying to ignore him and at least finish his bottle of Victoria.

Finally, exasperated that his incoherent ramblings had not provoked the American, the Slavic drunk leaned forward, propping himself on the richly upholstered bar, and blurted: "Just . . . who . . . do . . . you . . . think . . . you're . . . protecting . . . down . . . here?"

My Libyan friends giggled. "He funny," one of them said, referring to the drunk. The stoic American, his Victoria unfinished, tossed a fifty-córdoba note at the beefy *nica* bartender (who had remained noticeably indifferent to this contretemps) and left in an obvious huff. The drunken Russian, doubtless convinced he had scored one for his side, stumbled across the room and plopped down in an empty chair at a table of Nicaraguans. Shortly he lapsed into a stupor.

Even allowing for his combatively drunken state, the Russian had made a point: Whom are we protecting in Central America?

What are we safeguarding? And from whom? The left? The right? Do the governments we support and subsidize believe in the things we do? President Reagan has compared the Central American crisis with the momentous choices in 1947 that prompted the enunciation of the Truman Doctrine, one of the boldest and most consequential decisions in American foreign policy. And the Kissinger Commission on Central America has portrayed the isthmian situation as a "real" and "acute" crisis and urged this country to confront it because "the stakes are large, for the United States, for the hemisphere, and, most poignantly, for the people of Central America." Except for the order of those for whom the "stakes are large," the distinguished members of the commission were correct. But they needed a Central American variation of one of Frank Capra's World War II inspirational films to get the point across.

Consider the Kissinger Commission Report's explanation of why the Central American situation requires prompt attention. "Central America is our neighbor. Because of this, it critically involves our own security interests. But more than that, what happens on our doorstep calls to our conscience. History, contiguity, consanguinity—all these tie us to the rest of the western hemisphere. They also tie us very particularly to the nations of the western hemisphere."[1] These are bracing (and, I believe, credible) injunctions to action, yet the key to understanding what they really mean lies not so much in the words themselves but in the implication of their meaning. If the most important consideration for the United States in Central America is safeguarding our security interests, as Reagan and the joint chiefs define them, then that goal would apparently best be served by maintaining the status quo. This would be a singularly difficult feat if we respond to those conditions in Central America that "call to our conscience." As we have seen, the issues in Central America that "call to our conscience" are so entrenched and seemingly immutable that the prospects for changing them in any significant, lasting way by an outside power (the United States, Cuba, or the U.S.S.R.) are negligible.

If, by extrapolating from the Kissinger Commission Report and various other ruminations on the isthmian condition, what we want for Central Americans is political stability, individual freedom, economic opportunity, and societies that nourish those values, there is one—and *only* one—way to guarantee they will be achieved there: annex the Central American countries as states in the Union.

As preposterous as this sounds, it would *guarantee* American objectives in Central America. What American mother would despair of sacrificing her son's life to defend Tegoose or San José if Honduras or Costa Rica were states in the American Union? Certainly the joint chiefs of staff would have few doubts about public commitment to the "United States of North and Central America." Realistically, of course, few of the ruling elements in the isthmus would acquiesce in such a bizarre proposal. The only country in Central America that comes close to fulfilling our criteria for statehood is Costa Rica, and I encountered several *ticos* who after an initial expression of doubt warmed to the notion of Costa Rica as the fifty-second (after Puerto Rico, logically, became the fifty-first) state.

Presumably, then, the choices of action lie somewhere between annexing Central America as states and doing nothing. (Kissinger himself, perhaps jokingly, once remarked: "There is a case for doing nothing." This may have been prompted by another statement in the report: "A great power can choose what challenges to respond to, but it cannot choose where those challenges come—or when.") In any event, the second declaration of the report left no doubt about American resolve: "The [Central American] crisis calls out to us because we *can* make a difference." Why? Because Central America is close by and its states are small.

Running throughout the Kissinger Commission Report is the view that Central America's agonies derive from an explosive mix of internal discord and external meddling. Predictably, with Kissinger's towering intellectual presence, "linkage" served as explanatory device: "The tortured history is such that neither the military nor the political nor the economic nor the social aspects of the crisis can be considered independently of the others. . . . But unless the externally supported insurgencies are checked and the violence curbed, progress on other fronts will be elusive and would be fragile." In other words, every problem of Central America relates, ultimately, to the violence, which is fueled by domestic and foreign combustibles. Thus, to mix metaphors but retain the thought, the links of human misery, political discontent, and economic backwardness add up to inevitable revolution, which is no security threat to the United States but becomes one when the Cubans and the East Europeans and the Soviets and the Libyans (and assorted other global enemies) interfere.

It logically follows from this that a military response, limited to aid and perhaps some American advisers, makes sense if the United States is going to prevent the revolutionary momentum in Central America from falling under the sway of, as southern radio commentators used to say during the civil rights struggle, "outside agitators." But as the commission made clear after it had pleased Reagan with its pointed references to Soviet–Cuban intrusion in Central America, when the United States gets through spending several hundred *millions* now in military aid it should expect to spend eight *billions* over the decade for Central America's postwar reconstruction.

The Kissinger Commission spent precious little of its time actually in Central America. But its members did manage to absorb enough from the whirlwind tour to get a "feel" for what Central America is enduring. In Costa Rica the Americans found a "long-established democratic order" plagued by the world's highest per capita debt; in Honduras, hope for a more democratic society; and even in war-torn El Salvador, prospects for social reform and a more pluralistic political system. Guatemala, with one-third of isthmian peoples and the most diversified economy, offered a lesson in entrenched social injustice. And, of course, in Managua the bitterly anti-American Sandinistas, incensed over having to deal with the same Henry Kissinger who had "destabilized" Chile a decade earlier, subjected the commission to a Marxist litany.

And in spite of the region's complexities and the persistence of its troubles, the commission, in a flourish of "can-do" rhetoric, invoked the Central American agenda: "The encroachments of poverty must be stopped, recession reversed, and prosperity advanced. Adherence to this principle involves something deeper than meeting a short-term emergency. It means laying the basis for sustained and broad-based economic growth. There must be encouragement of those incentives that liberate and energize a free economy. There must be an end to the callous proposition that some groups will be "have-nots" forever. Any set of policies for the hemisphere must address the need to expand the economies of its nations and revive the hopes of its people." A persistent critic of Reagan's Central American policy, Senator Thomas Dodd of Connecticut, said after reading the Kissinger Commission Report, "I don't think there's going to be any great groundswell of support based on the Kissinger Commission recommendations." The report, he went on, lacks a "coherent policy" and "ideological index."

The senator from Connecticut was certainly right about the first. After three years of exhaustive rhetoric about the "grave crisis at our doorstep" the American people seemed as confused as ever, but their uncertainties about Central America did not translate into an expected "groundswell of support" for Reagan's tough stance.

Certainly, the president and his former secretary of state Alexander Haig had valiantly tried to explain the isthmian malaise as an example of Soviet subversion. In a widely quoted speech to the Organization of American States in February 1982, Reagan warned of "a new kind of colonialism" that had penetrated the western hemisphere and jeopardized the independence of the Americas.[2] Like Herbert Hoover's attributions of the U.S. depression to the breakdown of the European economy, Reagan's assignment of Central America's despair almost solely to external causes raised just as much doubt in the minds of the American people.

José Lopez Portillo, former president of Mexico, was much closer to the truth of the matter when he declared, in a speech aimed at placating the Nicaraguans, that what is happening in Central America "does not constitute an intolerable danger to the basic interests and the national security of the United States. What does constitute a danger is the risk of history's condemnation as a result of suppressing by force the rights of other nations." Implicit in his argument is the belief that changes are on the way for Central

America, and the United States should not fear them and, certainly, not make the mistake it did three-quarters of a century ago with the Mexican revolution and try to manipulate those changes. Mexico is hardly a model for a society where income is equitably distributed, but it has, as have Costa Rica and Panama, curbed its military and opened up the political arena to new recruits. These may not assure a significant rise in the standard of living (which, for those on the bottom in Mexico, has actually been getting worse) but at least makes for a more peaceful life.

What, then, are the causes of Central America's troubles— external subversion, internal discontent, or, as the Kissinger Commission suggested, a volatile mixture of both? There may be yet another explanation. The late Crane Brinton, in his study of revolution, argued persuasively that people rose in rebellion against the established order not when conditions were hopeless but, paradoxically, when things seemed to be getting better. (A parallel explanation held for the decade of the sixties in this country, when social programs doubtless benefited a generation of people that had never gotten much from government, yet accompanying this beneficence was an eruption of social discontent on a scale unmatched since the violent upheavals of the 1890s.)

Something roughly parallel has been going on in Central America for a generation. In one of its less sanguine passages, the Kissinger Commission Report noted the extreme poverty that prevails in Central America, especially in the countryside, where the quality of life rapidly diminishes from what one finds in the cities. Annual per capita income (in 1984) ranges from a paltry $675 in Honduras to more than $2,000 in relatively wealthy Costa Rica. But the untold story in these admittedly dismal statistics is the rapidly ascending economic indicators of the twenty-eight years after 1950, during which Central America's *real* growth rate averaged 5.3 percent and *real* per capita income doubled. Astonishingly, isthmian population in this era rose from 8.6 million to 23 million.

In the same period Central America diversified its economy, rapidly expanded its trade, and, at least in the cities and larger towns, dramatically improved social services. Nearing the end of the 1970s, Central America, measured by economic indices, had in one generation wrought revolutionary changes.

But the rapid improvement in the isthmus' economic condition had also spawned greater expectation among a new generation coming of age. Central America's equivalent of the baby-boom era that matured in the sixties in this country had more than its share of optimistic young who not only wanted a better life than their parents but expected the political system to open up as well.

The old order resisted. In Nicaragua in 1972 Somoza had the constitution altered so that he could succeed himself in the presidency. The generals in San Salvador played a similar trick on electoral propriety by denying José Napoleón Duarte the presidency he had rightfully won. Two years later, their Guatemalan associates committed a patently abusive electoral fraud. Among the alienated and discontented of this better-educated, politically conscious, and younger generation the guerrillas found new recruits. The overthrow of Somoza in 1979 demonstrated the effectiveness of an alienated generation once it had resolved to change the political situation by force of arms.

These confrontations came about just as the United States was undergoing a divisive debate over the impact the new Panama Canal treaties would have on its legitimate security interests in the region. About the political dislocation and social injustices of Central America, the United States professed only a nodding concern, amplified by Jimmy Carter's human-rights campaign. But even under Carter this vexing question was still tangential to American security concerns. When Washington's disapproval of the excesses of the military regimes failed to have much impact on their heavy-handedness (in Guatemala, Carter's disapprobation brought defiance from a once-compliant regime) the left grew bolder. In Nicaragua the Sandinistas seized the initiative in the civil war that toppled Somoza. Their refusal to bend to American wishes as long as Carter was offering them money and encouragement convinced his successors that a much tougher line was required in Central America.

The recalcitrance of the Central American left in its dealings with the United States persuaded Reagan and his advisers that if we were no longer calling the political tune in Central America, then some other outside power must be. Naturally, that was Cuba, acting as surrogate for the Soviet Union. Very little in the official American analysis of Sandinista policy, for example, gave much credence to the plausible argument that Nicaragua's somber experience had much more to do with its hostility toward the United States than the undeniably Marxist convictions of some of its more outspoken leaders.

In any event, if, as Secretary of State Haig posed the issue, we had been willing to engage American troops on the other side of the world to demonstrate American credibility, then surely we must be committed all the more to meet any challenges from the communist menace so close to our borders. And no persuasive commentary on the internal problems of Central America could obscure the "real" threat. As the director for the U.S. Army's Strategic Plans and Policy Staff bluntly put matters in testifying before the House of Representatives Armed Services Committee in March 1983: "Through direct and indirect provision of military aid, the Soviet Union exerts considerable influence in the western Hemisphere. Cuba, a key in the sphere of Soviet influence, is a base area for Communist operatives throughout the Western Hemisphere. . . . The threat . . . in El Salvador can easily result in denial to the United States of access to the Panama Canal. . . . What we are really witnessing in Central America . . . is a tremendous shift in the strategic alinement [sic] and relationships over the past few years. . . ." And if the Salvadoran war continues for another five years with no change in American efforts to assist the Salvadoran government in defeating the guerrillas, then "we could very easily find in the best case the kind of insurgency . . . that we are now witnessing in El Salvador on our . . . border with Mexico. . . . What that would do is send refugees like we have never seen before, in the millions, the tens of millions."[3]

In other words, the Soviets and the Cubans are winning the contest for credibility and we're getting the problems and the blame. With such a despairing view of Central American events, it's easy to see why the 1983 Grenada operation was such a powerful psychological boost to American military morale. Yet, as surprisingly costly as it was, the Grenada invasion was a relatively minor military excursion compared with what would be necessary to accomplish the same results in Central America, and the strategists of the Pentagon know it.

Plainly there are military stakes in Central America. But they are no longer so vital as they were three-quarters of a century ago when the Panama Canal opened and the United States depended on it for protection of both coasts. Certainly, through World War II and well into the postwar era, the Canal remained a central feature in American strategic calculation, to say nothing of its symbolic value in American imperial thinking. Disturbances in Central America, it was long argued, threatened American domination of the isthmian route.

But in accepting the new Canal treaties with Panama the United States recognized not only a long-standing Panamanian (and by implication, Central American) grievance against us but also a modern reality of strategic interests. We would have to accept eventual Panamanian control of the Canal, but the Panamanian government (and the other regional states that depend on the waterway much more than we do) assumed more responsibility in defending it. Despite the protestations of prominent (retired) military officers that the Canal remained as vital as ever to American continental defense, there were more persuasive arguments that the advent of a modern carrier fleet, whose ships are too large for the canal locks anyway, lessened its military value. The economic value of the Canal, of course, has not diminished as much, though, again, the countries of the region rely on it proportionately more than we do.

Certainly there are military threats in Central America that cannot be ignored. A hostile regime in Managua, determined to resist American pressures on it, has already drawn that country close to Soviet and Cuban influence, created by far the largest army of any state in the region, and seriously alarmed its neighbors with its menacing bellicosity. Nicaragua's transformation into an armed populace and its determined meddlesomeness in the Salvadoran civil war represent indisputable proof in Washington that compels the American government to respond forcefully.

And since the United States readily assumes that Central Americans cannot settle their own affairs without outside interference and that their governments cannot prevail against armed insurgencies without our assistance, it has matched the communist commitment to the Sandinistas and the Salvadoran rebels with significant (though highly debated) increases in military assistance to El Salvador and the virtual transformation of mountainous Honduras into a military base where American and Honduran soldiers practice counterinsurgency tactics and Nicaraguan exiles organize their raids against Sandinista outposts. Throughout, the administration retains a conviction that *enough* should be done (as the Kissinger Commission Report explained, to offer too little aid can be worse than offering none) to avoid confronting the dilemma that faced the United States in Vietnam in early 1965—send in much heavier doses of aid *and* use American troops or watch South Vietnam go under.

Those who fear a similarly tragic scenario in Central America if we persist in our present course have credible arguments for their case. In Central America, as in Vietnam, the American people find themselves locked in a political embrace with governments they consider repulsive and committed to the preservation of societies Americans neither admire nor understand. Architects of our isthmian policy contend just as persuasively that we don't have a choice: Central America is too close to our borders to ignore ("San Salvador is closer to Washington than Los Angeles . . .") and, to rehabilitate Kirkpatrick's thesis, if we have to choose between the (Marxist) totalitarians and the (rightist) authoritarians, naturally we have to choose the latter.

And in our desperation we have leaned more and more toward military solutions, because they appear to offer the quickest (and, presumably, the most reliable) answer to a perceived threat. The American military command has discovered a new ally in Honduras to take the place of the dramatic emergence of an independent

Panama, which will mean, ultimately, that the Southern Command must be shifted northward. Honduras, lying strategically on the bulge of Central America, has appeared willing (for a price) to play the role of America's surrogate in a troubled isthmus. American commanders boast that there is no army (nor military combination) between the Rio Grande and the Canal capable of stopping us.

President Reagan has continually reassured the American people that the administration sees no need for American troops to fight in Central America. This statement may be the modern variation of Lyndon Johnson's often-quoted utterance "American boys should not fight the wars that Asian boys should fight." The presumption is that as long as we keep open the supply lines to the Hondurans and Salvadorans and (if we don't insist on being too finicky about how they make war) to the Guatemalans, then they will hold the line against the insurgencies and somehow in the process rehabilitate themselves.

But let's presume the worst—that the governments we've taken on as disciples in our global struggle with the communists start to lose and only an urgent dispatch of American troops will save them. An anxious woman (who must have had a draft-age son) at a luncheon forum asked me if we had a war plan for Central America. About current war plans I confessed I knew only what had appeared in print but added, "We've had a Nicaraguan war plan since 1910." And, incidentally, the invasion it charted two years later was the last successful military campaign of American troops in Central America. The massive intervention of the late 1920s, which established the Somoza dynasty, failed in its ultimate purpose, the defeat of Augusto Sandino and his band.

Americans of an earlier era often permitted their overwhelming preponderance on the Caribbean Sea and their undeniable capability in seizing and, for a limited period, holding ports to delude themselves about our military superiority in the hemispheric tropics. In those days two or three shiploads of sailors and Marines could seize a coastal city and virtually dictate a political agenda for a captive government. Caribbean states were small, vulnerable, and virtually defenseless against a determined assault from America's naval force. An entire generation of Caribbean politicians acquired, Americans believed, a salutary lesson in political behavior because the U.S. military had been on hand to "chastise them," as Theodore Roosevelt liked to say.

The latest episodes in these policing operations occurred in Grenada and, before that, in the Dominican intervention of 1965. In the Dominican case the American goal was to prevent a putatively Marxist (and pro-Cuban) political element from getting power and at the same time to avoid a return to a rightist dictatorship. Though the brazen defiance of anti-interventionist credos by Lyndon Johnson severely damaged our prestige in the hemisphere, prompt American military action had arguably prevented "another Cuba." And despite the perpetuation of social inequities, the Dominican Republic, if not an unblemished "decent democratic regime," has in the two decades since achieved a modicum of political moderation. In Grenada, the Marxists are out, and the former strong man (Eric Gairy) staged a comeback but failed.

At first glance, Central America appears similarly vulnerable to American military pressures. It lies within the orbit of overwhelming American sea and air power, and its governments cannot escape the U.S. political shadow or the reach of its economic influence. But anyone who presumes that Central America's closeness to our borders automatically overcomes the major difficulty we would face in undertaking a military commitment there overlooks somes crucial *dissimilarities* between the Caribbean islands and the mainland.

The first is our comparable military records in both places. In Grenada and the Dominican Republic in our time (and in the era of American empire in TR's day), the landings of small numbers of troops in Caribbean ports or along the foreign-dominated Central American coastline had far greater impact in the islands, where a country's major seaport also happens to be its capital, than in the isthmus, where the seat of government in every country save Panama lies deep in the interior. Military expeditions inside Central America, just as those vaunted Marine campaigns in the Haitian and Dominican mountains in the heyday of American empire, required much larger numbers of soldiers. In the islands the American military ultimately suppressed the guerrilla opposition that defied its rule. In Nicaragua in the late twenties, the Marines, by then more adept at fighting "little wars," spent seven years chasing Sandino's band—and failed.

To be sure, the massive American involvement in Nicaragua prevented Sandino from coming to power and produced a pro-American regime in Managua headed by "an SOB but *our* SOB." But even if we're willing to bear the embarrassment of a democratic society's having to ally itself with another generation of undemocratic SOBs as a guarantee against a Marxist future for Central America, the likelihood of keeping them in power without ultimately much *greater* military commitment than we made to Somoza is bleak. The days of the Caribbean strong man who counts on American troops to sustain him are passing; neither the maturing Central American nor the present American generation will long tolerate such a notion. Central Americans remember all too well the ignominy (which is apparent today even in presumably subservient Honduras) that foreign troops symbolize, and Americans have not shaken themselves from the most persevering lesson of Vietnam. Reagan may remind them that "we fought for a noble cause," but such reassuring homilies do not dispel the memory of how much it cost and how little we got for the price of fifty-thousand dead.

The second lesson of our military experience in Central America should be equally sobering. While we have always had a tremendous impact on these countries, directly with the display of our military power or indirectly through our cultural and economic influence, our Central American allies have become noticeably reluctant to follow American guidelines. In the old days, as late as the Dominican crisis of 1965, we could exert our power rather forcefully in the region, knowing that our willingness to use troops to maintain our sway wouldn't make us many friends but at least would reinforce respect for our power. But nowadays even formerly compliant Honduras, whose *military* invited our troops into the country as a counterweight to the menacing buildup of the Sandinista militias, has the temerity to demand a higher price for its role as our military host in Central America. The Guatemalans made it clear a half-dozen years ago that they required neither our advice nor our aid to wage their counterinsurgency. Today the Salvadoran military, though still dependent on our reluctantly granted largesse, has expressed reservations about the usefulness of *our* advisers in *their* war. They will continue to take our money, as one disgruntled congressman said, "and then thumb their noses at us." Or, as another critic of American policy summed up the matter with a sarcastic reversal of FDR's quip: "They're not our SOBs, we're theirs."[4]

While the remark may be harshly overstated, it illustrates just how far Central America has come in its ability to influence American policy. We *must* react to events *now*, because if we delay, then the situation will worsen, and if the situation worsens anyway, then we must do more, always reminding ourselves about the dangers of plunging into "another Vietnam." Even one of the most caustic critics of the American policy in Central America, former ambassador to El Salvador Robert White, whom Reagan fired for being too soft on the Central American left, reluctantly acknowledged that a Marxist-dominated Central America would not be in American interests.

The result is that in Central America we're at a Mexican stand-off. We're resolved to commit enough aid so that the guerrillas don't win in El Salvador but doubt the ability of the Salvadoran military to quash the insurgency unless it wages the war with *our* methods. But we're determined not to commit ourselves to fighting *their* war with *our* boys. We have necessarily chosen the authoritarian governments of the Central American right because, as Kirkpatrick explained, they are preferable to the predictable totalitarian regimes of the left.

In reality we have not chosen the authoritarian regimes of Central America; they have chosen us. We have not selected the territory nor the principles to defend; they have been selected for us. We have not chosen the line to defend; our putative surrogates have marked it out for us. As fearful as we are about the military consequences of a more aggressive policy in Central America, we have reassured ourselves, because of the obvious economic desperation of our isthmian allies, that our aid will somehow rehabilitate their political and social systems, that it will bring a sufficient fair play and tolerance to their politics so as to render the left without a platform.

Nor are American economic interests in Central America so critical that a shrinkage of the isthmian market would jeopardize our security. Of the total amount of American trade with the entire world, only roughly 2 percent is with Central America, and our isthmian imports are made up largely of bananas, sugar, coffee, and beef—none of which could be even remotely considered a vital strategic resource. Doubtless the rise of "new Cubas" in Central America would not only harm American trade but more certainly affect the 2 percent of American investments abroad that Central America has absorbed. Almost 1,500 U.S. multinationals do business in Central America (counting Belize and Panama).

The real fear is that more "Cubas" in Central America would simply bring more obstacles to U.S. trade and investment, leading ultimately to the kind of economic nonrelationship we now have with Cuba, once thoroughly subordinated to the U.S. economy but since Castro almost completely cut off. A socialist state in Cuba has meant economic and political regimentation, and 80 percent of Cuba's economic ties are with communist countries. But Castro himself has repeatedly declared that the remaining 20 percent, which represents trade with capitalist countries (not just the United States), is vital for Cuba. If they have done nothing else for Nicaragua, the Cubans have given the Sandinistas some sobering advice—confrontations with the United States can lead to economic blockade. True, Cuban socialism has meant not only the nationalization of the considerable amount of pre-1959 American investments in that country but a closing of Cuban–American trade. It should be remembered however, that these conditions came about a generation ago when Cuba lay at the vortex of American–Soviet relations. Cuba accepted incorporation into the Soviet economic and military orbit in part because the United States tried to isolate Cuba in the hemisphere with an economic blockade, which has long since failed in its purpose of squeezing the Cubans into renouncing socialism. The Cubans would like more trade with us. No less dedicated a capitalist than David Rockefeller has said the biggest obstacle to American companies' doing business with communist nations is the American government. But neither the Cuban nor the American government is willing to meet the political demands the other makes as a price for some kind of economic reconciliation.

The most profound impact Central America now makes on this country is demographic. Even if we resolve ourselves to a policy of never committing American military forces to "save the isthmus from communism," Central Americans, like other Caribbean peoples, will continue to migrate north. We are rapidly becoming a society more noticeably influenced by events to the south for the simple reason that the entire Caribbean basin, including Mexico, provides the largest numbers of our immigrants and has been doing so ever since the mid-sixties, when fundamental changes occurred in the immigration laws.

In trying to find meaningful historical perspective for this sudden influx of new residents in this country, the American people naturally look back to the early years of the Cuban revolution, when Castro's economic programs scared the professional and middle-class Cubans into flight to the United States.

But to portray Central American revolution as the catalyst for a new wave of refugees is to simplify matters. Clearly, many thousands of isthmian peoples are fleeing to the United States because of the turbulence in their own countries. They represent a significant shift away from the islands in the origin of migrants. The numbers of Central Americans in the larger pool of illegal aliens within our borders had been rising even before the outbreak of the Salvadoran guerrilla war in 1979, an event that aggravated the political situation and escalated the figures on those escaping from that conflict. The latter represented mostly additions to an already high Salvadoran refugee population because of the crowded conditions in the country.

Barring a major alteration in our immigration law (as of now, by admission of its sponsors, the Simpson–Mazzoli bill appears dormant), the tide of Central America refugees is certain to continue to wash northward. The isthmian population, roughly 23 million today, will be pushing 40 million by the end of the century, and the existing Central American governments, whether right, left, or center on the political spectrum, will be hard-pressed to meet their basic economic needs. Denied the opportunities that the "revolution of rising expectations" has been promising for the last generation, they will join the Mexican and other Latin American migrants already en route to this country and form what is expected to be the nation's largest minority by century's end. For this reason alone, we are inextricably involved with Central America.

What kind of society will Central America be at the end of this century? A half-dozen impoverished countries burdened with social injustice and repressive political systems? Or a nation retaining the surprisingly rich cultural diversity of its European, African, and Indian ancestry yet guaranteeing basic political rights while creating economic and social opportunity for all its people? Surely no American, if given the power to determine Central America's destiny, would choose the former. Neither should we believe that Central Americans themselves really want to enter the twenty-first century with the political and social frailties they now seem to represent. Central Americans want a better future for their children; they simply have not agreed on the best way to achieve it. They are at war with themselves about which way to go because the price for changing appears so frighteningly uncertain that resisting change, however dismal their present situation, is somehow reassuring. Whatever their differences in political values, social traditions, or economic values, the Central Americans almost instinctively look to themselves and not the outsider for solutions to the issues plaguing this isthmus. Central Americans define *their* problems as they interpret them. This does not mean they reject the advice of outsiders. Quite to the contrary, isthmian leaders have been incorporating European and American political principles and economic theories for more than a century and a half, but they stubbornly insist on self-determination when applying those principles.

There is no American solution to Central America's problems. The reasons for this should be clear to us even if they are painful to accept. Of the nations that historically have interfered in isthmian affairs, the United States has contributed far more than any other toward Central American economic development, expressed largely through the activities of private American concerns. Lamentably the rapid expansion of export capitalism in the isthmus did little to advance the cause of republican government, and, if one follows the usually rigid Marxist interpretations of Central America's evolution in this century, has contributed to its political retardation. Certainly, American obsession with its security and its understandable choice of the stability associated with strong-man rule or military regimes over the political volatility of reformist governments have left little doubt among Central Americans about our priorities. We want more decent societies in Central America, but not if the price is "another Cuba." The frustration is aptly expressed in the summary comment often made about our position there: "We can't win, we can't lose, and we can't quit the game."

There are, I believe, some conclusions about Central America's political and cultural makeup relevant to shaping our future policy toward a region undergoing explosive political and social change:

The Central American left ranges across a surprisingly broad spectrum from doctrinaire Marxists to social democrats, uniformly critical of American imperialism and intensely concerned with social injustice but sometimes bitterly divided over the most appropriate path to power. El Salvador's fractious guerrilla bands, the volatile debates among the Sandinista leadership in Nicaragua, and the split among the Christian Democrats over civilian control of the military offer reinforcing evidence that Central America's future is not inevitably pro-Cuban or pro-Soviet. More than likely, as long as the United States is perceived as the villain in the region, the left in power will consciously pursue more independent policies in its dealings with the socialist regimes of the world, as the Sandinistas are already showing. This has less to do with a rigid devotion to Marx (who for most Latin Americans is a social philosopher whose teachings have validity but are not sacrosanct) than with a determination to resist American guidance.

Whatever the intensity of their ideological conviction, Central American leftists constitute a threat to the established order simply because they are more willing to alter the social structure than to tolerate the social injustices associated with political stability. The left cannot change society without power, and if denied power by peaceful means it will try to get it by violent means.

And with equal determination the Central American right, the inheritors of the Spanish patriarchal tradition, can be expected to resist, if necessary by a sanctified vigilantism, any political movement that threatens its primacy in the social structure. A besieged social order falling under the sway of a Central American variation of a Mussolini is as dreary a prospect as a Marxist isthmus.

These are the extremes, the visible antagonists of the Central American confrontation, and we find neither very palatable. Our fear of the left and what it portends for the isthmus is matched by the revulsion we experience by our association with the right.

This leaves us yearning for the triumph of the men and the political parties in the middle, like José Napoléon Duarte and the Christian Democrats, whose leaders speak of toughness against the guerrillas and compassion for the downtrodden, of respect for private property and a civilizing mission against the evils of unregulated capitalism. The Christian Democrats have, by virtue of the violence of those at the extremes, assumed in our estimation a role as critical as the major political parties in this society, providing a stabilizing force in an unstable polity and a protective embrace for divergent views in a culture gone berserk over political differences. They are looked to as the bond holding society together.

But what is at stake in Central America is not the breakdown of the political system, which has historically exhibited discontinuity, but the disruption of something that has proved far more cohesive— Central American culture. In this society we pride ourselves on political continuity, the preservation of a birthright in a heterogeneous and sometimes explosive culture. Central Americans, like most Latin Americans, have yet to achieve this political birthright granted to us by a generation of men of reason and enlightenment.[5] Their politics is an unending family quarrel. They cannot easily slough off the Hispanic tradition, rich in its cultural legacy, burdensome in its political and economic irrationalities, passed down through the ages to them. To do so means to reject also the cohesive benefits of their Hispanic past. Only one country in Central America, Costa Rica, has managed to fuse the paternalistic Hispanic tradition with the economic rationality of our times.

"We can't win, we can't lose, we can't quit the game" may be true for the next few years or so, but the real stakes for us and for Central Americans lie embedded in their past and the choices they make. As for the United States, so for the Cubans and the Soviets, what is going to count far more than what the big powers can do is what the Central Americans decide. Will forty million people in the year 2000 live in half a dozen countries ranging from the geographical expression of Honduras to the social experiment of Costa Rica? Or will they settle their family quarrels in another round of gruesome isthmian wars and finally achieve nationhood?

We can't prevent such a war, but we can do much to isolate it and allow the conflict to run its inevitable course. And we can plainly indicate now—by exhibiting military restraint and a decided preference for "decent democratic regimes"—what kind of nation we hope Central America chooses to be. At the same time we should be prepared to accept Central America for what kind of nation *it* chooses to be. The choice is theirs *and* ours.

Epilogue

I T IS DECEMBER 1984, CHRISTMAS IS FAST APPROACH-
ing, and seasonal conversation turns readily to
peace—even a momentary truce in the Salvadoran
civil war. A few days ago, the Napoleon of El Salvador, following a
dramatic overture in the United Nations, journeyed into the mountains
north of the capital to a village called la Palma to negotiate with rebel
chieftains. Back in San Salvador fearful rumors circulated to the effect
that "the decent guy up front" might be selling out to the rebels by the
expediency of "power-sharing." It is a compound word more appropriate
in this country, where the president and Congress "share" power and the
Supreme Court occasionally intrudes by determining the rules of governance, but singularly inappropriate for El Salvador or Guatemala or Honduras or Nicaragua. Except possibly in Costa Rica, where some consideration for American-style checks and balances between the branches of
government lends credence to the concept, there is no power-sharing in
our sense of the word in Central America. Either one has power or not, or
is in power or is not.

And in Nicaragua the Sandinistas have power. Their candidate for
president, Daniel Ortega, no charismatic like Fidel, has won a
stupendous electoral victory, in a campaign charged with controversy over
American meddling in Nicaraguan affairs. The Sandinistas have beaten
back the *contra* attacks on their northern flank, divided the Miskitos with
overtures to Brooklyn Rivera (the new leader of MISURASATA) and
stinging denunciations of Steadman Fagoth (who has established a rival
organization, MISURA) as a *contra*, and watched approvingly as the
organization of their enemy to the south, Señor Lone Ranger, Edén

Pastora, has disintegrated into contentious factions. Despite the bitterness of their own people over the demonstrable economic failures of the new order (the "project of transformation") the Sandinistas have rallied the country's youth to the defense of the *patria* with ominous warnings of American invasion. The youngsters were desperately needed for the coffee harvest, but the Minister of Agriculture, sensing the psychological benefits of a united show of force against the "yanquí monster" routinely vilified as the enemy of humankind, has proudly released them for the patriotic duty of resistance. The American "invasion" never came off, but the alacrity with which the *nicas* responded was a measure of their unity and the residue of anti-Americanism, an explosive mixture of hatred and determination.

Yet, in remote Manzanillo, Mexico, the Sandinistas have been negotiating as equals with the Americans, achieving a stature in confrontation with the United States that their predecessor never gained as American sycophant.

On December 1, 1984, a trio of Sandinistas descended on Lawrence, Kansas, a pleasant university town in the most Republican state in the Union, a state born of conflict and civil war, for a consortium on the "Contadora process" and the prospects for peace in Central America. The people who gathered there on a brisk December morning were no strangers to conflict. Their ancestors, armed with a Bible in one hand and a rifle in the other, fought off Missouri ruffians and made Kansas a free state. They know the cost of making a nation.

The conference had its proper sprinkling of academics to speak authoritatively about the Soviet presence in Nicaragua or Costa Rican aid to Pastora or the CIA's funneling of monies to the *contras*, but the dominating personalities here were the *nicas*. There was a last-minute cancellation. The vice-president-elect, Sergio Ramírez, citing "visa problems" with the State Department, detoured to Mexico City for a friendly chat with President Miguel de la Madrid. In his stead came the new Nicaraguan ambassador, Carlos Tunnermann, an educator whom I'd met at Kansas University in my graduate school days a generation ago. He was then associated with the national university in León, the seat of Nicaraguan Liberalism and suppressed anti-Somoza intellectuals. Being the representative of a revolutionary government to a hostile Washington, whose leaders look for your every misstep and subsidize your enemies, is a tough job for any Nicaraguan in these times. When the Sandinistas first took power in 1979 they virtually drafted somebody to go to the United States. Somoza's old family emissary, Guillermo Sevilla-Sacasa, had spent so much time in the dictator's service in the United States that he had become a Washington institution and dean of the diplomatic corps.

His successor, believing no true Sandinista should live in Somoza's palatial American outpost, sold the building and deposited the money in a local bank in the name of the Nicaraguan ambassador. One of *his* successors, a dashingly handsome and ambitious fellow, stayed just long enough at his post to withdraw the funds and, some say, to deliver them to Pastora. More cynical observers believe that he melted away into America's Hispanic countryside. ("Do you have any idea where this guy is?" the ambassador's aide queried me at lunch. "We really want to find him. He stole our money.")

Kansans are Reagan supporters, but these people, many of them older citizens lured on-campus from Topeka and Kansas City, proved unexpectedly skeptical about their president's tough stance in Central America. They responded enthusiastically to the fervent appeal from the head of the Nicaraguan electoral council (himself a KU grad) when he called for "peace with the United States," or laughed approvingly when he referred to the "Reagan regime" because, he explained, "your president is always talking about the 'Sandinista regime.' "

The ambassador made the most of this opportunity to reinforce the doubts of Reagan's America about Central America. The issue at hand was Contadora, but the scrappy *nica* ranged over as many of the salient features of the Nicaraguan–American relationship as time allotted. "Your government said we were afraid to hold elections," he declared, "but when we did then your government labeled us as unfair to the opposition." (There were, frankly, some rowdy incidents by Sandinistas aimed at embarrassing their principal opponent, Arturo Cruz, who succumbed to American pressures and withdrew from the campaign, saying the election was a "farce." All things considered, however, the Sandinistas won as much of a mandate as did Reagan in 1984.) "Your government said we were afraid to approve the Contadora treaty," the ambassador continued with his accusatory litany, as some in the audience, their consciences perhaps irritated by the detectable sarcasm, shifted uneasily in their seats, "but when we did then your government called us 'insincere.'

"We have to feel ourselves threatened," Señor Tunnermann said, referring to American aid to the *contras* and the still noticeable scars of U.S. military intervention in his country. "We need peace in order to rebuild our country. We want to be at peace with our neighbors."

The Central American crisis has been with us so long that the issues and the predictable discussion about them have assumed their own momentum and vocabulary. The ambassador spoke in rapid-fire Spanish, pausing after every two or three sentences to permit his translator, a handsome woman in her twenties with an authoritative presence, to convey his thoughts into Midwest-Americanese. But Señor Tunnermann has already learned which words to avoid in speaking to an American audience. Edén Pastora, who is routinely castigated in *Barricada*, the Sandinista newspaper, as a "traitor," was here in the American heartland simply dismissed as an "ex-comandante," somebody of the faith who has gone astray. And he obviously sensed that these people retain lingering doubts about the *morality* of their government's cause, and he (as did the other *nicas* in his entourage) continually distinguished between what the American government is doing in Central America and what the American people know is right.

But these appeals that bypass Washington to speak directly to the American people are fraught with dangers neither the *nicas* nor the other Central Americans who follow their example may fully appreciate. Ninety years ago Cuban revolutionaries lobbied in this country in order to win approval for a cause among a people with only the vaguest notions about its purpose and succeeded so well that decent Americans, resolved to "humanize" the conflict, marched in torchlight parades in tranquil towns like Lawrence and stampeded their president into a war he really didn't want. The Cubans, who desired only a genuine neutrality and a nearby source of weapons in the United States, wound up with a conquering army on their island and a pervasive American influence in their country that lasted for sixty years.

So far, the debate on Central America in Lawrence and the countless towns like it in this country has not reached the point where a "concerned citizenry," aroused by a unifying spirit of the crusader, suddenly dismisses all the good reasons for not getting involved in Central America's centuries-old quarrels and, with the most enthusiastic "we-can-solve-anybody's-problems" aplomb, plunges into the isthmian quagmire. This is a society that produces great engineers and impressive builders, but it does not naturally follow that we can rebuild other societies.

The American governmental bureaucracy is, apparently, institutionally ready for such a dramatic shift toward a military cum political solution. In a later response to my remarks at the conference, a distinguished consultant who served as an expert for the Kissinger Commission told me that the Kissinger Commission Report was a *political* document, intended for the president. The commission was a bipartisan group. In the beginning he conveyed many of the sentiments I expressed, mainly, that there really is no American solution to Central America's problems. When I interjected that the report's sometimes inspirational phrases (admittedly his) contrasted sharply with his words, he explained, in tones of one familiar with the proclivities of special commissions, that he tried to tell the commission members there is no American solution down there but *not one* wanted to hear that message. So, armed with the positive phrases that sound the call to action and with that understandable need to want to influence people who are called on to inform the leader of the most powerful government in history, he told the members of the commission what they wanted to hear.

The remark underscores much of our thinking about Central America and reinforces our conviction that its problems are much like those we have confronted in this country. If Central Americans would debate their political differences instead of shooting one another or innocent by-standers, if they would divide the economic pie in fairer proportions so as to satisfy all their interest groups, if they would adopt the notion of functional rather than authoritative government, if they would run their society the way we run ours . . ., then none of their problems would be insolvable. Some problems might require more time or cost more, but each ultimately would find a solution. After all, this country, which we believe is an infinitely more complex society than Central America, found, in one way or another, solutions to its "problems."

Central America is much smaller than the United States, but its social, economic, and political configurations are just as baffling and no more easily manipulated than those we have confronted. Indeed, given Central America's tortured history, its problems may be proportionally more awesome and less tractable.

If, for example, we measure any one of the Central American states (excluding Belize and Panama) in terms of the unifying strength of the political convictions of its leaders, or the size of its population, or its economic diversity—each a crucial yardstick for assessing a modern society—then Guatemala readily qualifies as a model. Yet Guatemala is permeated with social injustice and burdened with a repressive political system. The visible pattern of modern Guatemala—an Indian culture ruled by Spaniards and their *ladino* descendants—took form more than four centuries ago. Its social character has determined its rigid politics. Far from being a deterrent to economic progress, as its rulers have defined that term, Guatemala's notorious record of governmental repression and political uniformity has been unashamedly defended by its leaders as their only recourse. As one arrogant son of the establishment informed me: "What would be the political condition of the United States if the population were fifty percent Indian?"

If our measure of the worthiness of a society is the determination of its leaders to persevere despite the adversities of civil war and yet hold an election, supervised by international observers, that was as fair as any held in Maryland during the American Civil War, then El Salvador would readily meet that test. If, in addition, our criteria included a demonstrative patriotism coupled with a reputation for hard work, then El Salvador again would come as close as any of its neighbors in the ability of its people to express a palpable nationalistic pride. But the same country, if one gauges the worthiness of a society by its political diversity or opportunity for those on the bottom to improve their lot, is embarrassingly backward.

Yet its neighbor and former enemy, Honduras, remains lamentably the most laggard of the isthmian states, with its people still the poorest of all Central Americans despite the massive infusions of American monies and the transformation of the country, to use a popular phrase, "from an American banking center into a military base." But if our measure of a worthy society is one in which the guiding political philosophy is "that government which governs least, governs best" or that those on the bottom should not be tantalized with prospects of a better life, then lowly Honduras certainly rises to the top of our scale. It has the appearance, but not the reality, of a civilian, democratic state structure, and if style is more important than substance in our criteria for a model Central American state, Honduras is a superb candidate.

To continue with the analogy, if our test of an admirable society is one that is composed of deeply religious people who are capable of agreeing on little except their collective refusal to return to the crass dictatorship that ruled over them for fifty years and who are willing to risk international embarrassment by holding an election, internationally supervised, while their economy suffers from postwar dislocation and hostile American pressures (all the while fighting a two-front war against its enemies), then Nicaragua is the only Central American country that satisfies these criteria. The only parallel to its suffering and perseverance in our own history is the quarter-century after the American Revolution, when the monarchies of Europe, in retaliation for our creation of a republican government, applied the severest economic measures against us, meddled in our politics, and so humiliated us with retaliatory policies that we were compelled, in 1812, to fight a "second war for American independence."

Finally, if our criteria for an admirable society are political pluralism and economic rationality in a people paternalistic in their social philosophy yet egalitarian in their political principles, then Costa Rica represents the only Central American country that has achieved this happy union of sometimes antagonistic concepts. And it is the only isthmian culture with a sufficiently large middle class so as to nourish those political, social, and economic values to which the average American subscribes.

There is no American solution to Central America's problems, but this absolute statement does not mean that there can be no effective American policy toward Central America. Most assuredly, we can have an understandable and, more important, defensible posture toward that region, but it must incorporate some fundamental changes in our thinking.

First, the Central American crisis of our times reinforces the truism of Theodore Roosevelt's age that the circum-Caribbean is a region vital to our security, but it is not our empire anymore. Unlike the small Caribbean and Central American societies of Roosevelt's day, these countries can no longer be denied their rightful place in the larger community of world-states. They will no longer tolerate the subservient status of their predecessors, and where necessary, they will raise the flag of defiance against the outsider, even when the cause seems hopeless or they face overwhelming superiority. This is why Castro's stature has remained fairly high among his Caribbean neighbors. He has transformed Cuba into a rigid model of a Soviet-style economy (which Caribbean onlookers don't especially admire) and mortgaged his country to the Russians (which they will never forgive), but he has *defied* the United States, survived our economic boycott, and insisted that Cuba will enjoy at least some tactical autonomy (even under Soviet control) in its international behavior. In other words, he has gained the sullen respect of the *yanquís* by his defiance and perseverance.

Early on, the Sandinistas sensed the psychological advantages they would gain among their own people, particularly during the inevitably hard times after the revolution, by refusing to knuckle under to American pressure. Time and again they have persevered by exploiting the latent anti-Americanism among ordinary *nicas*—in the early days of the Reagan administration, when sorely needed American aid expired; and, most recently, in the 1984 political campaign, when the Sandinistas identified their enemies with the hated Americans and demonstrated to skeptical Europeans that they would hold an election when the American government said they wouldn't and that it could be, despite their troubles, a reasonably fair election. In their defiance of the American giant the Sandinistas, despite their woeful economic performance, have gained a respect for Nicaragua that Somozaland never enjoyed—not even from the United States.

Second, the political model of republican government has been adopted in form but not in substance in all but one state in Central America. People vote (and in much higher percentages than in the United States), assemblies deliberate and pass legislation, executives carry out laws (more or less), and the courts sit in judgment, but the process of governance has never worked the same way it does in this country and probably never will. The reasons are many: the inherited Hispanic tradition that values the authority of government more than its obligation to the citizenry, its needs, and its rights; that cherishes social more than political order; and that militates against the idea that a "public office is a public trust." Additionally, in modern times there is the woeful inadequacy of the Central American bureaucracy to meet social needs and demands. To ask any of the isthmian countries (except Costa Rica, which has a bloated state government) to perform for their people what, let us say, the state of New York does for its citizens, while still respecting fundamental civil liberties, is seen by them as a monumental undertaking beyond their economic capabilities and a great political risk. None of the Central American states can generate enough largesse to satisfy their populations—expectations run stronger than the capability of weak governments to satisfy them. Even what appears a *minor* alteration in the governing style may be a harrowingly dangerous undertaking for a Central American leader. In late 1984, José Napoleón Duarte, having pledged to bring at least a modicum of justice in dealing with the country's notorious death squads, shifted a few generals around and stripped the main culprit in the assassination of two American labor representatives in early 1981 of his *pension*. The brother of one of the slain Americans was incensed at this trivial punishment, and rightly so, but the point to remember is that Duarte took a big chance with his own life in levying this toll against the Salvadoran military.

Third, Central America's most debilitating problems are not only beyond our solution, but largely hidden from our view. These are the daily struggles of ordinary *centroamericanos* in countries that have slipped behind in their ability to feed their own people, in cultures where the reassurance of familial tradition and unity is rapidly disappearing, and in states where the promise of economic security often means the loss of political liberty. The Caribbean Basin Initiative, even if one added another zero to the sum, is not likely to deal very effectively with these fundamental issues that plague 23 million people.

Nor will American aid have much impact on the divisive struggle going on in the church between conservative clerics, who argue that it is man's soul and not his stomach that is the church's concern, and their liberal brothers, who just as fervently contend that God meant for His children to have a better life on this earth. The inseparable fusion of religion and politics in Central America has no counterpart in this country. Private American citizens and volunteer organizations, acting through their own churches or philanthropic societies, may alleviate some of the human suffering Central Americans are experiencing. They may shelter a Salvadoran refugee or serve mankind in a remote Honduran village, but the religious character of Central America's conflict will remain persistently baffling to even the most religious of isthmian intruders. In Central

America, the good, the bad, and the indifferent all convincingly invoke God's blessing for every humane and inhumane gesture.

Fourth, historically outsiders have been able to *influence* Central Americans, but even with considerable military backing the interlopers have not been able to *compel* isthmian peoples to accept a foreign model for their societies as their own. The Cubans and the Soviets are doubtless extending their influence into Sandinista Nicaragua, but however welcome their advice and aid in a time of adversity, the *nica* inclination, as that of "our" allies, is to manipulate its benefactors to Nicaragua's own needs. Americans who witnessed the gradual absorption of Cuba into the Soviet family will doubtless disagree. But what kind of society would Cuba be today had there been no Cuban–American confrontation in the early sixties that invited Soviet meddling? The Russians used Castro, it cannot be denied, but with equal credibility it can be argued that Castro has manipulated the Russians. So are the Sandinistas using the Cubans and the Soviets. Americans who fought for and then won independence two centuries ago by playing the European powers against one another, allying with a French against a British monarchy, and then for a quarter-century resisting the efforts of both to "guide" our political destiny would have understood what the Sandinistas are doing.

Fifth, the alarmist rhetoric about a guerrilla triumph in El Salvador sending "hordes of refugees" storming to our shores confuses most Americans about this increasingly controversial subject. The motivation of refugees from Central America and the insular Caribbean (*including* Cuba) has been *both* economic and political. Central America's political turmoil has exacerbated an already existing problem that reaches back for at least a generation. Certainly, Central America's strife has added significantly to the numbers of illegal aliens in this country *and* in Honduras, Costa Rica, and Mexico, all three of which are in much poorer shape than we are to absorb them. Senator Alan Simpson is undeniably correct when he argues that immigration reform is the most urgent issue facing this country, but for Mexico and Central America it is an equally pressing (and controversial) matter.

What we are witnessing is the re-Hispanicization of that once-Spanish domain in North America, and unless we are willing to dilute some of our cherished political and economic principles, the refugees from the Caribbean basin and Mexico, inspired by our political freedom and economic opportunity, will keep coming. Just as the millions of turn-of-the-century immigrants (who were *legal* entrants) frightened an older generation of Americans, so these recent waves of abused and alienated yet hopeful peoples from Hispanic cultures and authoritarian political climates prompt fearful murmurings for the future of American democracy. But the

Italians and Russians and Poles and Jews who came to this country a century ago ultimately helped make American democracy work for the betterment of all the people, and so have their Hispanic successors. Despite the Hispanic's persistent identity with the culture he has left behind, whether Cuba or Mexico or Nicaragua or El Salvador, his loyalties to the society that protects his civil liberty and offers him economic opportunity will be no less than those of native-born Americans. And any American who doubts this should look up the numbers of persons named García or Martínez or Rodríguez who have died in America's wars.

Finally, Central American *nationhood*, discounted by some as unrealistic and historically frustrated by the big powers, is in the long run to the advantage of the average *centroamericano* and would serve our interests as well. Central America must be a nation. The price of nationhood, as Americans well know, is high in human and material costs, but without it Central America's 23 million will continue to endure state governments incapable of meeting their needs and, more than anything else, of inspiring a deeper sense of identity and patriotism that only national governments can generate.

Students of the isthmus's history will quite rightly point out that Central Americans have always been too antagonistic and belligerent to form a lasting union. At the top, certainly, among the creole and *ladino* chieftains, the Central Americans have flailed away at one another. But among their peoples there exists a unity born of common suffering and want, and the isthmian political movement that speaks to these issues will find converts for its cause.

Given its tumultuous history, it is doubtful that Central America will achieve nationhood peacefully. A likelier prospect is a revival of that early-twentieth-century interstate conflict that American troops eventually crushed. If such a disturbing scenario takes place, our interest, some argue, would lie in protecting our newest isthmian ally, Honduras. Militarily this might make sense if we were prepared to sustain a *long* war *inside* Central America, but the American people do not now appear disposed to support such a crusade. They might be willing to dispatch a rescue operation to Costa Rica, whose people (as the English in 1940) may have to fight for those political and social values we cherish and may call for our support in defending them. If our political and military leaders are determined to defend "our way of life" *in* Central America, Costa Rica is the place to take our stand.

More realistically, our place in this future conflict should be *outside* Central America. From off its shores we can more capably shield the Central Americans from other meddlers, like the Cubans or Soviets, and carry out such a mission with considerably less cost in lives and materiél than by plunging into mountainous Honduras with an army to protect our "credibility." The real costs will be borne by Central Americans, who will suffer terribly in this struggle, as they have in their other wars, but who can in their suffering create a nation. Just as our own civil war ultimately demonstrated, a nation can arise from seemingly irreconcilable social and political disputes and fratricidal war. Central Americans want no less than nationhood, and they are willing to pay as high a price as we did to achieve it.

Notes

1: "TAKE YOUR REVOLUTION SOMEPLACE ELSE"

1. A brief account of the 1910–1912 intervention in Nicaragua appears in Lester D. Langley, *The Banana Wars: An Inner History of American Empire, 1900–1934* (Lexington, Ky., 1983), chap. 6.
2. The Cannon-Groce executions and their aftermath are based on José Joaquín Morales, *De la historia de Nicaragua, 1889–1913* (Granada, Nic., 1963), pp. 323–24; and Lester D. Langley, *The United States and the Caribbean in the Twentieth Century* (Athens, Ga., 1982), p. 51.
3. The Butler quotations are from "Old Gimlet Eye's" personal correspondence, part of which is at the Marine Corps History and Museums Division, Navy Yard, Washington, D.C.; the remainder is at the Butler home, Newtown Square, Pa.
4. For a summing-up of TR's general views on how we should treat Caribbean societies, see Langley, *The Banana Wars*, chap. 2.
5. For an assessment of the Walker intervention and its impact on Central America, see Thomas Karnes, *The Failure of Union: Central America, 1824–1860* (Chapel Hill, N.C., 1961).

2: "THEY MAY BE SOBS, BUT THEY'RE OUR SOBS"

1. See Hermann B. Deutsch, *The Incredible Yanqui: the Career of Lee Christmas* (London, 1931), pp. 117–18; and Ernest Baker, "United Fruit II: the Conquest of Honduras," Fortune, March 1933, p. 23.

2. For more on "the Banana Man," see Baker, "United Fruit II," *Fortune*, March 1933, pp. 25–33, which has an inside account of Zemurray's takeover of United Fruit; and Thomas McCann, *An American Company: the Tragedy of United Fruit* (New York, 1976).

3. This quotation is from Baker's article, cited above, which created quite a stir. Given Zemurray's legendary reputation for cursing, equally effective in English or Spanish, the expletive is probably correct.

4. This telling quote, sometimes attributed to FDR's secretary of state, Cordell Hull, has acquired a certain generic quality, referring not only to Somoza but his contemporaneous Caribbean tyrants, Fulgencio Batista in Cuba and Rafael L. Trujillo in the Dominican Republic.

5. Quoted in Robert and Nancy Heinl, *Written in Blood: The Story of the Haitian People, 1492–1971* (Boston, 1978), p. 514.

6. The aide was the historian Arthur M. Schlesinger, Jr., who elaborated on Kennedy's approach to the Caribbean in *A Thousand Days: John F. Kennedy in the White House* (Boston, 1965), pp. 226–56.

7. Ms. Kirkpatrick's controversial article "Dictatorships and Double Standards," which allegedly got Reagan's attention and Ms. Kirkpatrick the appointment as U.S. ambassador to the United Nations, appeared in *Commentary*, vol. 68 (November 1979), pp. 34–45.

8. Quoted in an article by Alan Riding in the *New York Times*, March 23, 1980.

3: "YOU CAN'T SHOOT HIM, HE'S MY BROTHER-IN-LAW"

1. Quoted in Frederick Palmer, *Central America and its Problems* (New York, 1913), p. 178.

2. Quoted in the spirited account in Harold Denny, *Dollars for Bullets: The Story of American Rule in Nicaragua* (New York, 1929). Afterward, Solórzano kicked the Liberals out of his cabinet, and Señor Rivas received a "donation" of $5,000, a house, and a membership in the International Club.

3. For a fuller account of Major Carter's experience, see his "The Kentucky Feud in Nicaragua," *World's Work 54* (July, 1927): 312–31.

4. Thomas and Marjorie Melville, *Guatemala: the Politics of Land Ownership* (New York, 1971).

5. For an incisive comment on Latin America's colonial heritage, see Stanley and Barbara Stein, *The Colonial Heritage of Latin America: Essays on Economic Dependence in Perspective* (New York, 1970).

6. The sociologist is Sam Stone, son of the archaeologist Doris Zemurray Stone, and the book is *La dinastía de los conquistadores* (San José, 1975).

7. True to his word, Wilson dispatched seven thousand troops to the Mexican port of Veracruz for six months in 1914, saying, "My ideal is an orderly and righteous government in Mexico." He got neither, but did earn the lasting enmity of every Mexican nationalist.

8. For a bitterly critical summary of American military efforts to rehabilitate the Salvadoran armed forces, see Richard Alan White, *The Morass: United States Intervention in Central America* (New York, 1984), esp. chap. 6.

9. In the presidential elections in El Salvador in 1984 one of the candidates, "Chico" Quiñónez, scion of one of the country's ruling families, ran on a platform that declared, "The Family [not *family*] is the basic unity that gives life to Society and without it we would cease to exist as a Democratic Society." Quoted from the political ad in *La Prensa Gráfica* (San Salvador), March 6, 1984.

4: "A PRETTY HOT NUMBER"

1. Samuel Griffith, Oral History, p. 22, Marine Corps History and Museums Division, Navy Yard, Washington, D.C.

2. Graves Erskine, Oral History, p. 95, Marine Corps History and Museums Division.

3. The classic account in English of Sandino's last days is Neill Macaulay, *The Sandino Affair* (Chicago, 1967), esp. pp. 242–56. A Marine captain with 75 Marines and 150 Nicaraguan guardsmen dispatched to crush Sandino in 1927 wrote: "I will become involved in a small real war." Quoted in Langley, *Banana Wars*, p. 197.

4. For an account of the literacy campaign by a priest, Fernando Cardenal, S. J., nominated for a Nobel Peace Prize for his efforts, see "Nicaragua 1980: the Battle of the ABCs," in *Revolution in Central America* (Boulder, Colo., 1983), pp. 447–57.

5. A former Sandinista official, Arturo Cruz Sequera, probes the internal debates among the Sandinistas and their impact on Nicaragua's relations with Cuba, the Soviet Union, and the United States, in "The Origins of Sandinista Foreign Policy," in Robert Leiken, ed., *Central America: Anatomy of Conflict* (New York, 1984), pp. 95–110.

5: *MATANZA:* THE LITTLE MAN WITH THE RED STAR IN HIS LAPEL

1. For a detailed account of the revolt, see Thomas P. Anderson, *Matanza: El Salvador's Communist Revolt of 1932* (Lincoln, Neb., 1971).
2. For a discussion of the modern Salvadoran guerrilla movement, see Tommie Sue Montgomery, *Revolution in El Salvador: Origins and Evolution* (Boulder, Colo., 1982).

6: A MAN NAMED NAPOLEÓN

1. This cogent summation of Christian Democratic philosophy is quoted in a superb biography, Stephen Webre, *José Napoleón Duarte and the Christian Democratic Party in Salvadoran Politics, 1960–1972* (Baton Rouge, La., 1979), p. 57.
2. Much of this story of a critical period in Duarte's political life is based on a highly analytical work by Thomas P. Anderson, *Politics in Central America: Guatemala, El Salvador, Honduras, and Nicaragua* (New York, 1982), esp. pp. 95–105.
3. Quoted in Christopher Dickey, "The Saving of El Salvador," *New York Review of Books*, June 4, 1984, p. 25.

7: DOWN IN TEGOOSE

1. Quoted in Walter LaFeber, *Inevitable Revolutions: The United States in Central America* (New York, 1983), p. 177.
2. Quoted in a pamphlet, "Honduras: A Democracy in Demise," published by the Washington Office on Latin America, February 1984.
3. The story appeared in *La Prensa* (Tegucigalpa), March 9, 1984.

8: OMAHA, CENTRAL AMERICA

1. Taken from an article by Christopher Dickey in the *Los Angeles Times*, November 17, 1983.
2. For a succinct account of *tico* politics in the 1940s, see Charles Ameringer, *Democracy in Costa Rica* (New York, 1982), esp. pp. 27–35.

3. He was also a big promoter of Costa Rican cultural life. "Why tractors without violins?" as Figueres often said. Quoted in the sympathetic biography by Charles Ameringer, *Don Pepe* (Albuquerque, N.M., 1978), p. 253.

4. For a tedious but revealing study of *tico* peasants, see Mitchell A. Seligson, *Peasants of Costa Rica and the Development of Agrarian Capitalism* (Madison, Wis., 1980), esp. pp. 153–72.

5. The story got much broader coverage in the leftist periodicals, especially *Libertad Revolucionaria* (March 9–17, 1984), p. 3.

6. The standard of living for the middle-class *ticos* has declined sharply in the past two or three years. In March 1984 the president of the Central Bank, Carlos Manuel Castillo, declared ominously: "We Costa Ricans are significantly poor nowadays." Quoted in *La República*, March 14, 1984, p. 16.

9: "WELCOME TO THE FREE REPUBLIC OF OLANCHO"

1. The account of the Santa Cruz waterwheel project is based on a scholarly paper delivered by the missionary's son at the University of Alabama, April 18, 1981, and recent correspondence between the author and both the missionary and his son.

2. "Food is . . . a weapon," stated Secretary of Agriculture John Block in January 1981, "but the way we use that weapon is to tie countries to us. That way they'll be reluctant to upset us." Quoted in Tom Barry, Beth Wood, and Deb Preusch, *Dollars and Dictators: A Guide to Central America* (New York, 1983), p. 97.

3. For a somewhat technical summary of Central American agricultural economics, see Peter Dorner and Rodolfo Quiros, "Institutional Dualism in Central America's Agricultural Development," *Journal of Latin American Studies*, vol. 5 (1973), pp. 217–32.

4. Joseph Collins, brought in to advise them, has provided an account of his Nicaraguan experience in *What Difference Could a Revolution Make?: Food and Farming in the New Nicaragua* (San Francisco, 1982).

10: PANZÓS

1. This account is based on Gabriel Aguilera (professor of political science and history at the University of San Carlos), "The Massacre at

Panzós and Capitalist Development in Guatemala," *Monthly Review*, December 1979, pp. 13–23.

2. On the "place" of the Indian in Guatemala, see the classic study by Eric Wolf, *Sons of the Shaking Earth* (Chicago, 1959), esp. pp. 211–32.

3. After the CIA plan succeeded and Arbenz fell, Dulles told the American people in a radio and television address: "The people of Guatemala have now been heard from." For two exhaustive summaries of this dreary affair that would later haunt the United States in Central America, see Stephen Schlesinger and Stephen Kinzer, *Bitter Fruit: the Untold Story of the American Coup in Guatemala* (Garden City, N.Y., 1982); and Richard Immerman, *The CIA in Guatemala* (Austin, Tex., 1983).

4. The account is taken from an article by Nancy Peckenham in Jonathan Fried et al., *Guatemala in Rebellion: Unfinished History* (New York, 1983), pp. 204–6.

5. Excerpts from Amnesty International's 1981 report, *Guatemala: a Government Program of Political Murder*, appear in *ibid.*, 139–45.

11: MY BROTHER'S KEEPER

1. The story appeared in the *Washington Post*, February 19, 1982.

2. Quoted in a story by Steve Weingarten (Cox News Service), *Atlanta Journal-Constitution*, July 1, 1984.

3. David Blundy's account of the Las Aradas massacre appeared in the *Sunday Times* (London), February 22, 1981.

4. Much of the account is based on testimony in *Salvadoran Refugees in Honduras*, Senate, Comm. on Foreign Affairs (Subcomm. on Inter-American Affairs), Hearings, 97th Cong., 1st Sess., December 17, 1981; and Centro de Documentación de Honduras, *Los refugiados Salvadoreños en Honduras* (Tegucigalpa, 1982).

5. Quoted in Reps. Gerry Studds, Barbara Mikulski, and Robert Edgar, "Conversations with Salvadoran Refugees," in Marvin Gettleman et al., *El Salvador: Central America in the New Cold War* (New York, 1981), p. 150.

12: NORTH TOWARD HOME

1. The story on refugees in New Orleans is based on articles in the New Orleans *Times-Picayune*, November 13 and 18, 1983.

2. Quoted in the *Christian Science Monitor,* August 22, 1983.
3. The story appeared in the *Christian Science Monitor,* October 25, 1983.
4. As Theodore Hesburgh, chairman of the Select Committee on Immigration and Refugee Policy, declared in congressional testimony in May 1981: "The open society does not mean limitless immigration." Quoted in *Final Report of the Select Committee on Immigration and Refugee Policy,* 97th Cong., 1st Sess. (Washington, 1981), p. 25.

13: "WE LOST THE WAR, BUT WE WON THE GAME"

1. Most of the details about the soccer war come from the first-rate account by Thomas P. Anderson, *The War of the Dispossessed: Honduras and El Salvador, 1969* (Lincoln, Neb., 1981).
2. For a probing assessment of war's origins from an ecological perspective see the study by William Durham, *Scarcity and Survival: Ecological Origins of the Soccer War* (Stanford, Cal., 1979).

14: THE MISKITO KING

1. Quoted in Lester D. Langley, *Struggle for the American Mediterranean: United States–European Rivalry in the Gulf-Caribbean, 1776–1904* (Athens, Ga., 1976), p. 92.
2. This account of Mocorón refugee camp appeared in *Christianity Today,* October 8, 1982, pp. 87 ff.
3. Based on Fagoth's testimony in Senate, Comm. on Appropriations, Hearings, 97th Cong., 2nd Sess., *Foreign Assistance and Related Programs, Appropriations, Fiscal Year 1983* (Washington, 1983), pp. 1–19.
4. From an article in *Libertad Revolucionaria,* March 9–17, 1984.

15: SEÑOR LONE RANGER

1. Much of this account of Pastora's guerrilla days is taken from Bernard Diederich, *Somoza and the Legacy of U.S. Involvement in Nicaragua* (New York, 1981).

2. For more on Pastora's Costa Rican sojourn, see *Christian Science Monitor*, August 4, 1981; *New York Times*, September 20, 1983; *Washington Post*, June 2, 1984; and an editorial, "More Respect, Señor Pastora," in the Costa Rican daily *El Debate*, March 16, 1984.
3. Quoted in an interview in the *Christian Science Monitor*, June 14, 1984.
4. Ibid.

16: GOD IS ON EVERYBODY'S SIDE

1. For a bitterly critical account of religious persecution in Latin America, see Penny Lernoux, *Cry of the People* (New York, 1980), esp. chaps. 3 and 4.
2. Quoted in a speech to the Tegucigalpa Rotary Club by Dr. Carlos Medina, March 1983, reprinted in *La Tribuna* (Tegucigalpa), March 8, 1984.
3. See Lernoux, *Cry of the People*, chap. 3.
4. Tommie Sue Montgomery, whose account appears in Martin Diskin, ed., *Trouble in Our Backyard: Central America and the United States in the Eighties* (New York, 1983), pp. 75–99.
5. On March 13, 1984, three Nicaraguan women, members of a base community, in an article in the pro-Sandinista paper *Barricada*, accused the Episcopal leader of Nicaragua and the archbishop of Managua of being "mouthpieces" for American imperialism.

17: THE REAL STAKES

1. This and other quotations from the Kissinger Commission Report come from the extract in the *New York Times*, January 12, 1984.
2. Quoted in an article by Robert Pastor, "Our Real Interests in Central America," *Atlantic Monthly*, July 1982, p. 28.
3. Quoted in U.S. Cong., H. R., Comm. on Armed Services (98th Cong., 1st Sess.), *Hearings* on Department of Defense Appropriations for Fiscal Year 1984 (Washington, 1984), pp. 5–6.
4. The statement is from Christopher Dickey, "The Saving of El Salvador," *New York Review of Books*, June 4, 1984, p. 28.
5. For more on this theme, see Carlos Fuentes, *High Noon in Latin America* (Washington, 1984), originally delivered by the distinguished Mexican novelist at the 1983 Harvard commencement.

Bibliographical Guide

TO UNDERSTAND MODERN CENTRAL AMERICA, IT'S vital to understand Central America's past. For a historical survey, rich in social and economic detail, Ralph L. Woodward, Jr., *Central America: A Nation Divided* (New York, 1976), is unsurpassed for its depth and offers in its concluding bibliographical guide a detailed comment on the literature.

The problem with most recent books on Central America is the understandable reluctance of authors in this age of specialization to integrate the social scientific technique with literary and journalistic "angles of vision." Central America looks different from different perspectives, and the following categories reflect the approach I've taken:

Culture. Probably the most *sensitive* interpreters of Central America are the anthropologists (and archaeologists), professional and amateur, going all the way back to the nineteenth-century diplomat John L. Stephens, who was more interested in Mayan civilization than American commercial advancement in the isthmus and published in 1841 the two-volume *Incidents of Travel in Central America, Chiapas, and Yucatán*, handsomely illustrated with the engravings of Frederick Catherwood. Stephens inspired successive generations of anthropologists to probe deep into Mayan culture. Among their works some of the best-known are Sylvanus Morley, *The Ancient Maya* (Stanford, 1946); Victor von Hagen, *Maya Explorer: John Lloyd Stephens and the Lost Cities of Central America and Yucatán* (Norman, Okla., 1947); Eric R. Wolf, *Sons of the Shaking Earth* (Chicago, 1959); and the multivolume *Handbook of Middle American Indians*, published by the University of Texas Press. For modern approaches to Guatemalan Indian cultures, see Richard Adams,

271

Crucifixion by Power (Austin, Tex., 1970); Sol Tax, *Heritage of Conquest* (Chicago, 1952); and Benjamin Colby and Pierre L. van den Berghe, *Ixil Country* (Berkeley, 1969). And for the Miskitos I have relied on Mary Helms, *Asang: Adaptations to Culture Contact in a Miskito Community* (Gainesville, Fla., 1971); and Bernard Nietschmann, *Between Land and Water: The Subsistence Ecology of the Miskito Indians, Eastern Nicaragua* (New York, 1973). A capsule summary of Costa Rican culture is Richard Biesanz et al., *The Costa Ricans* (Englewood Cliffs, N.J., 1982). John Augelli, *Middle America: Its Lands and Peoples* (Englewood Cliffs, N.J., 1976), is an exceptional text.

Literary.   Start with O. Henry, *Cabbages and Kings* (Garden City, N.Y., 1904), for turn-of-the-century Central American life; then follow with Miguel Ángel Asturias (Guatemalan), *Strong Wind* (New York, 1968), and *The President* (Baltimore, 1972); and Aldous Huxley, *Beyond the Mexican Bay* (London, 1934), for the Central America of fifty years ago. For a travel account of modern Central America, see the relevant chapters in Paul Theroux, *The Old Patagonian Express* (Boston, 1979).

Economics (including human ecology).   For the "big picture" the best accounts are Gary Wynia, *Politics and Planners: Economic Development Policy in Central America* (Madison, Wis., 1972); William R. Cline and Enrique Delgado, eds., *Economic Integration in Latin America* (Washington, 1978); and Tom Barry et al., *Dollars and Dictators: A Guide to Central America* (New York, 1983), which is mostly a diatribe but contains useful statistics on American multinationals in the isthmus. On the *critical* changes in isthmian agricultural life and their impact on rural people, see Mitchell A. Seligson, *Peasants of Costa Rica and the Development of Agrarian Capitalism* (Madison, Wis., 1980); Joseph Collins et al., *What Difference Could a Revolution Make? Food and Farming in the New Nicaragua* (San Francisco, 1982); and especially the suggestive work by William Durham, *Scarcity and Survival in Central America: Ecological Origins of the Soccer War* (Stanford, 1979).

Sociology (especially social structure and social change). For Latin America generally see Jacques Lambert, *Latin America, Social Structures and Political Institutions* (Berkeley, 1969); Claudio Veliz, ed., *Obstacles to Change in Latin America* (London, 1965); John Mander, *The Unrevolutionary Society: The Power of Latin American Conservatism in a Changing World* (New York, 1969), a breezy assessment; Seymour Martin Lipset and Aldo Solari, eds., *Elites in Latin America* (New York, 1967); and two important books by John Johnson, *Political Change in Latin America: The Emergence of the Middle Sectors* (Stanford, 1969), and *Continuity and Change in Latin America* (Stanford, 1967). Thomas and Marjorie Melville, in *Guatemala: the Politics of Land Ownership* (New

York, 1971), present a bitterly critical portrait of that country's social structure. Alistair White performs a similar (but less hostile) assessment in *El Salvador* (London, 1973). See Richard Millett, *The Guardians of the Dynasty* (Maryknoll, N.Y., 1977), for pre-Sandinista Nicaragua; and Sam Stone, *La dinastía de los Conquistadores* (San José, 1975), for Costa Rica.

Political Science (especially political parties and leaders). Thomas P. Anderson, a historian, provides the most compact summary in *Politics in Central America: Guatemala, El Salvador, Honduras, and Nicaragua* (New York, 1982). The exclusion of Costa Rica because of its *difference* is compensated for by Charles D. Ameringer, *Democracy in Costa Rica* (New York, 1982). For more on *tico* politics see his superb biography of Figueres, *Don Pepe* (Albuquerque, 1978). Enrique Baloyra, *El Salvador in Transition* (Chapel Hill, N.C., 1982); Stephen Webre, *José Napoleón Duarte and the Christian Democratic Party in Salvadoran Politics, 1960–1972* (Baton Rouge, La., 1979); Thomas Walker, *Nicaragua: Land of Sandino* (Boulder, Colo., 1981); and Bernard Diederich, *Somoza and the Legacy of U.S. Involvement in Nicaragua* (New York, 1981), assess the politics of two countries in turmoil from different perspectives.

On the background for Central America's present troubles I have relied heavily on Penny Lernoux, *Cry of the People* (New York, 1980), for the turmoil in the church; Thomas P. Anderson, *Matanza: El Salvador's Communist Revolt of 1932* (Lincoln, Neb., 1971), for the story of Augustín Farabundo Martí and the massacre; and the same author's *The War of the Dispossessed: Honduras and El Salvador, 1969* (Lincoln, Neb., 1981), for the "soccer war": Walter LaFeber, *Inevitable Revolutions: The United States in Central America* (New York, 1983), portrays modern isthmian revolution as a rebellion against the U.S. economic "system."

A surprisingly rich literature on the present Central American crisis has already appeared, with the promise of more to come. Among the recent books the most useful were as follows: For Central America generally see Thomas Buckley, *Violent Neighbors: El Salvador, Central America, and the United States* (New York, 1984), and Richard Alan White, *The Morass: United States Intervention in Central America* (New York, 1984), both of whom work the "another Vietnam" thesis into their presentations; and three collections—Martin Diskin, ed., *Trouble in Our Backyard: Central America and the United States in the Eighties* (New York, 1983); Robert S. Leiken, ed., *Central America, Anatomy of Conflict* (New York, 1984); and the Stanford Central America Action Network, ed., *Revolution in Central America* (Boulder, Colo., 1983). For El Salvador, see Raymond Bonner, *Weakness and Deceit: U.S. Policy and El Salvador* (New York, 1984), which castigates U.S. policymakers; and

Tommie Sue Montgomery, *Revolution in El Salvador: Origins and Evolution* (Boulder, Colo., 1982), and Marvin Gettleman et al., *El Salvador: Central America in the New Cold War* (New York, 1981), which assess the guerrilla war in that country. For Guatemala, Jonathan L. Fried et al., *Guatemala in Rebellion* (New York, 1983), contains documents and accounts of that country's turbulent history from the Conquest to the present. For Sandinista Nicaragua, see John A. Booth, *The End and the Beginning* (Boulder, Colo., 1982); and Thomas A. Walker, ed., *Nicaragua in Revolution* (New York, 1982).

Index